Short Takes

MODEL ESSAYS FOR COMPOSITION

Eighth Edition

Elizabeth Penfield

University of New Orleans

PEARSON
Longman

New York   San Francisco   Boston
London   Toronto   Sydney   Tokyo   Singapore   Madrid
Mexico City   Munich   Paris   Cape Town   Hong Kong   Montreal

Senior Vice President and Publisher: Joseph Opiela
Senior Acquisitions Editor: Lynn M. Huddon
Marketing Manager: Deborah Murphy
Senior Supplements Editor: Donna Campion
Production Manager: Charles Annis
Project Coordination, Text Design, and Electronic Page Makeup: Nesbitt Graphics, Inc.
Cover Designer/Manager: Wendy Ann Fredericks
Cover Photos (left to right): © Punchstock; John Bulmer/Dorling Kindersly; Jim Arbogast/
    Photodisc Red/Getty Images; and G. K. and Vicki Hart/Image Bank/Getty Images, Inc.
Manufacturing Buyer: Roy Pickering
Printer and Binder: R. R. Donnelley & Sons Company
Cover Printer: Phoenix Color Corporation

For permission to use copyrighted material, grateful acknowledgment is made to the
copyright holders on pp. 339–342, which are hereby made part of this copyright page.

Library of Congress Cataloging-in-Publication Data

Penfield, Elizabeth, 1939–
    Short takes: model essays for composition / Elizabeth Penfield.—8th ed.
        p. cm.
Includes index.
    ISBN 0-321-20779-3
    1. College readers 2. English language—Rhetoric—Problems, exercises, etc. 3. Report
writing—Problems, exercises, etc. I. Title.

PE1417.P43 2004
808'.0427—dc22

                                                                        2003026991

Please visit our website at http://www.ablongman.com

ISBN 0-321-207793-3

1 2 3 4 5 6 7 8 9 10—DOH—07 06 05 04

CONTENTS

lazily snapping up moths as they fluttered past. The other two frogs seemed content to stake out the sinks, which weren't quite as dependable a food source, though they weren't bad."

3 On Using Definition   **76**

4 On Using Example   **107**

beyond useless; we do work that takes energy and casts it to the wind like lint. And we don't even enjoy the work. Look at people in a health club. See anybody smiling?"

5 On Using Division and Classification   138

6   On Using Comparison and Contrast   171

but for its advice to the diggers of the world, a group to which I belong."

8 On Using Cause and Effect 237

"I know now that people need each other, and I wish I could tell the fourth grade that we could all be friends, that we could help each other with our problems. I wish that I could go back. But all I can do is apologize."

"All of us have all sorts of personal experiences with music: We find ourselves calmed by it, excited by it, comforted by it, mystified by it and often haunted by it."

"Wrestling may be a hybrid genre—the epic poem meets Marvel Comics via the soap opera—but its themes, with their medieval tone, could hardly be simpler: warrior kings doing battle after battle to see who is worthy, women pushed almost to the very edges of the landscape, Beowulf's heroic ideal expressed in the language of an after-school brawl: 'I wanna do what I wanna do. You gonna try to stop me?'"

"After dark, on the warrenlike streets of Brooklyn where I live, I often see women who fear the worst from me."

"If the world seems to be growing more, rather than less, nasty these days, it might have something to do with the images all of us now carry around in our heads."

THEMATIC GUIDE

Society

Science and Technology

Language and Education

Popular Culture and the Media

PREFACE

his book combines the old and the new. Back when the first edition was only an idea, I was teaching freshman English in a highly structured program that emphasized both the rhetorical modes and the final product. My dilemma then was one that many teachers still face: how to incorporate the modes with invention and the whole tangle of the writing process. But once I focused on the aims of discourse, the modes fell into place as means, not ends, and as patterns of organization used in combination, not just singly. There remained the problem of the textbooks, many of which contained essays of imposing length and complexity, essays that intimidated and overwhelmed many a student. Often, any essay that was short was so because it was an excerpt. *Short Takes* was the result of my frustrations. The Eighth Edition still reflects the rhetorical framework of the first one, but it is a flexible framework. You can even ignore it and use the thematic table of contents. But if you find the modes useful, you'll see them here.

This edition remains a collection of short, readable, interesting essays written by professionals and students, and the commentary continues to focus on reading and writing as interrelated activities. Much, however, is new. "Freeze Frame," the initial essay that sets the tone for the book by emphasizing reading and writing as active and interrelated processes, is aimed directly at the student and includes peer editing. Features new to this edition include

- Additional writing prompts after each selection and at the end of the chapter
- New writing prompts at the end of each chapter that call for evaluating two or more essays
- Discussion questions added to those that call for close reading, both under "Organization and Ideas"
- A selection of more challenging essays
- New essays, 25 of them, many of which deal with present events and issues

- "For Further Reading: Multiple Modes, Varied Opinions," which contains selections that mix the modes and offer differing views on contemporary topics

At the same time, those features that teachers particularly liked are still here.

- Introductions to each chapter directed to students and emphasizing the writing process (as well as the kinds of choices and decisions all writers face)
- Suggestions for writing journal entries and essays
- Descriptions of the author, the context for the essay, and its notable stylistic features
- Diversity of authors, styles, and subject matter
- Complete essays, not excerpts

As always, I welcome responses from students and teachers to this new edition, along with suggestions for the future. You can e-mail me direct <epenfiel@uno.edu> or write to me in care of Longman's Developmental English Editor at Longman, 1185 Sixth Avenue, 25th Floor, New York, NY 10036.

If you are familiar with previous editions, you'll also notice that the sequencing of the chapters has not changed. Description and narration are followed by definition because it plays such an important role in expository and argumentative writing. Each chapter builds on the previous one and leads to the one that follows, culminating in argument, but argument with a difference. The chapter on argument is a basic introduction, an extension of the kind of emphasis on thesis and evidence that exists throughout the text. Within each chapter, the essays are presented in order of difficulty. All the supplementary information—the chapter introductions, background information, notes on style, questions on the essays, and suggestions for writing—balance process and product, working on the premise that the two, like reading and writing, are so closely interrelated that one cannot be considered without the other.

The Essays

This edition contains 54 essays, 25 of which are new. Most are indeed short—about one thousand words at most—and as such should easily lend themselves to scrutiny and emulation, because most of the papers assigned in composition courses fall in the four hundred to one thousand word range. A few of the essays are longer and rely on the kind of research that students may be asked to carry out. And a few illustrate forms that differ from the classic short essay: the problem-solution organization often found in argumentative pieces; and essays that debate a single issue. Two essays also serve as a basic introduction to the Modern Language Association's system of documentation. All of the essays are complete pieces, not excerpts, illustrating the basic arms of discourse and standard rhetorical modes.

To write is to choose among alternatives, to select the most appropriate organization, persona, diction, and techniques for a given audience and purpose. Each of the essays included in this edition was chosen because it exemplifies the author's choices, and the apparatus emphasizes those choices and alternatives. The essays, therefore, serve as illustrative models of organization and stylistic techniques available to the writer. The essays were also chosen because their authors represent different genders, ages, and cultures; as a result, the subjects of the essays are accessible and their perspectives are lively, qualities that also allow them to serve as sources of invention, as jumping-off places for students to develop their own ideas in their own styles.

Rhetorical Modes and the Aims of Discourse

Anyone who has used a reader with essays arranged by mode has probably run into two problems: first, few essays are pure examples of a single mode; second, most collections of essays treat argument—an aim of writing—as though it were the equivalent of description, comparison/contrast, and so on. *Short Takes* addresses these inconsistencies by emphasizing the difference between mode—how an essay is organized—and purpose—how an essay is intended to affect the reader—and by pointing out how writing frequently blends two or more modes.

Because essays usually employ more than one mode, the essays here are grouped according to the *primary* rhetorical pattern that guides their organization; the questions that follow each essay point out the subordinate modes. As for the aims of discourse, the essays represent the various purposes for writing. The writers' self-expressive, informative, and persuasive purposes are underscored in the discussion questions. In addition, the apparatus connects academic writing and the kind of writing found outside the classroom.

Example, description, or other standard modes are used in developing all kinds of nonfiction prose—self-expression, exposition, and argument. Of these three types of writing, self-expression is the easiest and argument the most difficult. For that reason, argument has its own special chapter exemplifying the classical appeals: to reason, to emotion, and to the writer's credibility. Because lively discussion often leads to good writing, in the final chapter you'll find several essays on subjects that lend themselves to debate.

Apparatus for Reading and Writing

The apparatus makes full use of the essays. Chapters 1 to 9 begin with a brief introduction to the student that depicts the mode or purpose under discussion, showing how it can be used in formal essays and in practical, everyday writing tasks. The introductions point out specifically how the modes can be shaped by considerations of audience, purpose, particular strategies, thesis, and organization, ending with advice on finding a subject, exploring a topic, and drafting a paper. This division of the writing process approximates the classic one of invention, arrangement, and style but is not intended to imply that these are separate stages.

To emphasize both what a text says and how it says it, each essay in Chapters 1 to 9 is preceded by background information on the author and the text and a brief discussion of a stylistic strategy. Two sets of questions—"Organization and Ideas" and "Technique and Style"—follow the essay, along with ideas for journal entries and essays. Throughout, process and product, as well as reading and writing, are interrelated, emphasizing the recursive nature of the act of writing. Writers constantly invent, organize, and revise; the lines that distinguish those activities are narrow, if not downright blurred.

"Suggestions for Writing" follow each essay and contain a number of options for both journal entries and essays, all related by theme, organization, or ideas to the work that has just been read. The assignments allow a good deal of flexibility: some lend themselves to general information or personal experience, some to research papers, many to group work (outlined in the Instructor's Manual), some to the classic technique of imitation. In addition, at the end of Chapters 1–9 you'll find prompts for using the mode under discussion and for comparing and evaluating the essays.

Whether working alone or in groups, once students select their subjects, they will find flipping back to the introduction helpful. There the boxed section "Exploring the Topic" shapes questions so that no matter what type of paper they are writing, students can generate information about it. "Drafting the Paper" then helps students organize the material and points out some of the pitfalls and advantages inherent in a particular mode or aim.

The Instructor's Manual

An Instructor's Manual (ISBN 0-321-24483-4) includes key words and phrases, responses to the questions, and teaching suggestions for both the questions and the longer writing assignments. There are also additional thematic writing prompts and a sample student argument paper.

Acknowledgments

I have many people to thank for their help in bringing this book to publication: Lynn Huddon for her good advice and encouragement; Hope Rajala, Leslie Taggart, Karen Helfrich, and Liza Rudneva for their able assistance with past editions; James Postema, Nancy Braun, and Kim McDonald for their help and their students; and Theodora Hill for her sound recommendations, patience, and help with the more mundane aspects of preparing a manuscript. Mary Schoenung's careful copyediting of this edition is much appreciated. The following reviewers all provided guidance and advice that improved the manuscript: Phillip Ballard, South Arkansas Community College; Brenda Boudreau, McKendree College; Patrice Fleck, Northern Virginia Community College; Jill Karle Leahman, Piedmont Virginia Community College; Michael McDowell, Portland Community College; and Kate Mohler, Mesa Community College.

ELIZABETH PENFIELD

Freeze Frame

●●●●●●●●●●●●●●●●●●●●●●●●●●●●●●●●●●●●

Reading and Writing

This Book

In filmmaking, a "short take" is a brief scene filmed without interruption. Similarly, short essays move quickly toward their conclusions, with only the small breaks caused by paragraph indentations. Those are the kinds of essays you will find in this book, short essays that explain, argue, express the writer's feelings, or simply entertain. The essays carry out their purposes by drawing on various patterns of organization, patterns that can describe, tell a story, define a subject, provide examples, set up comparisons, or analyze a process or a cause and effect. These are the same patterns you will draw on when you write your own papers. The essays, then, can serve as models.

And just as the essays collected here are "short takes," this essay is a "freeze frame," as though you had stopped the film on one particular shot to get a better look at the details. That's just what this essay will do, stop and take a close-up look at what goes on when you read and when you write.

You, the Reader

A skilled reader interacts with the words on the page: reshaping, evaluating, selecting, analyzing. After all, you have your own world, one made up of everything you have experienced, from your first memory to your most recent thought—all of which you bring to what you read. An essay about why people love to walk on beaches, for example, will remind you of any beaches you know, and your associations will probably be pleasurable. As you begin the essay, you discover that the writer's associations are also pleasant ones, reinforcing yours. You read on, constantly reassessing your ideas about the essay as you add more and more information to your first impression. Now and then, you may hit a sentence that at first doesn't make much sense, so you stop, perhaps to look up an unfamiliar word, perhaps to go back and review an earlier statement, then read on, again reevaluating your ideas about what the author is saying and what you think of it. The result is analytical, critical reading—not critical in the sense of judging harshly but critical in the sense of questioning, weighing evidence, evaluating, comparing your world to the one the writer has created on the page.

The idea of revising and tinkering is usually associated with writing, less so with reading. Yet just as you tinker and wrestle with your own writing, you should do the same with what you read. You should scribble, underline, question, challenge. Reading in this way, reading critically with pen or pencil in hand, will give you a fuller appreciation of what you read and a better understanding of the techniques the writer used to create the essay.

If you're not used to reading in this manner, it may seem foreign to you. After all, what's printed on the page should be easy enough to understand. But because words only stand for things and are not the things themselves, different readers find different meanings. If, for instance, your only memory of a beach was of nearly drowning in the Atlantic Ocean, then you would have to suspend that association when you read an essay that praises beach walking. And if your skin turns bright red at the mere mention of the sun, that adds one more obstacle to understanding why others enjoy the seashore. How then can a reader comprehend all that an author is saying? More specifically, how can a reader go about reading an essay critically?

Identifying the Purpose   It helps to know what different kinds of writing have in common. Whether business letter, lab report, journal entry, news story, poem, or essay, all focus on a subject, address a reader, and have a point. And, too, all have a purpose and a style; they are written for specific reasons and in a certain way. These shared elements are perhaps more familiar as questions used to spark ideas for writing, the familiar journalistic *who? what? where? when? how? why?* Yet these questions can be equally useful for reading, and thinking about them will give you a general overview of what you are reading. To whom is an essay addressed? What is the writer's main point? How is the piece organized? Why is it structured that way? Where and when does the action take place? Many, many more inquiries can be spun off those seemingly simple questions, and they are useful tools for exploring an essay. Jotting down these questions and your answers to them in a notebook or journal can also sharpen your critical abilities and lead to a lively class discussion.

Looking for the Point   In much of the reading we do, we are looking for information. The election coverage reported in the newspaper, the syllabus for a course, and a set of directions all exemplify this kind of reading, but reading for information and reading for comprehension are as different as a vitamin pill and a five-course dinner. To understand not only what a writer is saying but also its implications and why that writer might have chosen to say it that way isn't easy.

The title of an essay is a good place to start, for most titles tip you off not only about the subject of the piece but also to the author's stand. You don't need to turn to the essay titled "Sweatin' for Nothin'" to figure out it may be about exercising and that the author doesn't see much point to fitness fads. Other titles, such as "Left Sink," just imply a subject and raise your curiosity. What about a left sink? What does it mean? Some titles focus clearly on their subject, as in "Living with Cancer." Still others tip you off to the author's tone, the writer's attitude toward the subject: if an essay were called "Tube E or Not Tube E," the play on the familiar line from *Hamlet* suggests a humorous discussion of a chemistry lab course. Now and then, however, a title may announce a bald version of the thesis, such as an editorial headlined "Your Vote Counts." The editorial then would expand the idea so that a full version of the thesis becomes, "Your vote counts because a single ballot can change the outcome of an election—and it has."

Knowing or at least having a hint about the subject is the first step to discovering an essay's thesis, the assertion the author is making about the subject. The first paragraph or set of paragraphs that act as an introduction will also help you form a tentative thesis. Sometimes the writer will place the thesis in the first paragraph or introduction, but sometimes a bare-bones version of the thesis will appear in the title. If you see it, you should mark it. If you don't spot a thesis, you should still write down a tentative version of your own so that you have a focus for what is to follow, an idea against which you can test other ideas.

This last option is a bit of a challenge. You must create the thesis by identifying key sentences and then mentally composing a statement that covers those ideas, a process that often takes more than one reading but is made easier if you underline the important sentences. Even then, you may well find that someone else who reads the essay comes up with a different thesis statement. And you both may be right.

What's happening here? If you think about how slippery words are and the different experiences that different readers bring to an essay, you can begin to see why there's more than one "correct" thesis. If you were to give the same essay to 10 critical readers, you would find that their versions of the thesis differ but overlap. Their readings would probably cluster around two or three central ideas. If an eleventh person read the essay and came up with a thesis that contradicted the 10 other readings, that version would probably be off base.

Sometimes writers unwittingly set traps, making it easy to mistake a fact for a thesis. If you keep in mind that a thesis is both a sentence and an assertion—a value judgment—those traps can be avoided. "The average American watches a lot of TV" states a fact most readers would shrug off with a "So what?" On the other hand, "Television rots the minds of its viewers" takes a stand that will probably raise hackles and a "Hey, wait a minute!"

Recognizing Patterns of Development

Once you've nailed down a thesis, go a step further to examine how that thesis is developed. Writers depend on various patterns of thought or modes of thinking that are almost innate. To tell a joke is to narrate; to convey what a party was like is to describe and to use examples; to decide which among many courses to take is to divide and classify; to figure out which car to buy is to compare and contrast (and if you think of your old car as a peach or a lemon, you are drawing an analogy); to give directions is to use process; to consider how to improve your tennis game is to weigh cause and effect; to explain how you feel is to define. Narration, description, example, division and classification, comparison and contrast, analogy, process, cause and effect, and definition are the natural modes of thinking upon which writers rely.

These patterns of thought provide the structure of an essay. A piece on the ethics of using prisoners to test new medicines might open with a brief narrative that sets the scene, go on to define what kinds of medicines are involved, and then explain the effects of such experiments on the prisoners, the development of new drugs, and society's concept of ethics. As you read, you should note each type of mode the writer uses so you can more fully understand how the thesis is developed and how the essay is organized. Though you may find an essay uses many types of modes, it's likely that one predominates.

You, the Writer and Editor

Central to any kind of writing is the question "Why am I doing this?" The obvious answer for most students is "Because it's assigned." Equally obvious is that writing and editing are hard work, involving both time and effort. While praise or a good grade can be rewards, they rarely seem equal to the thought and struggle that went into writing an essay; however, it is also true that writing can be its own reward. By writing, you learn about yourself and your subject, you sharpen your mind, and you increase your concentration. But once you have written something you like, you will find that fear is apt to replace enthusiasm, for the only thing scarier than putting words on paper is the idea that someone is going to read them. This kind of fear is something that most writers, students or professionals, experience. Yet you will find that having someone respond to your paper with "Hey, that was really good" or "I really liked that" more than makes up for the anxiety you experienced when you first sat down to write.

A blank sheet of paper or an empty computer screen can be a terrifying thing, so how should you begin? Off and on, you've been thinking about what to write, so in a sense you've already started your essay even though nothing is on paper. Or perhaps you've been able to talk about your topic with your classmates, generating ideas and finding a focus. Now you need to get those thoughts into print.

If you stare at a blank page and try to get that opening sentence just right, you're trying to edit too soon. Don't think of a finished piece or how your paper will begin or end; just start writing anything—notes, a title, a list of ideas, an outline, a paragraph—whatever comes to mind. At this stage, you're brainstorming, coming up with ideas and bouncing them off each other so that you can figure out what you are trying to say. Figuring out how you want your reader to respond, shaping your ideas, organizing and then polishing them, can come later. Now you just want to end up with ideas that can be loosely organized into a rough draft.

Thinking About Your Audience   If your class is run as a writer's workshop or uses peer groups, then at this point you have a draft of your essay, and your classmates can help you shape and refine it, keeping in mind questions of purpose, audience, thesis, and organization. Those are the same concerns that you will consider as you review your draft and those of your classmates.

You'll need to decide on the purpose of the essay. Should it inform, persuade, or entertain your reader, perhaps all three? In writing, as in speech, the purpose determines the relationship among the subject, writer, and reader. Most of the writing you will be doing in college is intended to inform. For that reason, most of the essays included in this book are expository; their primary purpose is to explain a subject, to inform the reader. In most of your other courses, you will find that your reading fits into this category, one occupied by stacks of textbooks. As for your writing, when you write a lab or book report, a précis, or an essay exam, you focus on your subject so that you explain it to your readers.

Though explaining may be your primary purpose, other aims enter in as well. In an essay exam about a historical event, you are also trying to convince your reader that you know what you are writing about. Your reader, of course, is your teacher, someone who knows more about your subject than you do, so you aren't trying to explain the subject; instead you're trying to persuade your teacher that your interpretation of it is sound.

If you're writing a journal or diary entry or a personal letter, however, your focus is on yourself, the writer. That's also true if you're writing an opinion piece in the newspaper or a meditative essay. If, for example, your teacher asks you to keep a journal in which you respond to what you read, your responses may range from fury over an opinion you disagree with to mild musings on what you think about the author's subject. What is important is what you feel, and your writing expresses those feelings by communicating them clearly to your reader. You, not the subject, are center stage.

Conveying what you feel about a subject and persuading your reader to share your opinion, however, are two different aims. Let's say you have a strong opinion about the "three strikes and you're out" policy of life imprisonment for a third felony. You decide to write a letter to the editor, and in it you rage on about the policy being a form of racism and claim that life imprisonment is "cruel and unusual punishment." While you may feel better for having let off some steam, few minds, if any, will have been changed; probably the only readers who finished your letter were those who agreed with you to begin with. The letter appeals to the emotions by waving the red flag of racism and the star-spangled banner of the Constitution.

Think about the difference if you were to recast your ideas into the genre of an editorial or guest opinion piece, a type of writing that leans on reason for its appeal. You might start by pointing out that the definition of what is or is not a felony differs from state to state, that many more prisons would have to be built and maintained, that judges—if allowed—can weigh the severity of the offense and the punishment it deserves, that the "three strikes" presents more problems than it resolves. You are careful to address a multiple audience of readers who agree, disagree, or have no opinion. You intend to make the reader think, and, ideally, to change opinions, so the argument's appeal rests primarily on reason, not emotion.

Discovering a Thesis   You will find that writing is a form of discovery, that writing about an idea helps clarify it. In your own experience, you have probably found that you usually don't have a clear grasp of your main point until you've written your way into it. You may start with an idea, a general focus, say, on professional wrestling, but that focus becomes clearer as you rethink your choice of a particular word or reread what is on the page to get a sense of what should come next. Gradually, your ideas become clearer and out of them an assertion emerges: professional wrestling may not be much of a sport, but it's splendid theater. And on you go, sometimes speeding, sometimes creeping, constantly revising.

Once your thesis is clear, then you must decide where to place it for the greatest effect. You may opt for placing it at the end of your introduction, but perhaps it would be best in your conclusion, or you may decide on a more subtle solution by weaving bits and pieces of the thesis into the essay as a whole. You may find it best to hold off a decision until you've worked some more on your essay's organization.

Organizing the Essay   Description, narration, cause and effect, and the like are modes that provide the structure of the essay, the means by which you support your major point, the thesis, and more often than not, you will draw upon several patterns of development to support your major point. Rarely does an essay rely solely on one pattern of development. In the example above, the thesis—professional wrestling may not be much of a sport, but it's splendid theater—suggests a paper that might begin with a brief introduction that describes the cast of wrestlers and their costumes, then develops the thesis by defining what makes a sport a sport, comparing professional wrestling with that definition, and presenting examples as evidence that professional wrestling is theater. Most of the essay would concentrate on examples, which would be its primary mode of organization.

When you are writing, modes such as example, definition, and the like provide ways to think about your topic as well as ways to organize your essay. With practice they become as much second nature as shifting gears in a manual-transmission car. At first you might be a bit tentative about knowing when to shift from first to second, but with time you don't even think about it. Similarly, you might wonder if your point is clear without an example; in time, you automatically supply it.

Knowing what you want to write and having a fair idea of how it should be organized still do not necessarily help you shape individual sentences so that they convey the desired tone, so that they *sound* right. That requires draft after draft. Even the idea of finishing is a shaky notion; many writers will continue to revise right up to their deadlines. Hemingway rewrote the last page of *A Farewell to Arms* 39 times, and Katherine Anne Porter spent 20 years writing and rewriting *Ship of Fools*. Writing nonfiction doesn't make the process any easier. Wayne Booth, a distinguished essayist and scholar, speaks for most writers: "I revise many, many times, as many times as deadlines allow for. And I always feel that I would have profited from further revision." Poet, novelist, essayist, journalist, student, or professional, all continue in the tradition expressed in the eighteenth century by a fellow writer, Samuel Johnson, who said, "What is written without effort is in general read without pleasure." Pleasurable reading derives from a pleasing writing style, and though some writers strive for elegance as well as clarity, most readers will happily settle for clarity.

Far from following a recipe, you will find that writing an essay is like driving a car while at the same time trying to impress the passengers, read a road map, recognize occasional familiar landmarks, follow scrawled and muttered directions, and watch for and listen to all the quirks of the car. You know vaguely where you are going and how you want to get there, but the rest is risk and adventure. With work and a number of dry runs, you can smooth out the trip so that the passengers fully appreciate the pleasure of the drive and the satisfaction of reaching the destination. That is the challenge the writer faces, a challenge that demands critical reading as well as effective writing.

Reading and Writing

Essays can be deceptive. What you see on the printed page resembles the writer's work about as much as a portrait resembles the real person. What you don't see when you look at printed pages are all the beginnings and stops, the crumpled paper, the false starts, the notes, the discarded ideas, the changed words. Instead, you have a finished piece—the result of the writer's choices. Don't be intimidated. The process most writers go through to produce their essays is very like your own. The writer Andre Dubus puts it another way: "There is something mystical [about writing] but it's not rare and nobody should treat it as though this is something special that writers do. Anybody born physically able in the brain can sit down and begin to write something, and discover that there are depths in her soul or his soul that are untapped."

As a writer and a reader, you tap into those depths, depths that help make meaning of the world we live in. The making of meaning is the heart of the essays contained in this book, together with its explanations, questions, and suggestions for writing. Stated concisely, this book reinforces a basic assumption: reading and writing are highly individual processes that are active, powerful, and interrelated ways to discover meaning.

To check out that statement, think of one day within the last week when something memorable happened to you. Isolate that incident so it's clear in your mind. Now think of all the other details of the day, from the time your eyes opened in the morning to the time they closed at night. That's a lot of detail, and most of it insignificant, meaningless, bits and pieces of information you would probably discard if you were to write about that day. What you would be left with is that memorable thing that occurred and a few details directly related to it, some preceding it, a few following. In writing about that day, you would reshape events—evaluating, selecting, and recreating what happened so that what was most meaningful comes through clearly. As a result, someone reading your description would be able to experience at a distance what you experienced firsthand.

To write, then, is to create and structure a world; to read is to become part of someone else's. And just as reading makes a better writer, writing makes a better reader.

POINTERS FOR READING

1. **Settle in.** Gather up a good dictionary and whatever you like to write with, and then find a comfortable place to read.
2. **Think about the title.** What sort of expectations do you have about what will follow? Can you identify the subject? A thesis? Can you tell anything about the writer's tone?
3. **Look for a specific focus.** Where is the essay going? What appears to be its thesis? At what point does the introduction end and the body of the essay begin? What questions do you have about the essay so far? Is the essay directed at you? If not, who is the intended audience?
4. **Look for a predominant pattern of organization.** What are the most important ideas in the body of the essay? Note the modes the writer uses to develop those ideas.
5. **Identify the conclusion.** Where does the conclusion begin? How does it end the essay? What effect does it have on you?
6. **Evaluate the essay.** Did the essay answer the questions you had about it? How effective was the support for the main ideas? Did the writer's choice of words fit the audience? What effect did the essay have on you? Why?

POINTERS FOR WRITING AND EDITING

1. **Settle in.** Get hold of whatever you find comfortable to write with—computer, pen, pencil, legal pad, note paper, notebook—and settle into wherever you like to write. Start by jotting down words that represent a general idea of your subject. As words cross your mind, write them down so that at this point you have a vague focus.
2. **Focus.** Try writing right away and quickly. Get your ideas down on paper without worrying about organization or punctuation or whether what you write is right. If you run out of steam, pause and read over what you have written and then summarize it in one sentence. Then start up again writing as quickly as you can. At some point you will have written your

way into a tentative thesis that will help you focus as you revise what you have written. Now you have a draft and are ready to edit your own paper and, perhaps, those of your classmates.

3. **Reread.** Go over what's written, looking for sentences that state an opinion. Mark them in some way (a highlighter is useful). These sentences can become topic sentences that lead off paragraphs and, therefore, help organize the ideas.

4. **Organize what's there.** Go through the paper asking questions. What would make a good introduction? A good conclusion? What order best suits what's in between? What examples do you have? Where would they work best?

5. **Think about purpose.** As you reread, think about the kind of effect the paper should have on readers. Does it explain something to them? Argue a cause? Tell them about feelings? Entertain? Some combination of purposes?

6. **Think about the readers.** What do they know about the subject? The answer to this question may help cut out some information; and what they don't know can be a guide to what needs to be included. Do they have a bias for or against the thesis? The answer will reveal whether those biases need to be accounted for and suggest how to do that.

7. **Revise.** You've probably been revising all along, but at this point you can revise more thoroughly and deeply. You know your purpose, audience, and thesis—all of which will help you organize your paper more effectively.

8. **Proofread.** Now look for surface errors, checking for spelling and punctuation. If you're using a word-processing program, run your text through the spelling checker. As for punctuation, if you have access to a grammar checker on your word processor, try it. You may find it useful, but probably a handbook of grammar and usage will be much more helpful because the explanations are fuller and you'll find lots of examples. The easiest way to use a handbook is to look up the key word in the index.

On Using
Description

1

Description turns up in various guises in all types of prose, for it is the basic device a writer uses to convey sense impressions. For that reason, it is as essential to **objective**[1] writing as it is to **subjective** prose and, of course, to everything in between. A quick sketch of a family gathering that you might include in a letter to a friend draws on the same skills as a complex report on the effectiveness of a new product. Both rely on the ability to observe, to select the most important details, to create a coherent sequence for those details, and then to convey the result by appealing to the reader's senses. To describe something, then, is to recreate it in such a way that it becomes alive again, so that the reader can see and understand it. Prose that depends heavily on description invites the reader to share the writer's initial sense of vividness and perception.

The role description plays in writing will vary. Personal narratives depend heavily on description to bring scenes and actions to life, to depict an outdoor wedding, for instance, or to convey what it feels like to have a toothache. Other types of expository essays use description in a less obvious role, perhaps to clarify a step in a process or make an example vivid. And persuasion often gets its punch from description, for it enables the reader to see the prisoner on death row or the crime that led to the death sentence. While no essay relies solely on description, each of the essays that follow uses description as its primary pattern of organization. The essays' general subjects are familiar—a sandwich, a place, a cold day, a person, a frog—but by selecting details, each author tailors description uniquely.

---

[1]Words printed in boldface are defined under "Useful Terms" at the end of each introductory section.

Audience and Purpose

Most writers start with a general sense of purpose and audience. Perhaps you want to explain an event or how something works or what you think about a particular place, person, or idea, in which case your purpose is expository and what you write is **exposition.** You focus on your subject so that you can explain it clearly to your reader. That's not as dull as it sounds. Odds are that if you wrote a description of your neighborhood in such a way that your readers felt as though they could see it, you'd have an interesting expository essay. Sure, it represents your opinion, how *you* see your neighborhood, but the focus is clearly on the subject; you are in the position of narrator, telling your readers about your subject, analyzing it, explaining it to them.

But imagine that as you begin to think about your neighborhood your thoughts turn to ways in which your life there could be improved. Perhaps the garbage could be picked up more frequently, the sidewalks could be repaired, or the property taxes lowered. All of a sudden you're off on an argumentative tear, one that can take a number of different forms—essay, letter to the editor, or letter to your city or state representative. But no matter who you write for, you're engaging in **persuasion** and your focus is on the reader, the person whose mind you want to change.

Writers who aim their work at a definite audience, say the readers of a particular magazine, have a head start by knowing the readership. One of the essays in this chapter comes from *Sierra*, the journal of the Sierra Club, an organization devoted to the preservation of American wildlife and nature. Writing for that audience, the author can assume a definite interest in animal life of almost any variety, so the only problem that remains is how to make the particular creature real and interesting.

If your audience is a more general one, say the readers of a newspaper or your classmates, the situation is quite different. The assumptions you can make must be more general. For a newspaper it's safe to assume, for instance, that most of the readers are educated and fall into a general age group ranging from young adult to middle-aged. Knowing that can help you estimate the distance between your subject and the audience. If your subject is old age, you will know that your readers are generally knowledgeable about the topic but that their experience is indirect. That means you must fill in the gap with descriptive details so that their experience becomes more direct, so that the readers can see and feel what it's like to be old. And if your audience is your classmates, a younger group, the gap between subject and audience is even wider so your description has to be even more full.

In addition to having a firm sense of what your audience does and does not know, it helps to know how your readers may feel about your subject and how you want them to feel. How you want them to feel is a matter of **tone,** your attitude toward the subject and the audience. Many readers, for example, are understandably squeamish about the subject of war, and that creates a problem for the writer, particularly one who wants to describe a scene realistically and at the same time elicit sympathy. One solution is to pretty it up, but that does a disservice to reality; however, too realistic a description can be so revolting that no one would read it. Nor would anyone want to read a dry, objective account. Rudyard Kipling, whom most of us know through his *Jungle Books,* faced this problem when he wrote *The Irish Guards in the Great War,* a history of a military unit in World War I. His description of the German positions before the British attack on the Somme can be summarized objectively by removing most of the details to create an intentionally flat, dull tone:

> The Germans had been strengthening their defenses for two years. It was a defense in depth, exploiting the smooth slopes ascending to their high ground. They fortified forests and villages and dug deep underground shelters in the chalky soil. They protected their positions with copious wire, often arranged to force attackers into the fire of machine guns. (Fussell 172).

Now compare that prose with how Kipling solves the problem of tone by finding a middle yet realistic ground:

> Here the enemy had sat for two years, looking down upon France and daily strengthening himself. His trebled and quadrupled lines of defense, worked for him by his prisoners, ran below and along the flanks and on the tops of ranges of five-hundred-foot downs. Some of these were studded with close woods, deadlier even than the fortified villages between them; some cut with narrowing valleys that drew machine-gun fire as chimneys draw draughts; some opening into broad, seemingly smooth slopes, whose every haunch and hollow covered sunk forts, carefully placed mine-fields, machine-gun pits, gigantic quarries, enlarged in the chalk, connecting with systems of catacomb-like dug-outs and subterranean works at all depths, in which brigades could lie till the fitting moment. Belt upon belt of fifty-yard-deep wire protected these points, either directly or at such angles as should herd and hold up attacking infantry to the fire of veiled guns. Nothing in

the entire system had been neglected or unforeseen, except knowledge of the nature of the men who, in due time, should wear their red way through every yard of it.[2]

Kipling's description is essentially an explanation, but note the argumentative twist he puts in his last sentence, his reference to the men of the Irish Guards and their valiant attack and huge losses, the blood of their "red way." There's no question about whose side Kipling is on. And there's no question about how he wants his readers to feel.

Details

No matter what the purpose or audience, descriptive essays are characterized by their use of detail. Note how many details are in the paragraph by Kipling, most of which are **concrete details.** The German defenses had not just been strengthened but "trebled and quadrupled." Nor is Kipling satisfied with **abstract words.** He tells us the quarries were "gigantic," an abstract word that has different meanings to different people, so he gives us a concrete sense of just how large those quarries are—they could hide whole brigades. We get a visual idea of their size. Visual detail also helps us see the wire defenses. Because Kipling's book, from which the passage was taken, was published in 1923, shortly after the end of World War I, a time when tanks, missiles, and bombers as we know them were unheard of, the general particulars of trench warfare were still fresh in his readers' minds; they would know, for example, that the wire he refers to is barbed wire, but Kipling makes his audience (both then and now) see it by saying that it was "belt upon belt" of wire, "fifty-yard-deep" wire.

Visual details make us see what a writer is describing, but using other appeals to the senses also brings prose to life. Once you start thinking about it, you'll find images that draw in other senses. For auditory appeal, for instance, you might think of a time when you walked in snow so dry that a snowball turns to powder and you could hear the small squeal of your footsteps; and if your climate goes to the other extreme, you might remember a blistering night and the chirps, bleeps, squeaks, and rasps sung by a chorus of summer insects.

---

[2]Quoted in Paul Fussell's *The Great War and Modern Memory.* New York: Oxford UP, 1977.

Comparison

Take any object and try to describe what it looks, feels, smells, sounds, and tastes like, and you'll quickly find yourself shifting over to comparisons. Comparisons enrich description in that they can produce an arresting image, explain the unfamiliar, make a connection with the reader's own experience, or reinforce the major point in the essay. Comparing the unfamiliar to the familiar makes what is being described more real. Even the computer-illiterate among us get the idea embedded in the term *World Wide Web*, immediately imagining an electronic spider web that encompasses the globe. The image is a metaphor, and often comparisons take the form of **metaphor, simile, or allusion.**

Simile and *metaphor* both draw a comparison between dissimilar things; the terms differ in that a simile uses a comparative word such as *like* or *as*. As a result, metaphor is often the more arresting because it is a direct equation. If you were writing and got stuck to the point where nothing worked—the classic writer's block—you might describe your state as "sinking in the quicksand of words." Then when you broke through and started writing again, you might think of it as being able to "open the locked door," even though the process of writing may be like the labors of Hercules, an allusion to the hero of Greek myths and his difficult and superhuman feats.

Unfortunately, the first comparisons that often come to mind can be overworked ones known as **clichés:** *green as grass, hot as hell, mad as a hornet, red as a rose*, and the like. While you can guard against them by being suspicious of any metaphor or simile that sounds familiar, clichés can sneak into your writing in less obvious ways. Watch out for descriptive words that come readily to mind—waves that pound or crash, clouds that are fluffy, bells that tinkle.

Analogy is another form of comparison. Think of it as a metaphor that is extended beyond a phrase into several sentences or a paragraph. You can understand how that can happen if you think of a metaphor for the way you write. Some may imagine a roller coaster; others might think of having to manage a busy switchboard; and for some it may be trying to build a house without having any blueprints or knowing what materials are needed. No matter which image, you can tell that it will take more than a sentence or two to develop the metaphor into an analogy.

Diction

The words a writer chooses determine whether the description is more objective or subjective, whether its tone is factual or impressionistic. Although total objectivity is impossible, description that leans toward the objective is called for when the writer wants to focus on the subject as opposed to emotional effect, on what something is rather than how it felt. Read the paragraph below by J. Merrill-Foster in which she describes an 85-year-old woman.

> She is frightened and distressed by letters from retired military men. They write that unless she sends $35 by return mail, the Russians will land in Oregon and take over America. The arrival of the daily mail looms large in her day. Once, every few weeks, it contains a personal letter. The rest is appeals and ads. She reads every item.

That passage comes from the first part of "Frightened by Loss," an essay by F. Merrill-Foster, which ends with this paragraph:

> I watch the woman—my mother—walking carefully down the frozen, snow-filled driveway to the mail box. She is a photograph in black and white, which only loving memory tints with stippled life and color.

The first description reports the unnamed woman's feelings and the facts that give rise to them and then generalizes on the importance of the daily mail, noting what it contains and the attention the woman gives it. The second description uses first person and identifies the woman as the author's mother, the words *I* and *mother* forming an emotional bond between reader and writer, overlaying with feeling the picture of the woman walking to the mailbox. On finishing the first passage, the reader understands the role an everyday event—the arrival of the mail—plays in the life of an old woman; on finishing the second, the reader knows and feels how old age has diminished a once vital person.

Organization and Ideas

All the details, all the comparisons are organized so that they add up to a single dominant impression. In descriptive essays, this single dominant impression may be implicit or explicit, and it stands as the **thesis.** An explicit thesis jumps off the page at you and is usually stated openly in one or two easily identifiable sentences. An implicit thesis, however, is more subtle. As reader, you come to understand what the thesis is even though you can't identify any single sentence that states it. If that process of deduction seems mysterious, think of reading a description of the ultimate pizza, a description that alluringly recounts its aroma, taste, texture. After reading about that pizza you would probably think, Wow, that's a really good pizza. And that's an implied thesis.

Whether implicit or explicit, the thesis is what the writer builds the essay around. It's the main point. The writer must select the most important details, create sentences and paragraphs around them, and then sequence the paragraphs so that everything not only contributes to but also helps create the thesis. In description, paragraphs can be arranged by **patterns of organization,** such as process and definition, and according to spatial, temporal, or dramatic relationships. The writer can describe a scene so that the reader moves from one place to another, from one point in time to another, or according to a dramatic order. If this last idea seems vague, think of how a film or novel builds to a high point, one that usually occurs just before the end.

The building block for that high point and for the essay itself is the paragraph. And just as the essay has a controlling idea, an assertion that is its thesis, so, too, does the paragraph, usually in the form of a **topic sentence.** Like the thesis, the topic sentence can be explicit or implied, and it can be found in one sentence or deduced from the statements made in several. A topic sentence often covers more than one paragraph, for paragraphs frequently cluster around a central idea, particularly in a longer essay, one over 600 words or so.

There's no magic number for how many words make up a paragraph and no magic number for how many paragraphs make up an essay, but it is safe to say that all essays have a beginning, middle, and end. The same is true of a paragraph or group of paragraphs that function under one topic sentence. As you read, ask yourself why a given paragraph ends where it does and what links it to the one that follows. You may discover that sometimes paragraph breaks are not set in cement, that they could occur in several different places and still be "right."

Useful Terms

Abstract words Words that stand for something that cannot be easily visualized and, therefore, may hold different meanings for different people. A box of cereal labeled "large" may be your idea of "small."

Allusion An indirect reference to a real or fictitious person, place, or thing.

Analogy A point-by-point comparison to something seemingly unlike but more commonplace and less complex than the subject. An analogy is also an extended metaphor.

Cliché A comparison, direct or indirect, that has been used so often that it has worn out its novelty, such as *cool as a cucumber* or *ice cold.*

Concrete details Words that stand for something that can be easily visualized and have fixed meaning. If you replaced the "large" on the cereal box with "8 ounces" or "two servings for moderately hungry people," you would be replacing the abstract with more definite, concrete details.

Exposition Writing that explains; also called expository writing.

Metaphor An implied but direct comparison in which the primary term is made more vivid by associating it with a quite dissimilar term. "Life is a roller coaster" is a metaphor.

Objective prose Writing that is impersonal.

Patterns of organization Paragraphs and essays are usually organized according to the patterns illustrated in this book: description, narration, example, division and classification, comparison, process, cause and effect, and definition. Although more than one pattern may exist in a paragraph or essay, often one predominates.

Persuasion Writing that argues a point, that attempts to convince the reader to adopt the writer's stand.

Simile A comparison in which the primary term is linked to a dissimilar one by *like* or *as* to create a vivid image. "Life is like a roller coaster" is a simile. Remove the linking word and you have a metaphor.

Subjective prose Writing that is personal.

Thesis A one-sentence statement or summary of the basic arguable point of the essay.

Tone A writer's attitude toward the subject and the audience.

Topic sentence A statement of the topic of a paragraph containing an arguable point that is supported by the rest of the paragraph.

POINTERS FOR USING DESCRIPTION

Exploring the Topic

1. **What distinguishes your topic?** What characteristics, features, or actions stand out about your subject? Which are most important? Least important?

2. **What senses can you appeal to?** What can you emphasize about your subject that would appeal to sight? Smell? Touch? Taste? Motion?

3. **What concrete details can you use?** What abstract words do you associate with each of the features or events you want to emphasize? How can you make those abstractions concrete?

4. **How can you vary your narrative?** Where might you use quotations? Where might you use dialogue?

5. **What can your audience identify with?** What comparisons can you use? What similes, metaphors, or allusions come to mind?

6. **What order should you use?** Is your description best sequenced by time? Place? Dramatic order?

7. **What is your tentative thesis?** What is the dominant impression you want to create? Do you want it to be implicit? Explicit?

8. **What is your relationship to your subject?** Given your tentative thesis, how objective or subjective should you be? Do you want to be part of the action or removed? What personal pronoun should you use?

Drafting the Paper

1. **Know your reader.** If you are writing about a familiar subject, ask yourself what your reader might not know about it. If you are writing about an unfamiliar subject, ask yourself what your reader does know that you can use for comparison.

2. **Know your purpose.** If you are writing to inform, make sure you are presenting new information and in enough detail to bring your subject to life. If you are writing to persuade, make sure your details add up so that the reader is moved to adopt your conviction. Keep in mind that your reader may not share your values and indeed may even hold opposite ones.

3. **Vary sensory details.** Emphasize important details by appealing to more than just one sense.

4. **Show, don't tell.** Avoid abstract terms such as *funny* or *beautiful*. Instead, use concrete details, quotations, and dialogue. Don't settle for vague adjectives such as *tall*; replace them with sharper details such as *6 feet 7 inches*.

5. **Use comparisons.** Make your description vivid with an occasional metaphor or simile. If you are writing about something quite unfamiliar, use literal comparison to make your description clear.

6. **Arrange your details to create a single dominant impression.** If you are writing descriptive paragraphs, check the order of your sentences to make sure they follow each other logically and support the impression you wish to create. If you are writing an essay that relies heavily on description, check for the same points from one paragraph to another. Is your topic sentence or thesis implicit or explicit? Reexamine your first paragraph. Does it establish the scene? The tone?

A Sandwich

Nora Ephron

Journalist, essay writer, novelist, screenwriter, and director, Nora Ephron has been busy. She started her career working for the New York Post *as a reporter, then did freelance work before she became a member of the staff at* New York *and* Esquire. *Her essays have been collected in* Wallflower at the Orgy *(1970) and* Crazy Salad *(1975), but she is probably best known for* Heartburn *(1983), a thinly disguised and funny "novel" about her marriage. As for films, her script for* Silkwood *was nominated for an Oscar, and in 1989, she was again nominated, this time for Best Original Screenplay with the film* When Harry Met Sally. *More recently, she directed* Sleepless in Seattle *(1993) and* You've Got Mail *(1998). Her essay "A Sandwich" appeared in the August, 2002, double issue (19 and 20) of the* New Yorker. *In it, you'll find she's quite familiar with Los Angeles and New York, to say nothing of pastrami.*

What to Look For   Not everyone knows about, much less likes, a hot pastrami sandwich, so when you read Ephron's essay, watch for the various ways she tries to get the reader's interest and attention.

1   The hot pastrami sandwich served at Langer's Delicatessen in downtown Los Angeles is the finest hot pastrami sandwich in the world. This is not just my opinion, although most people who know about Langer's will simply say it's the finest hot pastrami sandwich in Los Angeles because they don't dare to claim that something like a hot pastrami sandwich could possibly be the best version of itself in a city where until recently you couldn't get anything resembling a New York bagel, and the only reason you can get one now is that New York bagels have deteriorated.

2   Langer's is a medium-sized place—it seats a hundred and thirty-five people—and it is decorated, although "decorated" is probably not the word that applies, in tufted brown vinyl. The view out the windows is of the intersection of Seventh and Alvarado and the bright-red-and-yellow signage of a Hispanic neighborhood—bode-

gas, check-cashing storefronts, and pawnshops. Just down the block is a spot notorious for being the place to go in L.A. if you need a fake I.D. The Rampart division's main police station, the headquarters of the city's second-most-recent police scandal, is a mile away. Even in 1947, when Langer's opened, the neighborhood was not an obvious place for an old-style Jewish delicatessen, but in the early nineties things got worse. Gangs moved in. The crime rate rose. The Langers—the founder, Al, now eighty-nine, and his son Norm, fifty-seven—were forced to cut the number of employees, close the restaurant nights and Sundays, and put coin-operated locks on the restroom doors. The opening of the Los Angeles subway system—one of its stops is half a block from the restaurant—has helped business slightly, as has the option of having your sandwich brought out to your car. But Langer's always seems to be just barely hanging on. If it were in New York, it would be a shrine, with lines around the block and tour buses standing double-parked outside. Pilgrims would come—as they do, for example, to Arthur Bryant's in Kansas City and Sonny Bryan's in Dallas—and they would report on their conversion. But in Los Angeles a surprising number of people don't even know about Langer's, and many of those who do wouldn't be caught dead at the corner of Seventh and Alvarado, even though it's not a particularly dangerous intersection during daytime hours.

3   Pastrami, I should point out for the uninitiated, is made from a cut of beef that is brined like corned beef, coated with pepper and an assortment of spices, and then smoked. It is characterized by two things. The first is that it is not something anyone's mother whips up and serves at home; it's strictly restaurant fare, and it's served exclusively as a sandwich, usually on Russian rye bread with mustard. The second crucial thing about pastrami is that it is almost never good. In fact, it usually tastes like a bunch of smoked rubber bands.

4   The Langers buy their pastrami from a supplier in Burbank. "When we get it, it's edible," Norm Langer says, "but it's like eating a racquetball. It's hard as a rock. What do we do with it? What makes us such wizards? The average delicatessen will take this piece of meat and put it into a steamer for thirty to forty-five minutes and warm it. But you've still got a hard piece of rubber. You haven't broken down the tissues. You haven't made it tender. We take that same piece of pastrami, put it into our steamer, and steam

it for almost three hours. It will shrink twenty-five to thirty per cent, but it's now tender—so tender it can't be sliced thin in a machine because it will fall apart. It has to be hand-sliced."

5   So: tender and hand-sliced. That's half the secret of the Langer's sandwich. The other secret is the bread. The bread is hot. Years ago, in the nineteen-thirties, Al Langer owned a delicatessen in Palm Springs, and, because there were no Jewish bakers in the vicinity, he was forced to bus in the rye bread. "I was serving day-old bread," Al Langer says, "so I put it into the oven to make it fresher. Hot crispy bread. Juicy soft pastrami. How can you lose?"

6   Today, Langer's buys its rye bread from a bakery called Fred's, on South Robertson, which bakes it on bricks until it's ten minutes from being done. Langer's bakes the loaf the rest of the way, before slicing it hot for sandwiches. The rye bread, faintly sour, perfumed with caraway seeds, lightly dusted with cornmeal, is as good as any rye bread on the planet, and Langer's puts about seven ounces of pastrami on it, the proper proportion of meat to bread. The resulting sandwich, slathered with Gulden's mustard, is an exquisite combination of textures and tastes. It's soft but crispy, tender but chewy, peppery but sour, smoky but tangy. It's a symphony orchestra, different instruments brought together to play one perfect chord. It costs eight-fifty and is, in short, a work of art.

Organization and Ideas

1. Ephron makes a claim in her first sentence and echoes it in the last two sentences of the final paragraph. Which of the two is the more valid and why?

2. What reasons can you think of for Ephron's delaying a definition of a pastrami sandwich till paragraph 3?

3. Paragraphs 4–6 describe how the restaurant creates a pastrami sandwich. What reasons can you give for Ephron's sequencing the paragraphs as she does?

4. What effect does Ephron achieve by contrasting the negative aspects of the restaurant with the positive ones of the sandwich?

5. To what extent does Ephron persuade you about the excellence of Langer's pastrami sandwiches?

Technique and Style

1. Ephron mentions New York City in paragraphs 1 and 2, along with Kansas City and Dallas. What does her mention of these other cities add to her image of Pastrami Expert?
2. The second sentence of paragraph 2 is quite long. Try breaking it up into two or more sentences. What is gained? Lost?
3. Ephron quotes Norm Langer in paragraph 4 and Al Langer in paragraph 5. What do the direct quotations add to the essay?
4. How effective is Ephron's concluding metaphor—the "symphony orchestra"?
5. What senses does Ephron appeal to? Which one predominates?

Suggestions for Writing

Journal

1. Assuming you were in Los Angeles, explain why you would or wouldn't have a pastrami sandwich at Langer's.
2. Based on the essay, analyze the kind of person Ephron appears to be. Use examples from the essay to support your views.

Essay

1. Most people have a favorite food or restaurant that they regard a "work of art." It may be the ultimate cheeseburger or BLT, and the restaurant may be a fast-food franchise or nondescript diner, but "It's the best!" Write your own essay in which you describe, explain, and analyze your choice. Possible topics:
   Burger
   Hot dog
   BLT
   Fried chicken
   Pizza
2. Sooner or later almost everyone is confronted with a vegetable or fruit or dish that challenges the imagination of the diner, perhaps an artichoke, avocado, kiwi, clam, or whole fish. Think about such a time and write an essay in which you describe the situation, explain how you dealt with it, and analyze what you thought about it.

Deep Cold

Verlyn Klinkenborg

Given his name, Verlyn Klinkenborg might more likely be the author of a Scandinavian cookbook than a relatively regular contributor to the New York Times' *editorial pages. But the title of his column— "The Rural Life"—accurately reflects his close relationship with nature.* Making Hay *(1986), his first book, takes his readers to Iowa, Minnesota, and Montana, and established him as a writer who lyrically depicts and admires the small details of living and working on small family farms.* The Last Fine Time *(1992) is very different, an exploration of immigrant life in Buffalo, New York, and its suburbs. The essay that follows finds him in both worlds, this time in Cambridge and Boston and on a farm in upstate New York. It is from his most recent book,* The Rural Life *(2003), a collection of his columns published in the* New York Times, *where the essay appeared in a section titled "January." If you are familiar with Thoreau or Emerson, you'll find them echoed in Klinkenborg's writing, which, according to* Publisher's Weekly, *is "much closer to poetry than essay." His essays have also appeared in the* New Yorker *and* Harper's.

> **What to Look For**   While much description says to the reader "Picture this!," Klinkenborg says "Feel this!" As you read the essay, keep track of the senses he appeals to and the feelings and atmosphere his images create.

1   If deep cold made a sound, it would be the scissoring and gnashing of a skater's blades against hard gray ice, or the screeching the snow sets up when you walk across it in the blue light of afternoon. The sound might be the stamping of feet at bus stops and train stations, or the way the almost perfect clarity of the audible world on an icy day is muted by scarves and mufflers pulled up over the face and around the ears.

2   But the true sound of deep cold is the sound of the wind. Monday morning, on the streets of Cambridge, Massachusetts, the windchill approached fifty below zero. A stiff northwest wind

rocked in the trees and snatched at cars as they idled at the curb. A rough rime had settled over that old-brick city the day before, and now the wind was sanding it smooth. It was cold of Siberian or Antarctic intensity, and I could feel a kind of claustrophobia settling in all over Boston. People went about their errands, only to cut them short instantly, turning backs to the gust and fleeing for cover.

3   It has been just slightly milder in New York. Furnace repairmen and oil-truck drivers are working on the memory of two hours' sleep. Swans in the smaller reservoirs brood on the ice, and in the swamps that line the railroad tracks in Dutchess Country, you can see how the current was moving when the cold snap brought it to a halt. The soil in windblown fields looks—and is—iron hard. It's all a paradox, a cold that feels absolutely rigid but which nonetheless seeps through ill-fitting windows, between clapboards, and along uninsulated pipe chases. People listen superstitiously to the sounds in their heating ducts, to the banging of their radiators, afraid of silence. They turn the keys in their cars with trepidation. It's an old world this cold week.

Organization and Ideas

1. What reasons can you find for Klinkenborg beginning his essay as he does?
2. The description covers urban and rural landscapes. Why might Klinkenborg have included both?
3. The essay implies a number of conflicts: people versus nature, city versus country, misery versus comfort, threat versus safety. Which is the most effective and why?
4. The subject of the essay is obvious—deep cold. What assertion is Klinkenborg making about it?
5. To what extent does Klinkenborg's idea of deep cold match your own?

Technique and Style

1. What verbs strike you as particularly apt and why?
2. Klinkenborg spells out a paradox in paragraph 3. Explain whether it is effective.
3. What examples can you find of appeals to the senses? Which sense predominates?

4. Only in paragraph 2 does Klinkenborg use first person, placing himself in a scene, yet, obviously, all the observations are his. To what extent is the description objective? Subjective?

5. How would you characterize the emotional tone of the essay: Reserved? Admiring? Fearful? What?

Suggestions for Writing

Journal

1. Fill in the blanks and expand: If _____ made a sound, it would be _____ .

2. How do the scenes Klinkenborg describes add up to "an old world" (paragraph 3)?

Essay

1. Klinkenborg's essay is one of many in which he depicts particular days in the various seasons. Think about a particular day in a particular season that stands out in your memory and describe it. Like Klinkenborg, you should appeal to the senses yet distance yourself from the scene. You may remember:

    A blistering summer day
    The first cutting of hay
    The most brilliant time of fall foliage
    An ice storm in winter
    The first thaw in the spring

2. Think about the times when you experienced the full force of nature—heat wave, flood, hailstorm, tornado, hurricane—and write an essay in which you analyze just how mighty that force was and its effect on people. Like Klinkenborg, try to observe and analyze.

The Bridge

Jason Holland

Almost everyone has a special place, either in the present or past, that represents any number of emotions, pleasure being first among them. For Jason Holland, that place was a bridge and the time was when he was in high school. He is now a student at Valley City State University in Valley City, North Dakota, having decided on attending VCSU because of the academic and athletic opportunities the university provided. When he began his first-semester composition course, he says that he was "somewhat skeptical of my writing skills, but began finding it was easy to write about memorable moments," particularly those spent with his friends in high school. He used "writing about these incidents as an outlet as well as a coping device" to accommodate himself to the difficulties of college life. One of the results is what he characterizes "a short, descriptive essay," "The Bridge." Noreen Braun, his instructor, reprinted the essay on a Web page devoted to what she titled as "Some Fine Student Writing from Composition I, Fall Semester, 1997."

What to Look For   If you are having a difficult time giving your reader a vivid picture of your scene, you might try writing down as many adjectives and adverbs about various objects or people that you associate with the place. After you have done this, then you can choose the most appropriate ones. That is what Jason Holland did when he was coming up with his descriptive essay about his adventures with his friends on a condemned bridge. As you read the essay look specifically at the detail he uses to enhance his essay.

1   I can see it now. The four of us sitting out on the wood bridge puffing on our cheap, Swisher cigars. The smoke rising above the rusty, cast iron sides and filtering up to the full moon above. As the moon reflects off the Goose River my friends and I sit and talk about everything from girls to UFO theories. We sit without a worry on our minds.

2   The bridge looks like it's something from a surreal movie with a midnight atmosphere. Located two miles out of town, it's hidden on a winding, gravel road that sometimes gets washed out if it rains heavily. Because of the lack of maintenance the bridge has old oak and maple trees leaning against it. The wood tiling on the bottom is spaced far apart, almost to the point where our feet could fall through.

3   When we were at the bridge we felt as though nothing could go wrong. We thought that all our problems and fears would go away if we stayed out there long enough. We felt as though our parents, teachers, and coaches had no control over us. We could talk about

anything and anyone without even thinking about the consequences. No one could touch us. We were like 1920 bootleg gangsters that the law couldn't catch up with. We were almost invincible
as we smoked our cigars and talked about our dreams and aspirations.

4   As we sat and smoked it felt as though we were the only people
on earth. The world revolved around us. It was like we could control the world while we were out at the bridge. It was a rickety, old
bridge, but it seemed to empower us to the point where we felt as
though we could control our own destiny. My friend who didn't do
well in school was a smarter and more insightful person when he
was at the bridge. My friend who wasn't good at athletics felt like
he was as good an athlete as any professional. My friend who didn't
have a girlfriend seemed like he was a savvy, babe magnet. The
bridge had the power to give us confidence.

5   The bridge was county property, but my friends and I felt like
we were the owners. It was a mutual relationship. We owned the
bridge, and the bridge owned us. On the long, cool summer nights
we knew that the bridge needed company so we would get our
cigars and take a ride down the long, windy road and leave our
problems behind. We sat out at the bridge for hours basking in the
sounds of an occasional swat of a mosquito, the cooing of an owl
in the distance, the splashing of a fish in the river, with the cool yet
comfortable, windless night.

6   I haven't yet found a place where I could be so much in my own
world and in my own element as I could when I was at the bridge.
Having my best friends and cheap cigars made me enjoy it even
more.

Organization and Ideas

1. Paragraph 1 tells you where the scene takes place and who is there.
   What else does it do?
2. Examine paragraphs 2–5 and in one or two words list a subject or main
   idea for each one. What progression do you find?
3. Considering the ideas you identified in question 2, what does the
   bridge represent to the writer?
4. State the thesis of the essay in your own words. Where in the essay
   does the writer place the thesis? How effective do you find that
   placement?
5. How important is it to have a place where you can "be in [your] own
   world and in [your] own element"?

Technique and Style

1. In a handbook of grammar and style, look up *sentence fragment* and then reexamine Holland's second and third sentences. What are they missing? Explain whether the two sentences are acceptable fragments.
2. If you vary the length of your sentences, you'll find that your prose moves more smoothly and is apt to be of greater interest to the reader. What evidence can you find that Holland uses this technique?
3. Reread paragraph 2. Which sentence functions as a topic sentence? What words in the other sentences are related to it?
4. Repetition can be effective or ineffective. Explain how you judge Holland's similar sentence beginnings in paragraph 3.
5. Reread paragraph 5 looking for details that appeal to the senses. What are they?

Suggestions for Writing

Journal

1. Imagine that you are the narrator of "The Bridge." What "problems and fears" would you be leaving behind?
2. Holland describes the bridge as looking like "something from a surreal movie with a midnight atmosphere." Think about places you know about that match that description and describe one of them.

Essay

1. Almost everyone has at least one "special place" that represents a particular mood or feeling, either positive or negative. To write an essay about such a place that holds meaning for you, think first about an emotion and then about the place you associate with it. Here's one list to consider, but other ideas will probably occur to you as well:

   comfort
   fear
   happiness
   excitement
   curiosity

   Once you've decided on a topic, then you can start accumulating details that will make your scene and the way you feel about it come alive for the reader.
2. Holland's essay deals with two strong human bonds—to place and to a sense of community. Choose one of the two and analyze its importance to you. Try to distance yourself from your subject by limiting your use of the first person *I* so that what you write is a general thought-piece rather than a narrative or personal essay.

El Hoyo

Mario Suarez

When Mario Suarez returned from four years in the Navy, he enrolled at the University of Arizona and found himself taking freshman English. The essay that follows was written for that class and so impressed his teacher, Ruth Keenan, that she not only encouraged him to take other writing courses but also to submit "El Hoyo" to the Arizona Quarterly, *where it was published. That was a long time ago (1947), but it started Suarez on a successful writing career; it is a rare anthology of Chicano literature that doesn't include at least one of Suarez's works.*

What to Look For   Like many writers, Suarez faces the problem of explaining the unfamiliar, but for Suarez the problem is compounded. Many of his readers do not know the meaning of *barrio,* nor are they familiar with Latino culture. Those who do know the terms may have negative associations with them. As you read his essay, note the techniques he uses to combat these problems. Also note how Suarez uses repetition effectively to lend emphasis to his description. Read Suarez's second paragraph out loud so you can hear the repetition more clearly.

1   From the center of downtown Tucson the ground slopes gently away to Main Street, drops a few feet, and then rolls to the banks of the Santa Cruz River. Here lies the section of the city known as El Hoyo. Why it is called El Hoyo is not very clear. In no sense is it a hole as its name would imply; it is simply the river's immediate valley. Its inhabitants are chicanos who raise hell on Saturday night and listen to Padre Estanislao on Sunday morning. While the term chicano is the short way of saying Mexicano, it is not restricted to the paisanos who came from old Mexico with the territory or the last famine to work for the railroad, labor, sing, and go on relief. Chicano is the easy way of referring to everybody. Pablo Gutíerrez married the Chinese grocer's daughter and now runs a meat department; his sons are chicanos. So are the sons of Killer Jones who

threw a fight in Harlem and fled to El Hoyo to marry Cristina Mendez. And so are all of them. However, it is doubtful that all these spiritual sons of Mexico live in El Hoyo because they love each other—many fight and bicker constantly. It is doubtful they live in El Hoyo because of its scenic beauty—it is everything but beautiful. Its houses are simple affairs of unplastered adobe, wood, and abandoned car parts. Its narrow streets are mostly clearings which have, in time, acquired names. Except for some tall trees which nobody has ever cared to identify, nurse, or destroy, the main things known to grow in the general area are weeds, garbage piles, dark-eyed chavalos, and dogs. And it is doubtful that the chicanos live in El Hoyo because it is safe—many times the Santa Cruz has risen and inundated the area.

2   In other respects living in El Hoyo has its advantages. If one is born with weakness for acquiring bills, El Hoyo is where the collectors are less likely to find you. If one has acquired the habit of listening to Octavio Perea's Mexican Hour in the wee hours of the morning with the radio on at full blast, El Hoyo is where you are less likely to be reported to the authorities. Besides, Perea is very popular and sooner or later to everyone "Smoke in the Eyes" is dedicated between the pinto beans and white flour commercials. If one, for any reason whatever, comes on an extended period of hard times, where, if not in El Hoyo, are the neighbors more willing to offer solace? When Teofila Malacara's house burned to the ground with all her belongings and two children, a benevolent gentleman carried through the gesture that made tolerable her burden. He made a list of 500 names and solicited from each a dollar. At the end of a month he turned over to the tearful but grateful señora $100 in cold cash and then accompanied her on a short vacation. When the new manager of a local store decided that no more chicanas were to work behind the counters, it was the chicanos of El Hoyo who, on taking their individually small but collectively great buying power elsewhere, drove the manager out and the girls returned to their jobs. When the Mexican Army was en route to Baja California and the chicanos found out that the enlisted men ate only at infrequent intervals, it was El Hoyo's chicanos who crusaded across town with pots of beans and trays of tortillas to meet the train. When someone gets married, celebrating is not restricted to the immediate friends of the couple. Everybody is invited. Anything calls for a celebration and a celebration calls for anything. On

Memorial Day there are no less than half a dozen good fights at the Riverside Dance Hall. On Mexican Independence Day more than one flag is sworn allegiance to amid cheers for the queen.

3   And El Hoyo is something more. It is this something more which brought Felipe Suarez back from the wars after having killed a score of Japanese with his body resembling a patchwork quilt to marry Julia Armijo. It brought Joe Zepeda, a gunner, . . . back to compose boleros. He has a metal plate for a skull. Perhaps El Hoyo is proof that those people exist, and perhaps exist best, who have as yet failed to observe the more popular modes of human conduct. Perhaps the humble appearance of El Hoyo justifies the indifferent shrug of those made aware of its existence. Perhaps El Hoyo's simplicity motivates an occasional chicano to move away from its narrow streets, babbling comadres and shrieking children to deny the bloodwell from which he springs and to claim the blood of a conquistador while his hair is straight and his face beardless. Yet El Hoyo is not an outpost of a few families against the world. It fights for no causes except those which soothe its immediate angers. It laughs and cries with the same amount of passion in times of plenty and of want.

4   Perhaps El Hoyo, its inhabitants, and its essence can best be explained by telling a bit about a dish called capirotada. Its origin is uncertain. But, according to the time and the circumstance, it is made of old, new or hard bread. It is softened with water and then cooked with peanuts, raisins, onions, cheese, and panocha. It is fired with sherry wine. Then it is served hot, cold, or just "on the weather" as they say in El Hoyo. The Sermeños like it one way, the Garcias another, and the Ortegas still another. While it might differ greatly from one home to another, nevertheless it is still capirotada. And so it is with El Hoyo's chicanos. While being divided from within and from without, like the capirotada, they remain chicanos.

Organization and Ideas

1. Examine the essay using the standard journalistic questions. Which paragraph describes *where* El Hoyo is? What paragraphs describe *who* lives there? What paragraph or paragraphs describe *how* they live? *Why* they live there?

2. All of the questions above lead to a larger one: *What* is El Hoyo? Given the people and place, and how and why they live there, what statement is the author making about El Hoyo?

3. The essay ends with an analogy, and toward the end of paragraph 4, Suarez spells out some details of the analogy. What other characteristics of capirotada correspond to those of chicanos? Where in the essay do you find evidence for your opinion?

4. How would you describe the movement in the essay? Does it move from the general to the particular? From the particular to the general? What reasons can you give for the author's choice of direction?

5. It's obvious that Suarez likes and appreciates El Hoyo, but to what extent, if any, does he gloss over its negative qualities?

Technique and Style

1. The introductory paragraph achieves coherence and cohesion through the author's use of subtle unifying phrases. Trace Suarez's use of "it is doubtful." How often does the phrase occur? Rewrite the sentences to avoid using the phrase. What is lost? Gained?

2. What key words are repeated in paragraph 2? Why does he repeat them?

3. Paragraph 2 gives many examples of the advantages of living in El Hoyo. List the examples in the order in which they appear. The first two can be grouped together under the idea of El Hoyo as a sanctuary, a place where people aren't bothered. What other groupings does the list of examples suggest? What principle appears to have guided the ordering of the examples?

4. Why might the author have chosen not to use either first or second person? What is gained by using "one"?

Suggestions for Writing

Journal

1. Write a journal entry explaining why you would or would not like to live in El Hoyo. Use examples from the essay to flesh out your reasons.

2. Suarez compares the dish capirotada to El Hoyo, developing it as a metaphor. Think of a metaphor that would work for your neighborhood or for one of your classes. Write a paragraph or two developing your comparison and you will probably discover that using metaphor may also make you see the familiar in a new way.

Essay

1. If you live in an ethnic neighborhood, you can use the essay as a close model. If you do not, you can still use the essay as a general model by choosing a topic that combines people and place. Suggestions:
     family ritual at Christmas, Hanukkah, or Ramadan
     family ritual at Thanksgiving
     dinner at a neighborhood restaurant
     busy time at the university student center
2. Write an essay analyzing and explaining why you would or would not like to live in El Hoyo. Use examples from the essay to flesh out your reasons.

Left Sink

Ellery Akers

Ellery Akers is a writer, naturalist, and poet who lives near San Francisco. Knocking on the Earth, *her first book of poems, was published in 1989 by Wesleyan University Press, and her poems have been published in the* American Poetry Review, *the* Harvard Review, *and* Ploughshares *as well as other poetry journals. As you read the essay, you'll discover that her prose reflects a number of characteristics of poetry—imagery, concise language, and an acute eye for detail. You'll also see that the line between description and narration is a fine one. The essay won the 1990 Sierra Club Award for nature writing and was published the same year in* Sierra. *While the essay is longer than most in this book, you'll find its length is deceptive. You'll read it quickly.*

What to Look For   Writers who deal with familiar subjects face the challenge of making the familiar new or unusual, and to do that they rely on concrete detail. Ellery Akers knows her readers are familiar with bathrooms and frogs, but she goes on to individualize this particular bathroom and the frog she names Left Sink. Some writers might be content to state "The frog was small." Akers, however, takes the word small and gives it substance, "no bigger than a penny, and his round, salmon-colored toes stuck out like tiny soupspoons."

Remember as you write that one person's idea of a general term, such as *small,* may not be the same as another's, so it's best to use concrete details to show just what you mean.

1   The first time I saw Left Sink, I was brushing my teeth and almost spit on him by mistake. I wasn't expecting to find a frog in a Park Service bathroom, but there he was, hopping out of the drain and squatting on the porcelain as casually as if he were sitting beside a pond.

2   He was a small green tree frog, no bigger than a penny, and his round, salmon-colored toes stuck out like tiny soupspoons. For a few minutes I stared into his gold eyes, each pupil floating in the middle like a dark seed.

3   I was so close I could see his throat pulse, but I was probably too close, for he looked at me fearfully and leaped onto the silver "C" of the cold-water faucet.

4   Then he must have thought better of it, for he jumped down again, and sat, hunched over, by the soap. He kept making nervous little hops toward the safety of the drain, but my looming face was obviously in the way, so I ducked below the basin for a moment, and when I looked again he was descending into the hole, head first.

5   Feeling I'd disturbed his evening hunt, I decided to make amends. I grubbed around the floor for a dead moth, found one (though it was a little dried up), and offered it to the hole. The wing slanted into the drain, but nothing happened. I thought perhaps he'd hopped back down into the pipe. Trying to find something a little more appealing, I picked around the window sills until I discovered a really decent-looking moth, pushed it up to the drain, and waited. After a few minutes, I got discouraged and walked away. When I turned back to sneak one last look, I found both moths had vanished.

6   The next day was so hot I forgot Left Sink completely. It is always hot in the California chaparral in September, especially in the Gabilan Mountains. I spent the afternoon in the shade, lying on the cool pebbles of a dry wash and looking over my field notes. I had been camping for weeks, studying birds, and by now I had gotten used to the feeling of expectation in the landscape.

7   Everything seemed to be waiting for rain. The streambeds were dry, the fields were dry, and when the buckeye leaves hissed in the wind they sounded like rattlesnakes. Ravens flew overhead, croaking, their wings flapping loudly in the air, and the rocks baked. Once in a while a few thirsty finches fluttered up to a seep in a cliff and sipped from a damp clump of algae.

8   I leaned against the cool flank of a boulder and fanned myself with my hat. From far away I could hear the staccato drill of a Nuttall's woodpecker.

9   All the animals had some way of coping with the heat. The wrentits could last for several weeks without drinking. The deer found beds of shade and waited patiently until evening. Even the trees adapted. Though I couldn't see it, I knew that somewhere beneath my boots, 100 feet down, the root of a digger pine was twisting along a crevice in the bedrock, reaching far below the surface to tap into the permanent water.

10   And the frogs—the normal ones—were sleeping away the summer and fall, huddled in some moist spot in the ground in a kind of hot-weather hibernation.

11   That night, when I went back to the bathroom, I discovered Left Sink had a neighbor. Even before I turned on the water in the right-hand basin, I noticed a second frog, and when I stepped back to look at both of them in their respective sinks, I started to laugh: They reminded me of a couple of sober, philosophical old monks peering out of their cells.

12   Overhead was a third frog, puffy and well-fed, squatting on top of the fluorescent lights, surrounded by tattered moths. Light Buddha, I would call him.

13   In the world of the bathroom the light shelf was a delicatessen of the highest order. Light Buddha sat there night after glorious night, lazily snapping up moths as they fluttered past. The other two frogs seemed content to stake out the sinks, which weren't quite as dependable a food source, though they weren't bad. Almost every night I found a damp moth thrashing around in one of the basins, one little flopping death after another, leaving a trail of scales behind.

14   Right Sink was extremely shy, and spent most of his time crouched far back in the pipe. Usually I saw his gold eyes shining in the darkness, but that was all. Left Sink was more of an adventurer, and explored the whole bathroom, darting behind the mirror,

splatting onto the porcelain, hopping on the window sills, leaping on the toilet, and climbing the slippery painted walls toe pad by toe pad.

15   From time to time I was tempted to pick him up as he was climbing. But I didn't think it would be fair; I knew this geometrical universe, and he didn't. Besides, there was no place for him to hide on those smooth, painted bricks, so I let him be.

16   I was amazed at how few people noticed Left Sink, even when he was sitting on top of the faucet. Kids saw him right away, though, and I worried sometimes that one night a little girl would pop him into a jar and take him home to some confining terrarium.

17   Also, he stood out. Even though tree frogs can change color in ten minutes, there was nothing in Left Sink's repertoire that could possibly match white paint; the best he could do was a sickly pink.

18   I could always tell if he had just emerged from the drain because he would still be a murky gray-green. As the evening wore on he got paler and paler. Once I couldn't find him for half an hour. Finally I caught sight of him over my head. Plopped on a narrow ledge, he looked like a pale pebble in all that metal and paint. I climbed onto the toilet for a better look. To my horror he began hopping along the ledge, which was no wider than half an inch. It was a ten-foot fall to the floor—for a frog that small, an abyss. He bounded past me, his grainy throat quivering.

19   He headed toward a swarm of moths and flies that circled the fluorescent lights. A fly drifted down from the glare; Left Sink, his pink mouth flashing, snapped it up.

20   I was never quite sure just how skittish he really was. Sometimes he tolerated my watching him, sometimes he didn't. I got in the habit of sidling up to the plumbing, bent over so as not to be seen, and I must have looked pretty peculiar. One night a woman came into the bathroom and caught me hunched over like Quasimodo, staring intently at the drains, my hands full of dead moths.

21   "Left Sink! Right Sink!" I was saying. "Got a little treat for you guys!"

22   The woman bolted out the door.

23   For the next few weeks I checked on the frogs every morning and evening. Sometimes when I saw Left Sink skidding down a length of plastic, unable to hold on in spite of his adhesive toe pads, I worried. I couldn't help thinking there was something un-natural about a frog in a bathroom.

24   Of course, I knew there were a few oddballs that *had* managed to live with us in our artificial world, but they were mostly insects. One year in school I had learned about the larvae of petroleum flies: They lived in the gunk of oil fields, so numerous at times that, according to my textbook, they imparted "a shimmering effect to the surface of the oil." Their world was oil; if you deprived them of it, took them out and cleaned them off, they'd curl up and die in less than a day.

25   In that same class I'd learned that furniture beetles live in our table legs, and occasionally, in wooden spoons; drugstore beetles float happily in bottles of belladonna, mating, pupating, dying. We have cheese mites in our cheese, and flour mites in our flour.

26   As far as I knew no one had ever done any research on frogs and plumbing. Luckily, I always carried a trunkful of books and field guides in my car, and one night I flipped through every book I had to see if I could find any instances where humans and animals—wild ones—had actually gotten along. Arthur Cleveland Bent said that wrens nested in old clothes in barns, and swallows on moving trains. Edwin Way Teale said he had once read about a pigeon using rubber bands and paper clips in her nest on a window ledge off Times Square. One year, he wrote, a thrush spent the entire winter in a florist's shop on Madison Avenue, flitted about between the iced gladiolas and roses, and flew away in spring.

27   But no one mentioned anything about frogs.

28   Actually, considering the drought, Left Sink had a pretty good set-up. It was already October and still no rain. Once in a while a few drops would plop into the dirt and gravel, and I would catch a whiff of wet dust, soaked cheat grass, and buckwheat. But that was all.

29   All the other frogs were holed up in the dirt, huddled in a moist crack or an abandoned gopher hole, waiting for the first rains of winter to wake them up. There were probably a few hiding in the field next to Left Sink's bathroom, their eyelids closed, their toes pulled under them to conserve moisture, unmoving, barely breathing, their heartbeats almost completely stilled. If I dug them up they would look like small stones.

30   One night just before I was about to leave, I had a nightmare. It was a dream I had had many times, a dream of a city so polluted the air rose in black plumes above the granite and cement. I was at the entrance of a tunnel. Inside I could hear a whoosh of air:

Millions of butterflies were flashing in the dark, thousands of ducks, eagles, sparrows, their wings making a vast rustling as they flew off and vanished.

31   I heard a low shuffling. After a while I realized it was the sound of feet: the slow trudge of bears, the pad of badgers, the pattering of foxes, the rasp of a hundred million beetles, rabbits, ants, mice. I looked around, panicked, to see if any animals were left. There were still cockroaches scuttling over the window sills. There were pigeons, flies, starlings. I named them over and over in a kind of chant: the adaptable, the drab, the ones who could live with us, who had always lived with us.

32   A fox coughed close to my camp in the middle of the nightmare and woke me up. I unzipped the tent and looked out at the stars: Rigel, Algol, clear, cold, and changeless. A golden-crowned sparrow chirped from a nearby branch, then sputtered off into silence. For a while I tried to stay awake, but soon drifted off.

33   The next morning huge bluish clouds rolled across the sky. A couple of ravens sailed past the cliff in front of me. One of them jackknifed its wings, plummeted straight down, and then, at the last minute, unfolded them and flapped away. It was still early, but when I reached the bathroom it had already been cleaned. It reeked of ammonia, and a mop and bucket leaned against the door.

34   I rinsed off my face, brushed my hair, and looked sleepily into the drains. As usual, Right Sink was huddled far back into the dark pipe; he retreated still further when I bent over.

35   Left Sink, however, was gone. I wondered if he had slipped behind the mirror, or had come up in the world and was squatting above with Light Buddha. The shelf was empty. I looked on the window sill—not there either.

36   It was not until I opened the door to the toilet that I found him. There, in the center of the ammonia-filled bowl, his green bloated body turning gray, was Left Sink, splayed out in the milky liquid, dead. Floating in front of him was a dead damselfly. I suppose he must have jumped in after his prey, convinced he was at the edge of a strange-looking pond, his toe pads gripping the cold, perfectly smooth surface of the porcelain.

37   His skin looked curdled, and it occurred to me he might have been there all morning waiting to die. Then I remembered that frogs breathe through their skin; it must have been a hard, stinging death, but a quick one.

38   I flushed him down, wishing I could think of something to say as he made his way through the pipes and rolled out to the septic tank, some acknowledgment of the link between my kind and his, but I couldn't think of anything except that I would miss him, which was true.

39   When I opened the door, a couple of nervous towhees blundered into the bushes. It was beginning to rain.

Organization and Ideas

1. The story of Left Sink unfolds slowly. Which paragraphs provide the introduction? What reasons can you give for your choice?
2. An essay of this length tends to group paragraphs around a topic sentence or main idea rather than have a topic sentence for each paragraph. What groupings can you identify? What ideas tie those paragraphs together?
3. Paragraphs 30 and 31 stand out because they strike a very different note from the rest of the essay. What function do they serve?
4. Akers says "there was something unnatural about a frog in a bathroom" (paragraph 23). What does she imply in that paragraph and elsewhere about the relationship between humans and nature?
5. Many essays have an explicit thesis, one that you can spot in a complete sentence. Others, however, have an implied thesis, one that the writer suggests and the reader must deduce. That is the case with Akers' essay. What do you find to be its thesis?
6. Most people would find it difficult to cultivate affection for a frog, but that's what Akers tries to do. How well does she succeed?

Technique and Style

1. What does Akers think and feel about Left Sink? What details can you find to support your opinion?
2. What details can you find that lead to the conclusion that Akers is a naturalist?
3. Unlike many more formal essays, Akers uses lots of short paragraphs. Look up types of paragraphs in your handbook. What justification can you find for short paragraphs?
4. Akers' choice of verbs helps create the fast pace of the essay and its readability. Find a sentence that uses unusual verbs and rewrite it, substituting other verbs. What is gained? Lost?
5. At various places in the essay, Akers refers to rain or the lack of it. What does that contribute to the essay?

Suggestions for Writing

Journal

1. The tone of an essay can be tricky, particularly if it appeals to emotion. To pinpoint Akers' tone, explain how you feel about the frog at the start of the essay, in the middle, and at the end.

2. Take a moment to jot down all the words you associate with the word *frog*. Looking at your list, mark the associations according to whether they are positive, negative, or neutral. Then make another list of the adjectives you think Akers would use for Left Sink. What differences do you find between your list and Akers'?

Essay

1. Day-to-day life is apt to be full of contrasts, though not usually so striking as a frog in a bathroom. See how many contrasts you can spot in the course of a day when you're looking for them. Jot down what you see, and then choose from your notes to work the contrast into a descriptive essay. Like Akers' essay, yours should have a thesis, either implied or explicit. Suggestions:

   at a beach, look for a fully dressed person

   in a library, look for someone who is nervous or loud

   at a film, look for someone who has brought a baby

   in a cafeteria, look for someone who is studying

2. Write an essay in which you analyze your response to "Left Sink." Use examples and quotations from the essay to support your points, but remember to analyze any quotation you use rather than letting it speak for itself.

ADDITIONAL WRITING ASSIGNMENTS

Using Description

1. Describe a person so that you convey the person's character: friend, family member, student, teacher, coworker.
2. Describe a place so that you create a specific point about it: neighborhood, workplace, classroom, where you live, restaurant.
3. Describe a job so that you communicate exactly what it's like: part-time, summer, indoors, outdoors, household chore.
4. Describe a favorite article of clothing so that your attachment to it comes across to your reader: tee shirt, blue jeans, hat, running shoes, top.

Evaluating the Essays

1. The authors of "A Sandwich" and "Deep Cold" rely on descriptive language to convince their readers about their subjects. Ephron wants you to lust after one of Langer's pastrami sandwiches, and Klinkenborg wants you to feel that deep cold. Write an essay in which you compare the two pieces to determine which is the more effective. Use evidence from the essays to support your point.
2. Description is often used to bring scenes and events to life in such a way that the unfamiliar becomes familiar. That is the challenge facing the authors of "El Hoyo" and "Left Sink." Not many readers would know El Hoyo or a similar Chicano neighborhood, nor have many observed the life of a small frog in a sink. Reread the two essays noting the ways the writers depict their subjects and what they think about them. Which does the better job of describing the unusual?
3. Both "Deep Cold" and "Left Sink" examine various aspects of nature. Reread the two essays, looking for how the authors treat nature: What examples of nature are they writing about? What are their attitudes toward them? What is each writer saying and implying about nature? Consider your own relationship with nature and write an essay in which you compare your own views to those of Klinkenborg and Akers.

4. Think about the idea of community that is suggested by "The Bridge" and "El Hoyo." How would you define each writer's concept of community? How important is it? Who is involved in it? What values do those in that community share? What emotions are included? Which of the two is closer to your own idea of community? Write an essay in which you analyze your own definition of the word *community* and how your concept differs from those of Holland and Suarez.

On Using
Narration

2

Whether prompted by the child's "Tell me a story" or the adult's "What happened?" **narration** supplies much of our entertainment and information. But anyone who has asked "What happened?" only to be overwhelmed with every detail knows that telling everything can blunt the point and bore the listener. Effective narration takes more than telling a story; it calls for compressing and reshaping experience so that the listener or reader relives it with you and is left with a particular point. Shaping narrative draws on some of the same skills used in description: keen observation, careful selection of details, and coherent sequencing. But with a narrative you must go a step further: you must present a conflict and its resolution. A story with no point is indeed pointless; one with no conflict is no kind of story at all.

Often the narrative and the subject are the same: if you are writing about what happened to you when lightning struck your house, what happened is the subject of your narrative. Frequently, however, a writer chooses narrative to introduce or to conclude an essay or perhaps to do both, thus building a narrative framework. Or perhaps you would opt for narrative to emphasize a particular point. An essay that explains the dangers of toxic waste may be made more effective if it starts with a brief narrative of what happens at a place where pollution threatens the area and its residents; an essay on Los Angeles and its smog, for example, might begin with the story of an asthma attack. A paper on the same subject that argues for stricter federal and state controls may end by predicting what might happen without tougher regulation. The essays in this chapter, however, rely on narration for their primary structure. All present conflicts, build to a point, and spring from personal experience—from the something that happened.

Audience and Purpose

No one tells a story for the sake of telling a story, at least no one who wants to be listened to. Most of us will use a narrative to explain something, or to argue a point, or perhaps to entertain. If you think of a journal, the concepts of narration, audience, and purpose may become clearer. If you've ever kept a journal, then you realize that even though *you* are the audience, much of what you write may not make much sense later. It does, of course, right after you finish the journal entry, but two months or two years down the line, you can no longer supply the details from your memory. "Had a terrible argument," you might write, but unless you explain what the argument was about, you may be mystified when you reread that entry. And had you told the whole story behind the quarrel, you might have found that you could muster even more ammunition to support your side than you did in the heat of battle. In that case, you would not only have written about an argument, you would also have written one.

Much of what people write in journals, however, has explanation and entertainment as the goals. Writing in a journal helps many of us think through problems or events. Essentially, we are reliving the incident or situation so that we may examine and comprehend it more clearly: we retell our stories to understand them. A seemingly simple question (such as "Why did I feel so _____?") calls for a narrative that provides the context. Often, however, we record an event simply because it gave us pleasure, pleasure that we want to be able to relive, once as it is written and again and again as we reread it.

The need for details increases as the distance between the reader and the subject grows. Yet there are always general experiences held in common. Say, for example, you are writing an essay based on something that happened to you in high school. And say you went to a small, all-male Catholic high school in Chicago. You might well wonder how you can make your narrative speak to a general readership, people who attended public, private, or religious schools, schools large and small, rural and urban, some single sex but most coed. Big differences, yes, but when you start thinking about details, you may find yourself turning to description to tap into shared experience—the blurred hum and jangle of students gathered together before a bell rings, the stale, dusty smell of chalk, the squeal of rubber-soled shoes on a waxed floor.

Emotion also speaks across differences. Anyone who has ever been to school knows the panic of being called on by a teacher when you don't even know the question, much less the answer. Moments of praise are equally memorable, whether it be for a point scored on a test or on a basketball court. Joy, despair, fear, elation, anguish, frustration, boredom, laughter, embarrassment—all these and an almost infinite number of other emotions are interwoven in narratives, no matter what the topic, making the topic more interesting because the reader has experienced the same feeling.

Who, What, Where, When, How, Why

These are the standard questions used in journalism, and they are important in narrative essays as well. *What happened?* That's the essential question for narrative, and you'll probably find that the greater part of your essay supplies the answer. *How* and *why* will probably figure in as well, and *who* is obviously essential. But it's easy to neglect *where* and *when.*

If you think of both *where* and *when* as the **setting,** as ways to set the scene, you can remember them more easily and perhaps put them to good use. An essay that relates the tale of a job interview that began as a disaster and ended as a success, for example, might begin by describing the writer as a night person, barely human before 11 A.M. The time of the interview? Nine o'clock. Sharp. The office is impersonal to the point of being cell-like, and the interviewer is so buttoned into his three-piece suit that it looks like armor. Add to those descriptions so that the reader gets the impression that the interview itself will make the Spanish Inquisition look like the first Woodstock, and the writer will have set the tone for the essay as well as built up the readers' interest in what will happen next, the meat of the essay.

Conflict

Narratives are structured around a **conflict.** In its simplest form, conflict is *x* versus *y,* Superman versus the Penguin, the Roadrunner versus Wily Coyote. But rarely does conflict exist in such a clear-cut way. Put real people in place of any of those terms, and you begin to understand that what seemed so simple is not; the defense versus the prosecution, a Republican candidate versus a Democrat—these conflicts are complex. The issues become even more complex when you substitute ideas, such as reality versus illusion, a distinction that even a postcard can blur (how many of us have been disappointed when a scene didn't live up to its photograph?). Even distinguishing good from evil isn't always clear, as the debates over capital punishment and abortion constantly remind us. When a writer explores the complexity involved in a conflict, the essay gains depth and substance, making the reader think. That exploration can be direct, such as naming the opposing forces, or indirect, implying them.

The conflict that occurs in narrative essays is of two kinds and many layers. If, for instance, you were to write about leaving home for the first time—whether you were headed off to college, to the army, or just off—your initial conflict might have been **internal:** Should you go or should you stay? But it might have been **external** as well—what your parents wanted you to do versus what *you* wanted to do. And the conflict was probably also one of ideas—of freedom versus constraints, independence versus dependence.

And then if you generalize about your experience, using first person sparingly, you'll forge an even stronger link to your readers who have experienced similar conflicts. By minimizing first person, you'll also be writing the kind of prose expected in other college courses, prose that focuses more on the subject than the writer.

Point of View

A not-so-obvious question about any narrative you're about to write is "Who tells it?" This question identifies the **point of view,** the perspective from which the narrative is related. Probably the first pronoun that comes to mind is *I,* first-person singular, and that's a good choice if you want your readers to identify with you and your angle on the narrative you're relating. When a reader sees first person, an automatic psychological identification takes place, one that allows the reader to look through the writer's eyes. That sort of identification is strongest if you, as narrator, are part of the action. Obviously, there's a huge difference between "I was there" and "I heard about it."

But using first person can be a hazard, and that's why at some point in some classroom, you have probably been warned off using *I.* There are at least three reasons: it's easy to overuse the pronoun; it can modify your purpose in a way you hadn't intended; and it can lead to an overly informal tone. If you were to take a look at your first draft for an essay you wrote using *I,* odds are you used it too frequently. The result is apt to be short, choppy sentences that are similar in structure—subject (*I*) followed by a verb and its complement (the word or words that complete the sense of the verb). That's fine for a first draft, and you can revise your way out of the problem. You *need* to revise because too many *I*'s can shift the aim of your essay away from exposition or argument to self-expression; what becomes important is you, not your subject. Your tone may also change, becoming more informal than the assignment calls for, which is why you don't see many research papers that use first person.

Choosing to relate the narrative from the position of *he* or *she* (rarely *they*) puts more distance between the subject and the reader. Think of the difference between "I fell out of the window" and "He fell out of the window." With the latter, the reader's sympathies are at one remove. That's not the case with the second person, *you. You* is direct and that's what makes it a somewhat slippery choice. If you're going to use a second-person point of view, make sure the reader understands exactly who is meant by *you.* Many a teacher has been stopped short when reading an essay that has a sentence such as "When you graduate, you'll start looking for a job that can turn into a career"; if that sentence occurred in an essay on surviving an important job interview, its author had too narrow an audience in mind, one composed only of classmates and ignoring everyone else interested in the topic—including the teacher. One way around that problem is to specify the audience in your paper. "All of us who are now in college worry about jobs" tells the reader just who the audience is, and the teacher then reads the essay from the perspective of a college student.

Organization and Ideas

Narratives often begin with the setting, which is the context for the conflict, then establish the nature of the conflict and move toward its resolution. Setting, conflict, and resolution all reinforce the essay's thesis, one that can be explicit or implicit. If the thesis is explicit, it's apt to occur in the introduction; sometimes, however, the writer will reserve it for the conclusion. That kind of placement puts an extra burden on the writer, in that everything in the essay must build to the conclusion. If the organization isn't tight, the reader wonders where the story is going; with a delayed thesis, the reader needs to have the feeling that the story is going somewhere, even though the final destination isn't apparent till the very end.

With narrative essays, as with short stories, the thesis is often implied and the reader must deduce it. If you opt for an implied thesis, make sure that the reader can easily identify your subject and then, without too much effort, move on to infer your thesis. The question that the reader needs to ask is "What is the writer saying about the subject?" The answer, phrased as a complete sentence, is the thesis.

One way to control what the reader infers is to work with the narrative's chronology. The sequence of events can be shaped to emphasize different elements. It may help to list the most important incidents in the narrative on a scrap of paper; then you can review them to check that each one is essential and to figure out the best order in which to present them. Writers often disrupt exact chronology, opting for dramatic placement over actual time sequence. The **flashback** is a technique that allows the writer to drop from the present into the past and bring in an event that occurred prior to the narrative's action. You may be most familiar with this device from seeing it in films, the moment when the camera fades out on a scene and then fades into a past event.

You can also reinforce your thesis, implicit or explicit, by underscoring the relationship between what happens and where it happens. If the two are incongruous, for example, then the resulting irony will probably emphasize your main point. A narrative of the job interview that began badly but ended well, for example, may use the turn from bad to good to imply that "all's well that ends well."

Useful Terms

Conflict An element essential to narrative. Conflict involves pitting one force, a force that may be represented by a person or a physical object or abstract concept, against another.

External conflict Conflict that is outside of a person in the narrative though it may involve that person, as in St. George versus the Dragon.

Internal conflict Conflict that takes place within a person, as in "Should I or should I not."

Flashback A break in the narrative that takes the reader to a scene or event that occurred earlier.

Narration Narration tells a story, emphasizing what happened.

Point of view In essays, point of view usually refers to the writer's use of personal pronouns. These pronouns control the perspective flow from which the work is written. For example, if the writer uses *I* or *we* (first-person pronouns), the essay will have a somewhat subjective tone because the reader will tend to identify with the writer. If the writer depends primarily on *he, she, it,* or *they* (third-person pronouns), the essay will have a somewhat objective tone because the reader will be distanced from the writer. Opting for *you* (second person) can be a bit tricky in that *you* can mean you the reader, quite particular, or you a member of a larger group, fairly general. In both cases, *you* brings the reader into the text.

Setting   The *where* and *when* in the narrative, its physical context.

POINTERS FOR USING NARRATION

Exploring the Topic

1. **What point do you want to make?** What is the subject of your narrative? What assertion do you want your narrative to make about the subject? Is your primary purpose to inform, to persuade, or to entertain?
2. **What happened?** What are the events involved in the narrative? When does the action start? Stop? Which events are crucial?
3. **Why and how did it happen?** What caused the events? How did it cause them?
4. **Who or what was involved?** What does the reader need to know about the characters? What do the characters look like? Talk like? How do they think? How do others respond to them?
5. **What is the setting for your story?** What does the reader need to know about the setting? What features are particularly noteworthy? How can they best be described?
6. **When did the story occur?** What tense will be most effective in relating the narrative?
7. **What was the sequence of events?** What happened when? Within that chronology, what is most important: time, place, attitude?
8. **What conflicts were involved?** What levels of conflict exist? Is there any internal conflict?
9. **What is the relationship between the narrator and the action?** Is the narrator a participant or an observer? What is the attitude of the narrator toward the story? What feelings should the

narrator evoke from the reader? What should be the attitude of the reader toward the narrative? What can be gained by using first person? Second person? Third person?

Drafting the Paper

1. **Know your reader.** Try to second-guess your reader's initial attitude toward your narrative so that if it is not what you want it to be, you can choose your details to elicit the desired reaction. A reader can be easily bored, so keep your details to the point and your action moving. Play on similar experiences your reader may have had or on information you can assume is widely known.

2. **Know your purpose.** If you are writing to inform, make sure you provide enough information to carry your point. If you are writing to persuade, work on how you present yourself and your thesis so that the reader will be favorably inclined to adopt your viewpoint. If you are writing to entertain, keep your tone in mind. A humorous piece, for instance, can and probably will vary from chuckle to guffaw to belly laugh. Make sure you're getting the right kind of laugh in the right place.

3. **Establish the setting and time of the action.** Use descriptive details to make the setting vivid and concrete. Keep in mind the reaction you want to get from your reader, and choose your details accordingly. If, for instance, you are writing a narrative that depicts your first experience with fear, describe the setting in such a way that you prepare the reader for that emotion. If the time the story took place is important, bring it out early.

4. **Set out the characters.** When you introduce a character, immediately identify the person with a short phrase such as "Anne, my sister." If a character doesn't enter the narrative until midpoint or so, make sure the reader is prepared for the entrance so that the person doesn't appear to be merely plopped in. If characterization is important to the narrative, use a variety of techniques to portray the character, but make sure whatever you use is consistent with the impression you want to create. You can depict a person directly—through appearance, dialogue, and actions—as well as indirectly—through what others say and think and how they act toward the person.

(Continued)

5. **Clarify the action.** Narration is set within strict time limits. Make sure the time frame of your story is set out clearly. Within that time limit, much more action occurred than you will want to use in your narrative. Pick only the high points so that every action directly supports your thesis. Feel free to tinker with the action, sacrificing a bit of reality for the sake of your point.

6. **Sharpen the plot.** Conflict is essential to narration, so be sure your lines of conflict are clearly drawn. Keeping conflict in mind, review the action you have decided to include so that the plot and action support each other.

7. **Determine the principle behind the sequence of events.** Given the action and plot you have worked out, determine what principle should guide the reader through the events. Perhaps time is the element you want to stress, perhaps place, perhaps gradual change. No matter what you choose, make sure that the sequence has dramatic tension so that it builds to the point you want to make.

8. **Choose an appropriate point of view.** Your choice of grammatical point of view will depend on what attitude you wish to take toward your narrative and your audience. If you can make your point more effectively by distancing yourself from the story, you will want to use *he, she,* or *they.* On the other hand, if you can make your point most effectively by being in the story, use first person and then decide whether you want to be *I* the narrator only or *I* the narrator who is also directly involved in the story.

9. **Make a point.** The action of the narrative should lead to a conclusion, an implicit or explicit point that serves as the thesis of the piece. If explicit, the thesis can appear in a single sentence or it can be inferred from several sentences, either in the introduction or conclusion of the essay. Ask yourself if everything in the narrative ties into the thesis.

Designer of Audio CD Packaging Enters Hell

Steve Martin

Anyone who has watched television or been to the movies in the last few years is familiar with the wacky world of Steve Martin. Best known as a comedian, he is also becoming a familiar name to the readers of the New Yorker, *where his writing often appears in the "Shouts & Murmurs" slot. Martin got his start in television as a writer, turning out material for Sonny and Cher and the Smothers Brothers, among many others. From there, he went on to stand-up comedy and made frequent and memorable appearances on* Saturday Night Live *as well as various talk shows. More recently, he starred in dramatic as well as comic films and is also the author of* Picasso at the Lapin Agile, *a play that opened off-Broadway in 1995,* Shopgirl *(2001), a novel, and* Pure Drivel *(1999), a collection of short pieces, some of which were published in the* New Yorker. *Firmly grounded in the absurd, his comic sense runs from slapstick to sophistication, both of which can be found in the essay that follows, one published in the April 19, 1999, issue of the* New Yorker.

What to Look For   Dialogue is often used in narrative writing because it adds a sense of realism and also provides variety. As you read Martin's essay, keep track of who is speaking and note how the dialogue matches the speaker. Also keep track of how Martin breaks up a quoted sentence so that the emphasis is right where he wants it. That's a technique that can work well any time you use dialogue.

1   The burning gates of Hell were opened and the designer of CD packaging entered to the Devil's fanfare. "We've been wanting him down here for a long time," The One of Pure Evil said to his infernal minions, "but we decided to wait, because he was doing such good work above, wrapping the CDs with cellophane and that sticky tape strip. Ask him to dinner and be sure to invite the computer-manual people too."

2   The Devil vanished, missing the warm display of affection offered the inventor. "Beelzebub himself opened a nasty cut on his finger trying to unwrap a Streisand best-of," whispered an imp. A thick snake nuzzled closer, and wrapped itself around the inventor's leg. "He used to be enamored of the remote-control people, with their tiny little buttons jammed together, and their enigmatic abbreviations," the snake said, "but now all he ever talks about is you, you, you. Come on, let's get you ready for dinner. We can talk about your assignment later."

3   As the snake led the way to the dressing halls of Hell, a yearning, searching look came over its face. "How did you do it?" the snake asked. "You know, invent the packaging? Everyone wants to know."

4   The inventor, his feet comfortably aflame, and flattered by all the recognition, relaxed into his surroundings. "The original plastic CD 'jewel box' was just too damn easy to get into," he explained. "I mean, if we're going to prevent consumer access, for God's sake, let's prevent it! I wanted a packaging where the consumer would run to the kitchen for a knife, so there was a chance to at least slice open his hand."

5   "Is that when you got the idea for shrink-wrap?" said the snake.

6   "Shrink-wrap was nice for a while. I liked that there was absolutely no place to tear into it with a fingernail, but I knew there was further to go. That's when I hit on cellophane, cellophane with the illusion of an opening strip, where really none exists."

7   That night, at the celebratory dinner held once an aeon to honor new arrivals, the inventor sat to the Devil's right. On his left sat Cerberus, the watchdog of Hades and noted designer of the pineapple. The Devil chatted with the inventor all night long, then requested that he open another bottle of wine, this time with a two-pronged, side-slip corkscrew. The inventor perspired, and an hour later the bottle was uncorked.

8   At first, no one noticed the muffled disturbance from above, which soon grew into a sustained clamor. Eventually, the entire gathering looked toward the ceiling, and finally the Devil himself noticed that their attention had shifted. He raised his head.

9   Hovering in the ether were three angels, each holding an object. The inventor knew clearly what the objects were: the milk carton, the Ziploc bag, and the banana, all three perfectly designed packages. He remembered how he used to admire them before he fell

into evil. The three angels glided toward the dais. One held the Ziploc bag over the aspirin-bottle people, and bathed them in an otherworldly light. A yellow glow from the banana washed over the hellhound Cerberus, designer of the pineapple, and the milk carton poured its white luminosity in the direction of the CD packager. The Devil stood up abruptly, roared something in Latin while succubae flew out of his mouth, and then angrily excused himself.

10   After the fiasco, the inventor went back to his room and fiddled with the five remotes it took to operate his VCR. Frustrated, he closed his eyes and contemplated the eternity to come in the bleakness of Hell, and how he would probably never again see a snowflake or a Fudgsicle. But then he thought of the nice meal he'd just had, and his new friends, and decided that snowflakes and Fudgsicles weren't that great anyway. He thought how the upcoming eternity might not be so bad after all. There was a knock at the door, and the snake entered.

11   "The Devil asked me to give you your assignment," the snake said. "Sometimes he gets powerful headaches. He wants you to be there to open the aspirin bottle."

12   "I think I could do that," the inventor replied.

13   "Just so you know, he likes a fresh aspirin every time, so you'll have to remove the tamper-resistant collar, the childproof cap, *and* the aluminum sealer," said the snake.

14   The inventor breathed easily. "No problem."

15   "Good," the snake said, and turned to go.

16   Just then a shudder rippled through the inventor's body. "Say"— his voice quavered with nervousness—"who will remove the cotton wad from the inside of the bottle?"

17   The snake turned slowly, its face contorted into the mask of Beelzebub. Then its voice deepened and transformed itself, as though it were coming from the bowels of Hell:

18   "Why, *you* will," he said. "HA HA HA HA HA!"

Organization and Ideas

1. What paragraph or paragraphs introduce the essay? What reasons do you have for your choice?

2. Trace the essay's organization. What paragraphs mention articles that can be grouped with CD packaging? What articles are contrasted with it?

3. What paragraph or paragraphs make up the essay's conclusion? How effective do you find the conclusion?

4. Reread the essay keeping track of the various conflicts in it. How universal are they?

5. Unlike many essays, Martin's has an implied thesis. Think about the various conflicts in the essay and state his implied thesis in your own words.

Technique and Style

1. Jot down the various items Martin mentions. Why might he have presented them in the sequence he does?

2. The main person in the essay is never named but instead referred to as "the inventor." What does the essay gain by not naming him?

3. "Hot as Hell" is a common expression, so common that it has lost any freshness it might have had. How does Martin breathe life into what has become a cliché?

4. For a narrative as short as this one is, it has a surprisingly large cast of characters. How does Martin make them easy to keep track of?

5. Often, humor arises from the linking of unlikely objects. Where do you find Martin using this technique? How else does he create a comic effect?

Suggestions for Writing

Journal

1. Write an entry in which you describe your own battle with a product or machine.

2. Think of a time when you expected one thing but got another. Perhaps you were dreading a particular event and then found it was fun, or perhaps you thought you had done badly on a test only to find you did well. The difference between expectation and reality can become the central conflict for a narrative in your journal.

Essay

1. Write your own narrative of Hell, either serious or comic, replacing "the inventor" with a choice of your own. The list below gives you some categories to think about:

former friend
political figure
music group

historical figure
celebrity

You can use Martin's essay as a fairly close model if you like, incorporating dialogue and using much the same devilish cast.

2. If you responded to the first suggestion for the journal entry, you have a rough draft of an essay. Given the mechanical and technological world we live in, it's likely that you have been frustrated by one of its products. Turn that frustration into an essay, either a fictional narrative similar to Martin's or a straightforward one that relates and analyzes the situation.

Learning, then College

Meg Gifford

When Meg Gifford was considering taking a year off before college, her peers and high school guidance counselor opposed the idea, but she had her parents' support. Her mother even suggested she write the essay that follows and send it in to her local newspaper, the Baltimore Sun. *Not only did the* Sun *publish it, but it was reprinted in the New Orleans* Times-Picayune *on April 10, 2002. After taking her year off, Gifford enrolled at the University of Maryland, majoring in Family Studies and spending one semester at the University of Edinburgh in Scotland. By the time you read this note, she will probably be enrolled in graduate school, working on a master's degree in public health. She reports, "I received several emails thanking me for speaking up on the issue—one from as far away as Mexico."*

What to Look For   A major flaw in some narratives that use first person is the failure to generalize about an individual experience. As you read Meg Gifford's essay, notice how often she uses *I* and how she broadens her experience so that it connects with the experience of others.

1   As my younger friends receive their college acceptance letters this time of year, I think about my senior year at Western High School in Baltimore City and the decision I made that changed my life forever: taking time off before college.

2   In Britain, it's called a gap year—the sabbatical that most students take between high school and college.

3   This is a time for young people to discover themselves before their devotion to another four years of intensive schoolwork. Not a bad idea, considering that a good number of college freshmen flunk out because of the overwhelming temptations of extracurricular college life.

4   Most gap year students take a job or an internship to get a better grasp on the real world and pick up some life skills along the way. Some students understand that they are just not ready for college.

5   I chose to take a gap year for this very reason. I knew I wasn't ready to settle down and work. And because college is so expensive, I wanted to be sure that I would take that investment seriously.

6   I acknowledge that postponing college is not easy. Few people supported my decision, telling me that once I stopped my education I'd never get back on track. My classmates were especially doubtful, thinking that my time off was just an excuse for being lazy. It was infuriating to think that people could and would not associate my travels or internship as an extension of my education.

7   I learned more in my gap year than I have in two years of college. I discovered life skills that continue to help me through the hardest of times. I found independence and a new self-esteem. I learned the value of a dollar, and then I learned the value of not having a dollar. I learned that eggs are cheap and easy to cook.

8   Being 18 is wonderful. There's a whole world waiting to be discovered with a lifetime to do it. The average person doesn't retire until he is well into his 60s, and he probably has been working since he graduated from college. As I see my friends now settling down with careers and families, many of them express regrets at not having seen the world before taking on such unyielding responsibilities.

9   My advice to high school seniors is this: Now is your chance to explore. Do it before you have devoted your life to something else.

10   By the age of 20, I delivered three babies as part of my mid-wifery internship in Hyden, Ky., and learned how to cook a fine Kentucky rattlesnake. After teaching a 90-year-old-man the alphabet, he showed me how to make furniture.

11   I also have attended two years of college so far, making the dean's list every semester. What story will you be able to tell?

Organization and Ideas

1. In what ways does paragraph 1 prepare you for what follows in the rest of the essay?
2. Work out a timeline for the essay, noting when each paragraph takes place. What happens when?
3. How effective is Gifford's use of time?
4. Consider the pros and cons Gifford outlines and summarize them in one sentence. What is her thesis?
5. To what extent does Gifford persuade you that a gap year is a good idea?

Technique and Style

1. Reread the essay, paying particular attention to Gifford's audience. Who is it? What reasons do you have for your choice?
2. Consider the tone of the essay, the author's attitude toward her audience and subject. Is she earnest? Supercilious? Know-it-all? Caring? What?
3. To what extent is Gifford someone you would like to know? Why?
4. In paragraph 7, Gifford uses a lot of repetition. How effective is it?
5. Paragraph 10 summarizes Gifford's experience by presenting the highlights of her year off. How effective are her examples?

Suggestions for Writing

Journal

1. Did you consider taking a year off before entering college? Use your journal to explore why or why not.
2. Paragraph 7 summarizes what Gifford learned during her gap year. To what extent do you believe her and why?

Essay

1. One way to view Gifford's essay is to think of it as describing the kind of learning that is vital yet can take place out of the classroom. Consider what Gifford learned that she states in paragraph 7. Where have you learned knowledge that you value? Narrow down your choice to one example and write an essay in which you explore what you learned, where, and why. Suggestions:

> working part-time
> working full-time
> participating in a sport
> participating in an extracurricular activity
> being responsible for someone

2. Gifford cites the "overwhelming temptations of extracurricular college life" as a reason some students flunk out. Flunking out aside, consider the various "temptations" you face in college and write an essay in which you analyze the most hazardous one and how you dealt with it.

The Night of Oranges

Flavius Stan

Flavius Stan was 17 years old when this piece was published on Christmas Eve day, 1995, in the New York Times. *At the time, he was an exchange student at the Fieldston School in the Bronx, one of New York City's five boroughs. The time and place he writes about, however, is Christmas Eve in the city of Timisoara in the Romania of 1989, when the country was emerging from Communist rule. It had been an incredible month. On December 16, government forces opened fire on antigovernment demonstrators in Timisoara, killing hundreds. The President, Nicolae Ceausescu, immediately declared a state of emergency, but that did not stop antigovernment protests in other cities. Finally, on December 22, army units also rebelled, the President was overthrown, and civil war raged. The new government quickly won out, and Ceausescu was tried and found guilty of genocide. He was executed on December 25.*

What to Look For   Few of us reading this essay have had first-hand experience of a revolution, nor have many of us lived under

Communism or a dictatorship, much less a government whose leader was not only overthrown but also executed. But all of us know oranges. What is familiar to us was strange to Stan, and what is strange to us was his everyday world. The resulting gap between Stan's society and ours is huge, yet in this essay he is able to bring his readers into the cold, postrevolution world of a city in Romania and make us see our familiar orange in a new way. Read the essay once for pleasure and then read it again, looking for the ways in which he makes the unfamiliar familiar and vice versa.

1   It is Christmas Eve in 1989 in Timisoara and the ice is still dirty from the boots of the Romanian revolution. The dictator Nicolae Ceausescu had been deposed a few days before, and on Christmas Day he would be executed by firing squad. I am in the center of the city with my friends, empty now of the crowds that prayed outside the cathedral during the worst of the fighting. My friends and I still hear shots here and there. Our cold hands are gray like the sky above us, and we want to see a movie.

2   There is a rumor that there will be oranges for sale tonight. Hundreds of people are already waiting in line. We were used to such lines under the former Communist Government—lines for bread, lines for meat, lines for everything. Families would wait much of the day for rationed items. As children, we would take turns for an hour or more, holding our family's place in line.

3   But this line is different. There are children in Romania who don't know what an orange looks like. It is a special treat. Having the chance to eat a single orange will keep a child happy for a week. It will also make him a hero in the eyes of his friends. For the first time, someone is selling oranges by the kilo.

4   Suddenly I want to do something important: I want to give my brother a big surprise. He is only 8 years old, and I want him to celebrate Christmas with lots of oranges at the table. I also want my parents to be proud of me.

5   So I call home and tell my parents that I'm going to be late. I forget about going to the movie, leave my friends and join the line.

6   People aren't silent, upset, frustrated, as they were before the revolution; they are talking to one another about life, politics and the new situation in the country.

7   The oranges are sold out of the back doorway of a food shop. The clerk has gone from anonymity to unexpected importance. As he handles the oranges, he acts like a movie star in front of his fans.

8   He moves his arms in an exaggerated manner as he tells the other workers where to go and what to do. All I can do is stare at the stack of cardboard boxes, piled higher than me. I have never seen so many oranges in my life.

9   Finally, it is my turn. It is 8 o'clock, and I have been waiting for six hours. It doesn't seem like a long time because my mind has been flying from the oranges in front of me to my brother and then back to the oranges. I hand over the money I was going to spend on the movie and watch each orange being thrown into my bag. I try to count them, but I lose their number.

10   I am drunk with the idea of oranges. I put the bag inside my coat as if I want to absorb their warmth. They aren't heavy at all, and I feel that it is going to be the best Christmas of my life. I begin thinking of how I am going to present my gift.

11   I get home and my father opens the door. He is amazed when he sees the oranges, and we decide to hide them until dinner. At dessert that night, I gave my brother the present. Everyone is silent. They can't believe it.

12   My brother doesn't touch them. He is afraid even to look at them. Maybe they aren't real. Maybe they are an illusion, like everything else these days. We have to tell him he can eat them before he has the courage to touch one of the oranges.

13   I stare at my brother eating the oranges. They are my oranges. My parents are proud of me.

Organization and Ideas

1. Paragraphs 1–3 introduce the essay. Explain how they do or do not fit the journalistic questions establishing *who, what, where, why, when, how.*

2. The central part of the essay takes the reader from the time Stan decides to buy the oranges to his presenting them to his brother. What is the effect of presenting the narrative chronologically?

3. The last paragraph functions as the essay's one-paragraph conclusion, a conclusion presented in three short sentences. Explain whether you find the ending effective.

4. On the surface, Stan's essay has a simple thesis—that finding the rare and perfect gift for his brother fills him with pride, pride also reflected

by his family. If you dig a bit, however, you may also discover other less obvious theses. What, for instance, might Stan be implying about Christmas? About Romania's future?

5. How would you characterize the conflict or conflicts in this essay?

Technique and Style

1. Although the essay was written in 1995, it is set at an earlier time, 1989. Many writers would, therefore, opt for the past tense, but Stan relates his narrative in the present. What does he gain by this choice?

2. Trace the number of contrasts Stan has in his essay. What do you discover? How do they relate to the thesis?

3. Paragraphs 7 and 8 describe the clerk in charge of selling the oranges in some detail. What does this description add to the essay?

4. Why is it important that the money Stan spends on the oranges is the money he was going to spend on the movies?

5. Reread the first paragraph, one that sets not only the scene but also the atmosphere, the emotional impression arising from the scene. In your own words, describe that atmosphere.

Suggestions for Writing

Journal

1. Choose a common object and describe it as though you were seeing it for the first time.

2. In a sense, Stan's essay is written from the perspective of an 11-year-old, the age he was at the time of the narrative. Leaf through your journal to find a short narrative and then try rewriting it from the perspective of a much younger person.

Essay

1. Sift through your memory to find several times when you felt proud. Choose one to turn into a narrative essay. Perhaps, like Stan, you may want to retell the event in the present tense, placing yourself in the position of reliving it. If you do, check your draft to see if you have an implied thesis that is larger than the apparent one, for you want your essay to have some depth to it. For ideas of what might have made you feel proud, consider something you

> did
> didn't do
> saw
> owned
> said

2. For a more generalized essay, consider the times you felt pride and list them. What were the occasions? What do they have in common? In what ways are those examples similar? Different? Write an essay in which you define *pride*, using your experiences as examples and keeping first person to a minimum so that you emphasize the subject, not yourself.

Time to Look and Listen

Magdoline Asfahani

Newsweek *runs a regular column called "My Turn," and to celebrate its thirtieth anniversary, the magazine reexamined some earlier pieces and updated them. If you were to click on <www.newsweek.com> and then scroll to the bottom of the page, you would find "My Turn at 30" and a listing of various columns. There, under December 2, 1996, you would find this essay along with a brief biography titled "Magdoline Asfahani: An American Story." At the time the piece was published, Asfahani was a student at the University of Texas at El Paso, trying to balance her identity in ways that honored her parents' Syrian and Lebanese cultures while embracing her American-born values. It wasn't easy. Reflecting on what she wrote then, Asfahani finds "the piece is probably more meaningful now than it was when I wrote it." See if you agree.*

What to Look For   If you have ever written about a painful experience, you know that it's hard to keep your emotions under control. Anger, resentment, pain can break through and overwhelm what you are trying to portray in a cool, rational manner. As you read Asfahani's essay, look for the ways she keeps her emotions from engulfing her ideas.

1   I love my country as many who have been here for generations cannot. Perhaps that's because I'm the child of immigrants, raised with a conscious respect for America that many people take for

granted. My parents chose this country because it offered them a new life, freedom and possibilities. But I learned at a young age that the country we loved so much did not feel the same way about us.

2   Discrimination is not unique to America. It occurs in any country that allows immigration. Anyone who is unlike the majority is looked at a little suspiciously, dealt with a little differently. I knew that I was an Arab and a Muslim. This meant nothing to me. At school I stood up to say the Pledge of Allegiance every day. These things did not seem incompatible at all. Then everything changed for me, suddenly and permanently, in 1985. I was only in seventh grade, but that was the beginning of my political education.

3   That year a TWA plane originating in Athens was diverted to Beirut. Two years earlier the U.S. Marine barracks in Beirut had been bombed. That seemed to start a chain of events that would forever link Arabs with terrorism. After the hijacking, I faced class-mates who taunted me with cruel names, attacking my heritage and my religion. I became an outcast and had to apologize for myself constantly.

4   After a while, I tried to forget my heritage. No matter what race, religion or ethnicity, a child who is attacked often retreats. I was the only Arab I knew of in my class, so I had no one in my peer group as an ally. No matter what my parents tried to tell me about my proud cultural history, I would ignore it. My classmates told me I came from an uncivilized, brutal place, that Arabs were by nature anti-American, and I believed them. They did not know the hours my parents spent studying, working, trying to preserve part of their old lives while embracing, willingly, the new.

5   I tried to forget the Arabic I knew, because if I didn't I'd be for-ever linked to murderers. I stopped inviting friends over for dinner, because I thought the food we ate was "weird." I lied about where my parents had come from. Their accents (although they spoke English perfectly) humiliated me. Though Islam is a major monotheistic religion with many similarities to Judaism and Christianity, there were no holidays near Chanukah or Christmas, nothing to tie me to the "Judeo-Christian" tradition. I felt more ex-cluded. I slowly began to turn into someone without a past.

6   Civil war was raging in Lebanon, and all that Americans saw of that country was destruction and violence. Every other movie seemed to feature Arab terrorists. The most common questions I was asked were if I had ever ridden a camel or if my family lived in tents. I felt burdened with responsibility. Why should an adolescent

be asked questions like "Is it true you hate Jews and you want Israel destroyed?" I didn't hate anybody. My parents had never said anything even alluding to such sentiments. I was confused and hurt.

7   As I grew older and began to form my own opinions, my embarrassment lessened and my anger grew. The turning point came in high school. My grandmother had become very ill, and it was necessary for me to leave school a few days before Christmas vacation. My chemistry teacher was very sympathetic until I said I was going to the Middle East. "Don't come back in a body bag," he said cheerfully. The class laughed. Suddenly, those years of watching movies that mocked me and listening to others who knew nothing about Arabs and Muslims except what they saw on television seemed like a bad dream. I knew then that I would never be silent again.

8   I've tried to reclaim those lost years. I realize now that I come from a culture that has a rich history. The Arab world is a medley of people of different religions; not every Arab is a Muslim, and vice versa. The Arabs brought tremendous advances in the sciences and mathematics, as well as creating a literary tradition that has never been surpassed. The language itself is flexible and beautiful, with nuances and shades of meaning unparalleled in any language. Though many find it hard to believe, Islam has made progress in women's rights. There is a specific provision in the Koran that permits women to own property and ensures that their inheritance is protected—although recent events have shown that interpretation of these laws can vary.

9   My youngest brother, who is 12, is now at the crossroads I faced. When initial reports of the Oklahoma City bombing pointed to "Arab-looking individuals" as the culprits, he came home from school crying. "Mom, why do Muslims kill people? Why are the Arabs so bad?" She was angry and brokenhearted, but tried to handle the situation in the best way possible through education. She went to his class, armed with Arabic music, pictures, traditional dress and cookies. She brought a chapter of the social-studies book to life and the children asked intelligent, thoughtful questions, even after the class was over. Some even asked if she was coming back. When my brother came home, he was excited and proud instead of ashamed.

10   I only recently told my mother about my past experience. Maybe if I had told her then, I would have been better equipped to deal

with the thoughtless teasing. But, fortunately, the world is changing. Although discrimination and stereotyping still exist, many people are trying to lessen and end it. Teachers, schools and the media are showing greater sensitivity to cultural issues. However, there is still much that needs to be done, not for the sake of any particular ethnic or cultural groups but for the sake of our country.

11   The America that I love is one that values freedom and the differences of its people. Education is the key to understanding. As Americans we need to take a little time to look and listen carefully to what is around us and not rush to judgment without knowing the facts. And we must never be ashamed of our pasts. It is our collective differences that unite and make us unique as a nation. It's what determines our present and our future.

Organization and Ideas

1. In paragraphs 3–6, Asfahani recreates her experiences as a seventh-grader. How well does she do it?

2. It's possible to find a number of subjects in Asfahani's essay: discrimination, education, American values, hasty generalization. Which is the most important? What evidence can you find to support your opinion?

3. What statement is Asfahani making about that subject?

4. How would you characterize the essay's aim? Is Asfahani trying to persuade the reader? Explain her position? Let off steam? If some combination, which dominates?

5. The essay was published in 1996 just after Thanksgiving. To what extent, if any, is it dated?

Technique and Style

1. Asfahani describes her "political education" (paragraphs 2–9). Which example is the most telling and why?

2. In paragraph 8, Asfahani asserts that she comes "from a culture that has a rich history." How well does she back up that claim?

3. Asfahani never told her parents what she was going through when she was in the seventh grade, keeping it to herself. How realistic is that reaction?

4. According to Asfahani, "Education is the key to understanding" (paragraph 11). What evidence does she present to back up that idea?

5. What examples can you find of Asfahani appealing to the reader's emotions? To reason? Which predominates?

Suggestions for Writing

Journal

1. Use your journal to record the time you first recognized or experienced discrimination.
2. Think of how culture is expressed through language, food, celebrations, dress, gestures, relationships, and the like. Write a brief entry in which you tell of a time when you first experienced a culture different from your own.

Essay

1. "Know thyself" was a basic belief of the ancient Greeks, and it is as difficult to do today as it was then. You can define yourself, for example, in any number of ways by associating yourself with a group or belief or heritage, to name just a few. Think about the various ways in which you define yourself and write an essay in which you explain who you are. To generate some ideas, try thinking about who you are in relation to

   family
   ethnic heritage
   friends
   religion
   political beliefs

   Choose one of these ideas, or any other, and consider the conflicts you encountered in becoming who you are. The danger here is taking on too much so that you have the first chapter of your autobiography instead of an essay, so be sure you narrow down your topic.
2. Asfahani says that in high school, she reached a "turning point" and "would never be silent again" (paragraph 7). Think of such turning points in your own life and select one to explore in an essay. Like Asfahani, you should try to distance yourself from the time so that you can balance the emotional and the rational.

The Pie

Gary Soto

Gary Soto grew up in the San Joaquin Valley, and as he describes it, "We had our own culture which was more like the culture of poverty." Thinking he couldn't get into the University of California system, he applied to California State University, Fresno, where he soon changed his major from geography to English after being particularly struck by a poem by Edward Field, "Unwanted," that depicted the alienation Soto himself felt. Since then, he has earned an MFA at the University of California, Irvine, and taught at a number of universities, including Berkeley. Now, he devotes himself full-time to writing. The results are apparent in Books in Print, *where you will find that Soto has a very long list indeed. In 2003 alone, four of his books were published, and four others are slated for publication. Soto is also well known for his poetry, as numerous awards attest. The essay that follows was first published in his collection* A Summer Life *(1990). Though the essay is hardly "poetic" in the stereotypical sense, you'll find he uses a number of techniques that also characterize his poetry: precise diction, strong verbs, and imagery that appeals to the senses.*

What to Look For   To make writing memorable, the first draft of an essay will frequently depend more on adverbs and adjectives than on verbs, yet it is verbs that have muscle and can best get the job done—but not just any verb. All too often that same first draft is sprinkled with various forms of the verb *to be,* usually in its most simple form *is.* Soto shows you how to avoid that trap by using action verbs that convey far more precisely exactly what he is feeling.

1   I knew enough about hell to stop me from stealing. I was holy in almost every bone. Some days I recognized the shadows of angels flopping on the backyard grass, and other days I heard faraway messages in the plumbing that howled underneath the house when I crawled there looking for something to do.

2   But boredom made me sin. Once, at the German Market, I stood before a rack of pies, my sweet tooth gleaming and the juice of guilt wetting my underarms. I gazed at the nine kinds of pie, pecan

and apple being my favorites, although cherry looked good, and my dear, fat-faced chocolate was always a good bet. I nearly wept trying to decide which to steal and, forgetting the flowery dust priests give off, the shadow of angels and the proximity of God howling in the plumbing underneath the house, sneaked a pie behind my coffee-lid frisbee and walked to the door, grinning to the bald grocer whose forehead shone with a window of light.

3   "No one saw," I muttered to myself, the pie like a discus in my hand, and hurried across the street, where I sat on someone's lawn. The sun wavered between the branches of a yellowish sycamore. A squirrel nailed itself high on the trunk, where it forked into two large bark-scabbed limbs. Just as I was going to work my cleanest finger into the pie, a neighbor came out to the porch for his mail. He looked at me, and I got up and headed for home. I raced on skinny legs to my block, but slowed to a quick walk when I couldn't wait any longer. I held the pie to my nose and breathed in its sweetness. I licked some of the crust and closed my eyes as I took a small bite.

4   In my front yard, I leaned against a car fender and panicked about stealing the apple pie. I knew an apple got Eve in deep trouble with snakes because Sister Marie had shown us a film about Adam and Eve being cast into the desert, and what scared me more than falling from grace was being thirsty for the rest of my life. But even that didn't stop me from clawing a chunk from the pie tin and pushing it into the cavern of my mouth. The slop was sweet and gold-colored in the afternoon sun. I laid more pieces on my tongue, wet finger-dripping pieces, until I was finished and felt like crying because it was about the best thing I had ever tasted. I realized right there and then, in my sixth year, in my tiny body of two hundred bones and three or four sins, that the best things in life came stolen. I wiped my sticky fingers on the grass and rolled my tongue over the corners of my mouth. A burp perfumed the air.

5   I felt bad not sharing with Cross-Eyed Johnny, a neighbor kid. He stood over my shoulder and asked, "Can I have some?" Crust fell from my mouth, and my teeth were bathed with the jam-like filling. Tears blurred my eyes as I remembered the grocer's forehead. I remembered the other pies on the rack, the warm air of the fan above the door and the car that honked as I crossed the street without looking.

6   "Get away," I had answered Cross-Eyed Johnny. He watched my fingers greedily push big chunks of pie down my throat. He swal-

lowed and said in a whisper, "Your hands are dirty," then returned home to climb his roof and sit watching me eat the pie by myself. After a while, he jumped off and hobbled away because the fall had hurt him.

7   I sat on the curb. The pie tin glared at me and rolled away when the wind picked up. My face was sticky with guilt. A car honked, and the driver knew. Mrs. Hancock stood on her lawn, hands on hip, and she knew. My mom, peeling a mountain of potatoes at the Redi-Spud factory, knew. I got to my feet, stomach taut, mouth tired of chewing, and flung my frisbee across the street, its shadow like the shadow of an angel fleeing bad deeds. I retrieved it, jogging slowly. I flung it again until I was bored and thirsty.

8   I returned home to drink water and help my sister glue bottle caps onto cardboard, a project for summer school. But the bottle caps bored me, and the water soon filled me up more than the pie. With the kitchen stifling with heat and lunatic flies, I decided to crawl underneath our house and lie in the cool shadows listening to the howling sound of plumbing. Was it God? Was it Father, speaking from death, or Uncle with his last shiny dime? I listened, ear pressed to a cold pipe, and heard a howl like the sea. I lay until I was cold and then crawled back to the light, rising from one knee, then another, to dust off my pants and squint in the harsh light. I looked and saw the glare of a pie tin on a hot day. I knew sin was what you take and didn't give back.

Organization and Ideas

1. What does the first paragraph lead you to expect in the rest of the essay?
2. The time sequence traces Soto's guilt. What stages can you identify?
3. How would you describe the nature of the conflict in the essay? How real does it seem?
4. What emotions does Soto feel in the course of his narrative?
5. What does Soto learn? How real does it seem?

Technique and Style

1. Soto relates his narrative from the perspective of his six-year-old self. What is the first clue about his age?
2. Reread paragraph 4. What images appeal to what senses?
3. Paragraphs 5 and 6 bring in Cross-Eyed Johnny. What does that incident add to the narrative?

4. What other titles can you think of for the essay? What is gained? Lost?
5. Choose two sentences from paragraph 3 and rewrite them, using different verbs. Which versions do you prefer and why?

Suggestions for Writing

Journal

1. Place yourself in the position of Cross-Eyed Johnny and retell the scene (paragraphs 5 and 6) from his perspective.
2. The area under the house and its howling plumbing hold special significance for Soto. Think of a place that holds similar significance for you and describe it. Like Soto, you may want to use that place to frame a narrative.

Essay

1. Soto's experience probably reminds you of a similar one of your own or of a friend's. Recall a time when, directly or indirectly, you lived through such an event and use your memory of it as the basis of a narrative. Like Soto, you will want to describe not only what you or your friend did but also how it made you feel. Suggestions:
   being embarrassed
   feeling guilty
   getting caught
   getting away with "it"
2. As a child or young adult, you probably took a number of risks. Jot down a short list of the more memorable ones and then select one to analyze in an essay. What were the circumstances? Who and what were involved? What did you risk and why? How "typical" was your experience? What did you learn? After you have written a rough draft, revise it so that you step back a bit from your experience and put it in a larger perspective.

ADDITIONAL WRITING ASSIGNMENTS

Using Description

1. Write a narrative about an event that changed your opinion: product, music group, person, place, political candidate.
2. Write a narrative explaining a conflict: parent vs. child, brother vs. sister, boss vs. worker, human vs. animal, human vs. nature.
3. Write a narrative about a crucial decision that you made: going to college, choosing a major, getting married (or divorced), joining an organization or club, getting a job, leaving home.
4. Write a narrative about confronting prejudice. Perhaps it was based on gender, age, race, ethnic background, looks.

Evaluating the Essays

1. The essays by Flavius Stan and Gary Soto use material objects as symbols to represent something greater than the objects themselves and thus provide greater meaning as well as dramatic effect. For Stan, it's the oranges; for Soto, the pie. Which of the two writers uses the symbol more effectively? Quote from both essays to support your opinion.
2. Reread Meg Gifford's "Learning, then College" and Magdoline Asfahani's "Time to Look and Listen," paying particular attention to what each of the writers values. Which of the two comes closer to what you value? Write an essay in which you explain your answer and use evidence from the essays to support your thesis.
3. Dialogue and characterization add to the essays by Steve Martin and Gary Soto, though the essays differ in tone and purpose. Martin tells a fictional story to satirize a technological "advance"; Soto recounts an experience to explain his first understanding of sin. Martin is humorous; Soto is serious. Select either dialogue or characterization to explore how it operates in the narratives and argue for its more effective use.
4. Flavius Stan and Magdoline Asfahani grew up in cultures that differ from mainstream America, and their essays explore some of those differences and their effects. Both writers deal with conflict, external and internal. Which of the two writers do you identify with and why? Quote both to make your point.

On Using
Definition

3

"When I use a word," said Humpty Dumpty, "it means just what I choose it to mean—neither more nor less." To that Alice replied, "The question is whether you can make words mean so many different things." Humpty Dumpty then pronounced, "The question is which is to be the master—that's all." Writers are the masters of their words, although not to the extent that Humpty Dumpty would like, and often a discussion or argument boils down to the meaning of a crucial word. *Liberty, justice, civil rights, freedom,* and other similar concepts, for example, are all abstractions until they are defined.

If you had to write a paper on what *freedom* means to you, you might be tempted first off to look up the word in a dictionary, but you will discover more to say if you put aside the dictionary and first think about some basic questions, such as "Whose freedom?" If it's your freedom you are writing about, who or what sets limits on your freedom? The law? The church? Parents? Family responsibilities? After you mull over questions such as these, you are in a better position to make use of a dictionary definition. The dictionary is the most obvious place to find what the word means, but what you find there is only explicit meaning, the word's **denotation.** Look up *freedom* in a collegiate dictionary, and you'll see the different ways in which the word can be used, and also its etymology, but that won't convey the rich layers of meaning that the word has accumulated through the years.

What the dictionary does not reveal is the word's associative or emotional meanings, its **connotation.** One way to discover connotation is to ask yourself questions about the word, questions similar to those above that get at how the concept of freedom touches your life. The more specific your examples, the more concrete your definition can be, and the less the danger of slipping into clichés. Unless the word you are defining is quite unusual, most readers will be familiar with its dictionary definition; your own definition and your speculations on the word's connotation are of much greater interest.

A paper that defines a familiar word can hold just as much interest as one that examines an unfamiliar word or a word that is particularly powerful. "What does boredom mean?" "Why is synergism a useful concept?" "What does it mean to be called handicapped?" Questions such as these can be explored through almost any mode of thinking and writing. You can use those that you have already studied both to probe your subject as you think about it and to develop your ideas as you write.

> *Description*   What details best describe it? What senses can you appeal to?
> *Narration*   What story might best illustrate it? What kind of conflict might the word involve?

And even though you may not have read essays that use the other modes discussed in this book, they are already familiar to you as ways of thinking and can, therefore, also be useful to you as you think and write about your central term.

> *Example*   What sorts of examples illustrate it? What different times and sources can you use to find examples?
> *Comparison and contrast*   What is it similar to? What is it different from?
> *Analogy*   What metaphor would make it vivid? What might the reader be familiar with that you can draw an analogy to?
> *Division and classification*   How can it be divided? What types or categories can it be broken into?
> *Process*   What steps or stages are involved in it? Which are crucial?
> *Cause and effect*   What are the conditions that cause it? What effect does it have?

When questions such as these are tailored to the particular word or concept under scrutiny, they will help you develop your ideas.

Audience and Purpose

Unless your subject is unusual, you can assume that your audience has a general understanding of the word or phrase to be defined. The nature of that general understanding, however, differs. For instance, the word *spinster* most often raises an image of "little old lady," a picture possibly fleshed out with a cat or two and fussy furnishings. Short of those associations, a spinster is an unmarried woman of a certain age, but that age varies from one decade to another. Forty years ago, a single woman who was 26 might well have been considered a spinster. These days, the term—when used at all—would be applied to someone considerably older. Even so, the negative image remains, and those who use the word probably assume that the spinster leads a lonely, narrow life. Such an image, however, is a far cry from the likes of Katharine Hepburn, who never married but who, up to her death at the age of 94, was still being asked about her long-term love affair with her married Hollywood costar, Spencer Tracy. Were you to write an essay arguing against the stereotype and focusing on the Katharine Hepburns of our time, you might introduce your subject by reminding your readers of the word's usual connotations.

Sometimes you not only want to change the reader's understanding but also want to make the reader aware of how the meaning of a word has changed, a change that has an effect on our society. In that case you may choose to argue for a redefinition of the word or go a step further and attack the effects of the term's changed meaning. Words such as *amateur, dilettante,* and *gay* have all undergone major shifts in meaning within a relatively short period of time, at least short in the linguistic sense. *Amateur* used to refer to someone engaged in an activity for pleasure, not pay, but it now has the common meaning of inexperienced, unskilled. *Dilettante* also had a positive connotation, someone who was a lover of the arts; now it is more likely associated with someone who dabbles at them. As for *gay,* today it is associated with the word *homosexual,* which puts a very different spin on the nineteenth century and its Gay Nineties.

Definition can also be used to explore what people know and don't know about a place. If you were to write an essay that explains what your neighborhood means to you, you would essentially be presenting a personal definition of it. The same would be true if you were to write about any favorite spot, whether it be a tree house from your childhood or a park bench. To some, a park bench may be an eyesore or a necessity or a plain park bench, whereas to you it may hold particular meaning as the place where you find peace and quiet.

Perhaps you merely want your readers to reexamine a term and consider its importance. *Education* is a word familiar to all, and you and your classmates have had years of experience with it, but it may well mean different things to different people. Were you to write about the word within the context of your college education, you might begin by chasing down its etymology, which would bring you to the Latin *educatus*, meaning brought up, taught. From there you might speculate on how the meaning of education has shifted, slipping from the general—conveying general knowledge and developing reason and judgment—to the particular—emphasizing skills and preparation for a profession. At that point, you would have the makings of a good argument against or in favor of the change.

Using Other Modes

Definition, perhaps more than any other rhetorical pattern, depends on other modes to serve its purpose. Were you to write an essay on *honesty,* for example, you might begin your discussion with a narrative, a brief story about a friend who bought a magazine at a newsstand and received too much change for a 20-dollar bill. The narrative can then lead to comparison and contrast, making a distinction between honest and dishonest. And if the friend kept the money but feels guilty about it, then you would be dealing with cause and effect. Make your reader feel that guilt, and you'll be using description.

While an essay that depends primarily on definition can be developed as a personal narrative, one that is organized as straightforward exposition will also involve other patterns of organization. If you were writing a short research paper on the common cold, comparison would help you distinguish it from the flu and process would enable you to trace its progress from first sore throat to last sniffle. In between you might discuss possible ways to relieve symptoms, which would bring in classification. Although you may use many different modes, your primary one would still be definition.

To flesh out the definition of a term, you can draw upon a number of sources. You might make a quick connection with your reader's experience, for instance, by drawing examples from the world of athletics. An essay defining *grace* can cite Michael Jordan's drive to a basket, just as one on *bizarre* might well put Dennis Rodman at the head of the list for his habit of dyeing his hair different colors and cross-dressing. Citing examples of well-known figures from film, television, the arts, and politics is also a quick way to remind your readers of what they know and to make use of that to explain the unfamiliar. While contemporary figures are probably the first to come to mind, historical ones will serve just as well with the additional advantage of broadening the base of your information and adding to your credibility, your **persona,** the image of self that you create and then present through the prose in your essay. A brief mention of the grace of a Donatello bronze or the bizarre world of Hieronymus Bosch extends the range of your definition while also revealing the depth of your knowledge, portraying you as someone who knows the fine arts. Combining those references with a formal vocabulary, varied sentence structure, and wit, you will create a sophisticated, informed persona.

Organization and Ideas

Although a definition can play a key role in an essay, it is not the essay's thesis. The thesis rises from the author's assertion about the definition. Sometimes your title can serve as your thesis or at least hint at it, as in "Honesty Isn't Easy" or "No Cure for the Common Cold." The explicit thesis is also obvious, usually found in one sentence in the introduction. Sometimes, however, you want the reader to infer the thesis by combining the ideas in two or more sentences. Far more subtle is the implied thesis, which is what you have here:

> Pile on onions, lettuce, tomato, cheese, even mushrooms and jalapeño peppers, douse it with ketchup, mustard, mayonnaise, and still you can't hide the classic American hamburger—a quarter pound or so of relatively lean grilled beef snuggled into a soft but not spongy round roll. If the meat's too lean, the hamburger's too dry, but if it's not lean enough, the juice soaks the bun and the whole creation falls apart.

The thesis? Several are possible but two come quickly to mind, variations on "You can't spoil the classic American hamburger" and "The classic American hamburger is a splendid creation." Either way, what you have is a definition and an assertion about it.

Like the thesis, an essay's organization can be straightforward or somewhat complex. At times, you may want to use a roughly chronological pattern of organization, starting at one point in time and moving forward to another. Structuring an essay so that it moves from the least to the most important point is another obvious pattern, one used by several of the writers in this chapter. You might also consider organizing your paper by question/answer, the introduction posing a question and the body of the essay answering it. A variation on that pattern is one in which one part of the essay poses a problem that is then discussed and analyzed in terms of possible solutions. Both those ways of organizing an essay are relatively uncomplicated. Perhaps the hardest to handle successfully is the organization that goes from the particular to the general. Were you to write a paper on the American flag, for example, you might start with the particular—a description of the modern flag—and then discuss the general—what it means as a symbol.

Useful Terms

Connotation The associations suggested by a word that add to its literal meaning. *Home* and *domicile* have similar dictionary meanings, but they differ radically in their connotation.

Denotation The literal meaning of a word, its dictionary definition.

Persona The character of the writer that comes through from the prose.

POINTERS FOR USING DEFINITION

Exploring the Topic

1. **What are the denotations of your term?** You should consult an unabridged dictionary and perhaps a more complete or specialized one, such as the *Oxford English Dictionary* or a dictionary of slang.
2. **What are the connotations of your term?** What emotional reactions or associations does it elicit from people? What situations evoke what responses and why?
3. **What other words can be used for your term?** Which are similar?
4. **What are the characteristics, qualities, or components of your term?** Which are most important? Are some not worth mentioning?
5. **What other modes are appropriate?** What modes can you draw on to help support your definition and the organization of the essay? Where can you use description? Narration? What examples can you use to illustrate your term?

6. Has your word been used or misused? If so, might that misuse be turned into an introductory narrative? A closing one?

Drafting the Paper

1. Know your reader. Review your lists of denotations and connotations together with the characteristics related to your term to see how familiar they are to your reader. Check to see if your reader may have particular associations that you need to redirect or change. Or if your reader is directly affected by your topic, make sure your definition does not offend.

2. Know your purpose. Unless your term is unusual, one of your biggest problems is to tell the reader something new about it. Work on your first paragraph so that it will engage the reader from the start. From that point on, keep your primary purpose in mind. If you are writing a paper that is basically self-expressive or persuasive, make sure you have an audience other than yourself. If your aim is informative, consider narration, example, cause and effect, and analogy as possible ways of presenting familiar material in a fresh light.

3. Use evidence. Provide examples as evidence to illustrate what your key term means. Also consider using negative examples and setting out distinctions between the meaning of your word and other, similar words.

4. Draw on a variety of sources. Define your term from several perspectives. Perhaps a brief history of the word would be helpful, or maybe some statistical information is in order. See if a brief narrative might provide additional meaning for the term.

5. Make a point. Don't mistake your definition for your thesis. The two are certainly related, but one is an assertion; the other is not. Perhaps your definition is a jumping-off place for a larger point you wish to make or a key part of that point. Or perhaps your term evokes a single dominant impression you want to convey. Whatever purpose your definition serves, it needs to support your thesis.

Chocolate Equals Love

Diane Ackerman

As an undergraduate at Boston University and then Pennsylvania State University, Diane Ackerman studied both science and literature, twin interests she would pursue as a writer while earning an MFA and PhD. A staff writer for the New Yorker, *Ackerman often writes on nature and its inhabitants.* The Moon by Whale Light, *a collection of her essays, was published in 1991; it is subtitled* and Other Adventures among Bats, Penguins, Crocodiles, and Whales. *Another nonfiction book,* A Slender Thread *(1997), grew out of her volunteer work as a counselor at a suicide prevention and crisis center. Three of her books are* Natural Histor[ies] . . . of The Senses *(1990), of* Love *(1995), and of* My Garden *(2001). The essay below was published in* Parade Magazine *on February 9, 2003. Reading it, you will be able to tell that Ackerman is also a well-respected poet, for in "Chocolate Equals Love" she manages to combine the vivid detail and compression characteristic of poetry with the precise detail and keen observation associated with science.*

What to Look For   Good writers have a way of listening to words so that they are aware of a word's sound as well as sense. If you read Ackerman's second paragraph out loud, for instance, you'll hear a lot of *s* sounds that help make the prose flow smoothly. Reading your own work out loud will help you develop your own ear for the sound of good writing.

1   What food do you crave? Add a hint of mischief to your desire, and the answer is bound to be chocolate, Dark, divine, sense-bludgeoning chocolate. A wooer's gift. A child's reward. A jilted lover's solace. A cozy mug of slumber. Halloween manna. A gimme-more that tantalizes young and old alike. Almost every candy bar. Chocolate.

2   We can thank the Indians of Central and South America for chocolate's bewitching lusciousness. As the Spanish explorer Hernán Cortés found, the Aztecs worshiped chocolate (which they named *cacahuatl*) as a gift from their wise god Quetzalcoatl. Aztec soldiers and male members of court drank as many as 2000 pitchers

of chocolate every day. They spiked their drink with vanilla beans and spices, then drank it bubbly thick from golden cups. Adding chili peppers gave it bite. The Aztec leader Montezuma required a chocolate ice, made by pouring syrup over snow that runners brought to him from the nearest mountain.

3   Invigorating and dangerously sublime, chocolate dominated every facet of Aztec life, from sexuality to economy. Cocoa beans even served as currency: You could buy a rabbit for 10 beans, a slave for 100 beans.

4   At first, Cortés hated chocolate's shocking taste, which mingled bitter, spicy, pungent, silky, dank and dusty flavors. But in time its magic seduced him, and it is said that he introduced it to Spain, flavoring it with sugar instead of hot chili peppers.

5   By the 17th century, chocolate was thrilling Europeans with its sensory jolt—less devilish than liquor but still stimulating, luxurious and pleasantly addictive. Those who could afford it drank it thick and hot, as the Indians did, sometimes adding orange, vanilla or spices. Society ladies sipped several cups a day and even insisted on drinking it during church services. Doctors prescribed chocolate as a flesh-and-bone rejuvenator that could lift the spirits, hasten healing and raise a flagging libido.

6   Forget Viagra. Think bonbons.

7   Casanova, it is said, swore by chocolate and ate it as a prelude to lovemaking. The French King Louis XV's principal mistress Madame du Barry, served exquisitely refined but essentially drug-level chocolate to her various suitors. Unknowingly, they were following the custom of Montezuma, who was believed to have consumed extra chocolate before visiting his harem.

8   A liquid treasure until the 19th century, chocolate suddenly changed shape and personality when a Dutch chemist discovered how to separate cocoa butter, leaving powdered cocoa. The public clamored for portable, ever-ready chocolate, and confectioners obliged with pyramids of chocolate bars. Joining the chocolamania, the Cadbury brothers introduced chocolate in heart-shaped boxes in 1868. Milk chocolate appeared in Switzerland in 1875, thanks to Peter Daniel and Henri Nestlé. Then American mass-production provided cheap chocolates for the multitudes, thanks to the foresight of Milton Hershey. And the rest is history.

9   Is chocolate a health food? Chocolate is chemically active—a mind-altering drug that's good for you in moderation. The higher the cocoa content, the more antioxidants and other nutritious

bonuses. Cocoa powder contains the most antioxidants, followed by dark chocolate and milk chocolate.

10   What delivers the chocolate buzz? Chocolate contains more than 300 chemicals, including tiny amounts of anandamide, which mimics the active ingredient in marijuana, plus such stimulants as theobromine and phenylethylamine. A 1.4-ounce bar of chocolate also can provide 20 milligrams of caffeine. That's jitters away from the 140 milligrams of an average cup of coffee, not to mention a thimbleful of espresso. But it's rousing enough, combined with the rest of chocolate's chemical bag of tricks. And the full sensory and nostalgic saga of eating chocolate—the mouth feel, the aroma, the taste, the memories—can calm the brain or lighten one's thoughts, for a while anyway.

11   If we luxuriate in a memory framed by the heaven of chocolate—say, eating s'mores around a campfire with a giggling Girl Scout troop or receiving a box of chocolates from a sappy beau and then sampling them with him—a small constellation of pleasure will attach itself to the idea of chocolate lifelong. That happens early on to nearly everyone.

12   For example, when I was a child, each year my mother and I would choose a colossal chocolate Easter rabbit with pink candy dot eyes. Together, we would sit on the floor in the aptly named "den" and devour most of the hollow rabbit—always starting with the ears and working our way down—until we went way beyond sated and started to feel a little sick. We would laugh with shared delight as we gobbled and afterward lounged about in a chocolate haze.

13   It was a cherished bonding ritual more visceral than verbal, reminding me how much we adore our senses. They're our houseguests, our explorers, our pets—and we love to give them treats. So how do you reward the sense of taste? For ages, the delicacy of choice has been rich, sensuously inviting chocolate.

Organization and Ideas

1. Paragraph 1 announces the subject and describes it with quick images, all to interest the reader. How well does it succeed?

2. Ackerman chooses to begin the body of the essay (paragraphs 2–8) with a brief history of chocolate. How does that history help define it?

3. Paragraphs 9 and 10 provide a scientific view of chocolate. What information surprises you and why?

4. Think of the ideas Ackerman presents in paragraphs 2–10 and how chocolate can cause an emotional attachment, as described in paragraphs 11–13. State her thesis in one sentence.
5. To what extent does Ackerman's account of and appreciation for chocolate mesh with your own?

Technique and Style

1. Consult a handbook of grammar and usage for what it says about a sentence fragment, and then take another look at paragraph 1. To what extent, if any, are those fragments effective?
2. You are probably used to paragraphs as units that extend an idea, but Ackerman's sixth paragraph is quite different. What is its function?
3. In the last paragraph, Ackerman uses several metaphors for our senses. Which do you prefer and why?
4. In paragraphs 1, 9, 10, and 13, Ackerman uses questions. What purpose do they serve?
5. Most of the essay can be categorized as expository and objective, but in paragraphs 12 and 13, Ackerman switches to the personal. Why might she have chosen to do that and what effect does it have?

Suggestions for Writing

Journal

1. Use your journal to explore how the senses can be viewed as pets.
2. Write a description that defines the kind of chocolate you like or dislike the most.

Essay

1. Think of the senses as possible topics for an essay that explains and defines the one you depend upon the most: sight, smell, hearing, touch, or motion. Like Ackerman, you will want to include some scientific information, so you should do some research to be able to explain how that sense functions (a medical encyclopedia or medical Web page would be a good source). And, of course, use your own experience to explain why that sense is important to you.
2. Think about a kind of snack or food that you like a great deal, and write an essay that defines it. Like Ackerman, you can point out its history, how it is produced, the various forms it comes in, and your experiences with it. No matter what your topic, you can find a great deal of information about it from the Web by using a search engine.

I Was a Member of the Kung Fu Crew

Henry Han Xi Lau

New York City is still in many ways a city of neighborhoods, many of which are ethnic ones. The Chinatown that Henry Han Xi Lau writes about is one of the oldest, and it's where you can still walk down the street and not hear a word of English. To Lau, it's also home, even though he and his family have moved to Brooklyn, which like Manhattan, is one of the city's five boroughs or districts. A sophomore at Yale University at the time he wrote this essay, Lau describes the people and places of Chinatown, defining it as "ghetto." The piece was published in the New York Times Magazine *on October 19, 1997. After the essay came out, Lau objected to the way it had been edited, calling it a "warped presentation" in a later piece he wrote for* Discourses, *an undergraduate journal at Yale (you can find his critique reprinted in* Microcosm, *a Web journal published by Rice University). What's missing, according to Lau, is the "resourcefulness and hard-working side of ghettoness." See what you think.*

What to Look For   Lau relies heavily upon definition to convey what it's like to be a member of the Kung Fu Crew and to be "ghetto." Many of the techniques he uses are ones that can carry over to your own writing, so be on the lookout for the details that define the Crew's physical prowess, hair, pants, attitudes, accessories, and language, all of which add up to being "cool."

1   Chinatown is ghetto, my friends are ghetto, I am ghetto. I went away to college last year, but I still have a long strand of hair that reaches past my chin. I need it when I go back home to hang with the K.F.C.— for Kung Fu Crew, not Kentucky Fried Chicken. We all met in a Northern Shaolin kung fu class years ago. Our *si-fu* was Rocky. He told us: "In the early 1900's in China, your grand master was walking in the streets when a foreigner riding on a horse disrespected him. So then he felt the belly of the horse with his palms and left. Shortly thereafter, the horse buckled and died because our grand master had used *qi-gong* to mess up the horse's internal organs."

Everyone said, "Cool, I would like to do that." Rocky emphasized, "You've got to practice really hard for a long time to reach that level."

2   By the time my friends and I were in the eighth grade, we were able to do 20-plus pushups on our knuckles and fingers. When we practiced our crescent, roundhouse and tornado kicks, we had 10-pound weights strapped to our legs. Someone once remarked, "Goddamn—that's a freaking mountain!" when he saw my thigh muscles in gym class.

3   Most Chinatown kids fall into a few general categories. There are pale-faced nerds who study all the time to get into the Ivies. There are the recent immigrants with uncombed hair and crooked teeth who sing karaoke in bars. There are the punks with highlighted hair who cut school, and the gangsters, whom everyone else avoids.

4   Then there is the K.F.C. We work hard like the nerds, but we identify with the punks. Now we are reunited, and just as in the old days we amble onto Canal Street, where we stick out above the older folks, elderly women bearing leaden bags of bok choy and oranges. As an opposing crew nears us, I assess them to determine whether to grill them or not. Grilling is the fine art of staring others down and trying to emerge victorious.

5   How the hair is worn is important in determining one's order on the streets. In the 80's, the dominant style was the mushroom cut, combed neatly or left wild in the front so that a person can appear menacing as he peers through his bangs. To gain an edge in grilling now, some kids have asymmetrical cuts, with long random strands sprouting in the front, sides or back. Some dye their hair blue or green, while blood red is usually reserved for gang members.

6   Only a few years ago, examination of the hair was sufficient. But now there is a second step: assessing pants. A couple of years ago, wide legs first appeared in New York City, and my friends and I switched from baggy pants. In the good old days, Merry-Go-Round in the Village sold wide legs for only $15 a pair. When Merry-Go-Round went bankrupt, Chinatown kids despaired. Wide-leg prices at other stores increased drastically as they became more popular. There are different ways of wearing wide legs. Some fold their pant legs inward and staple them at the hem. Some clip the back ends of their pants to their shoes with safety pins. Others simply cut the bottoms so that fuzzy strings hang out.

7   We grill the opposing punks. I untuck my long strand of hair so that it swings in front of my face. Nel used to have a strand, but he

chewed it off one day in class by accident. Chu and Tom cut their strands off because it scared people at college. Jack has a patch of blond hair, while Tone's head is a ball of orange flame. Chi has gelled short hair, while Ken's head is a black mop. As a group, we have better hair than our rivals. But they beat us with their wide legs. In our year away at college, wide legs have gone beyond our 24-inch leg openings. Twenty-six- to 30-inch jeans are becoming the norm. If wide legs get any bigger, they will start flying up like a skirt in an updraft.

8   We have better accessories, though. Chi sports a red North Face that gives him a rugged mountain-climber look because of the jungle of straps sprouting in the back. Someone once asked Chi, "Why is the school bag so important to one's cool?" He responded, "Cuz it's the last thing others see when you walk away from them or when they turn back to look at you after you walk past them." But the other crew has female members, which augments their points. The encounter between us ends in a stalemate. But at least the K.F.C. members are in college and are not true punks.

9   In the afternoon, we decide to eat at the Chinatown McDonald's for a change instead of the Chinese bakery Maria's, our dear old hangout spot. "Mickey D's is good sit," Nel says. I answer: "But the Whopper gots more fat and meat. It's even got more bun." Nel agrees. "True that," he says. I want the Big Mac, but I buy the two-cheeseburger meal because it has the same amount of meat but costs less.

10   We sit and talk about ghettoness again. We can never exactly articulate what being ghetto entails, but we know the spirit of it. In Chinatown toilet facilities we sometimes find footprints on the seats because F.O.B.'s (fresh off the boats) squat on them as they do over the holes in China. We see alternative brand names in stores like Dolo instead of Polo, and Mike instead of Nike.

11   We live by ghettoness. My friends and I walk from 80-something Street in Manhattan to the tip of the island to save a token. We gorge ourselves at Gray's Papaya because the hot dogs are 50 cents each. But one cannot be stingy all the time. We leave good tips at Chinese restaurants because our parents are waiters and waitresses, too.

12   We sit for a long time in McDonald's, making sure that there is at least a half-inch of soda in our cups so that when the staff wants to kick us out, we can claim that we are not finished yet. Jack positions

a mouse bite of cheeseburger in the center of a wrapper to support our claim.

13   After a few hours, the K.F.C. prepares to disband. I get in one of the no-license commuter vans on Canal Street that will take me to Sunset Park in Brooklyn, where my family lives now. All of my friends will leave Chinatown, for the Upper East Side and the Lower East Side, Forest Hills in Queens and Bensonhurst in Brooklyn. We live far apart, but we always come back together in Chinatown. For most of us, our homes used to be here and our world was here.

Organization and Ideas

1. The essay is set out in chronological order. What paragraphs cover what times?

2. What categories of kids does Lau describe? Where does the Crew fit?

3. Lau describes "grilling" in paragraphs 4–8. What is his point?

4. Lau may have moved away from Chinatown, but he is still very much a part of its community. How would you characterize that community and its values?

5. Is Lau's thesis explicit or implicit? How can you phrase it in your own words?

Technique and Style

1. Look up the term *comma splice* in a handbook of grammar and usage, and check what you find against Lau's first sentence. Why is it a legitimate comma splice?

2. Lau uses dialogue in paragraphs 8 and 9. What does it add to the essay?

3. The essay piles on details and information that lead up to a definition of *ghetto*. State that definition in your own words.

4. *Ghetto* usually has a negative connotation. How does Lau make it positive?

5. The essay is written in standard American English. Why might Lau have chosen to write it that way instead of in "ghetto"?

Suggestions for Writing

Journal

1. If you met the Kung Fu Crew on the street, you might find yourself ignoring them, "grilling" them, admiring them, but no matter what, you'd have some sort of reaction. Describe how you would react.

2. Look up the word *intimidation* in an unabridged dictionary, and think about times in your experience when you were intimidated or intimidated someone. Use your journal to define how you felt.

Essay

1. People spend a lot of time analyzing what's in and what's out. For some, those in advertising or fashion, for instance, it's a business, but all of us are affected by it. Perhaps you would find a lot to say in an essay about what it means to be "in" or "cool" or the opposite. Think about a category (some suggestions are listed below), choose a subject, and then start jotting down details such as the particulars of language (spoken and body), appearance, attitudes, and likes and dislikes that define your central term.

> music
> films or television shows
> dates
> schools
> cars

As you draft your essay, try to keep your focus on definition. It's natural to lean toward comparisons, but, like Lau, make sure you use them to support what you are defining.

2. Each generation usually ends up with at least one label or tag—the Baby Boomers, the Yuppies, or some such. What label works for your generation? Write an essay that explains your choice, providing examples to prove your point.

The Handicap of Definition

William Raspberry

William Raspberry left the small and segregated town in Mississippi where he grew up to take a summer job with the Indianapolis Reporter, *moving on in 1962 to the* Washington Post. *Although he now teaches at Duke University, where he is the Knight Chair in Communications and Journalism, he is better known as a writer for the* Washington Post *and as the author of a syndicated column that runs in more than 200 newspapers. His commentary on issues such as rap music, crime, and AIDS earned him a Pulitzer Prize in 1994. In the essay that follows, he writes about the terms* black *and* white, *words that have connotations we don't often think about. Raspberry shows us that if we stop to think about* black, *we'll see that it has so narrow a definition that it is "one of the heaviest burdens black Americans—and black children in particular—have to bear." Not much has changed since 1982, when this essay first appeared in Raspberry's syndicated column.*

What to Look For   Somewhere along the line, we've all been warned never to begin a sentence with a conjunction such as *and, but,* and the like. But as long as you know how to avoid the trap of a sentence fragment, beginning a sentence with a conjunction can lend a conversational tone to your essay. As you read Raspberry's essay, notice how often he uses this technique.

1   I know all about bad schools, mean politicians, economic deprivation and racism. Still, it occurs to me that one of the heaviest burdens black Americans—and black children in particular—have to bear is the handicap of definition: the question of what it means to be black.

2   Let me explain quickly what I mean. If a basketball fan says that the Boston Celtics' Larry Bird plays "black," the fan intends it—and Bird probably accepts it—as a compliment. Tell pop singer Tom Jones he moves "black" and he might grin in appreciation. Say to Teena Marie or The Average White Band that they sound "black" and they'll thank you.

3   But name one pursuit, aside from athletics, entertainment or sexual performance in which a white practitioner will feel complimented to be told he does it "black." Tell a white broadcaster he talks "black," and he'll sign up for diction lessons. Tell a white reporter he writes "black" and he'll take a writing course. Tell a white lawyer he reasons "black" and he might sue you for slander.

4   What we have here is a tragically limited definition of blackness, and it isn't only white people who buy it.

5   Think of all the ways black children can put one another down with charges of "whiteness." For many of these children, hard study and hard work are "white." Trying to please a teacher might be criticized as acting "white." Speaking correct English is "white." Scrimping today in the interest of tomorrow's goals is "white." Educational toys and games are "white."

6   An incredible array of habits and attitudes that are conducive to success in business, in academia, in the nonentertainment professions are likely to be thought of as somehow "white." Even economic success, unless it involves such "black" undertakings as numbers banking, is defined as "white."

7   And the results are devastating. I wouldn't deny that blacks often are better entertainers and athletes. My point is the harm that comes from too narrow a definition of what is black.

8   One reason black youngsters tend to do better at basketball, for instance, is that they assume they can learn to do it well, and so they practice constantly to prove themselves right.

9   Wouldn't it be wonderful if we could infect black children with the notion that excellence in math is "black" rather than white, or possibly Chinese? Wouldn't it be of enormous value if we could create the myth that morality, strong families, determination, courage and love of learning are traits brought by slaves from Mother Africa and therefore quintessentially black?

10   There is no doubt in my mind that most black youngsters could develop their mathematical reasoning, their elocution and their attitudes the way they develop their jump shots and their dance steps: by the combination of sustained, enthusiastic practice and the unquestioned belief that they can do it.

11   In one sense, what I am talking about is the importance of developing positive ethnic traditions. Maybe Jews have an innate talent for communication; maybe Chinese are born with a gift for mathematical reasoning; maybe blacks are naturally blessed with athletic grace. I doubt it. What is at work, I suspect, is assumption, inculcated early in their lives, that this is a thing our people do well.

12   Unfortunately, many of the things about which blacks make this assumption are things that do not contribute to their career success—except for that handful of the truly gifted who can make it as entertainers and athletes. And many of the things we concede to whites are the things that are essential to economic security.

13   So it is with a number of assumptions black youngsters make about what it is to be a "man": physical aggressiveness, sexual prowess, the refusal to submit to authority. The prisons are full of people who, by this perverted definition, are unmistakably men.

14   But the real problem is not so much that the things defined as "black" are negative. The problem is that the definition is much too narrow.

15   Somehow, we have to make our children understand that they are intelligent, competent people, capable of doing whatever they put their minds to and making it in the American mainstream, not just in a black subculture.

16   What we seem to be doing, instead, is raising up yet another generation of young blacks who will be failures—by definition.

Organization and Ideas

1. Examine paragraphs 1–4, 5–7, and 8–11. Each functions as a unit. What sentence is the major assertion for each group of paragraphs?

2. Examine paragraphs 12–16 as a concluding paragraph block. What is the relationship between paragraph 12 and the preceding paragraphs?

3. Consider the controlling ideas that guide the paragraph blocks and the conclusions Raspberry draws from the examples that support those assertions. Stated fully, what is Raspberry's thesis?

4. A militant who read this essay would argue that Raspberry is trying to make blacks "better" by making them white. Is there any evidence to support this view? Explain.

5. A feminist who read the essay would argue that it is sexist. Is there any evidence to support this view? Explain.

Technique and Style

1. This essay was one of Raspberry's syndicated columns; as a result, it appeared in a large number of newspapers with equally large readerships, mostly white. What evidence can you find that Raspberry is trying to inform his white audience and persuade his black readers?

2. How and where does Raspberry establish his credibility as a writer on this subject? What grammatical point of view does he use?

3. Where in the essay does he qualify or modulate his statements? What is the effect of that technique?

4. Paragraphs 3, 7, 13, and 14 all begin with a conjunction. What effect does this technique achieve? Consult a handbook of grammar and usage for a discussion of this device. To what extent does Raspberry's usage conform to the handbook's advice?

5. Paragraph 16 is an example of a rhetorical paragraph, a one-sentence paragraph that gives dramatic emphasis to a point. If you eliminate the dash or substitute a comma for it, what happens to the dramatic effect? What does the pun add?

Suggestions for Writing

Journal

1. Raspberry's essay was published in 1982. Write a journal entry explaining whether his point holds true today.

2. Write down any examples you can think of that can substitute for those Raspberry uses, but focus on women. In a paragraph or two, explain how the substitutions would add to or detract from his point.

Essay

1. Find a word that has accumulated broad connotations and then see what definitions have evolved and their effect. Like Raspberry, you may want to consider two terms but emphasize only one. Possibilities:

man
hero
student
woman
worker
lover
politician

2. Raspberry says "we have to make our children understand that they are intelligent, competent people, capable of doing whatever they put their minds to . . ." (paragraph 15). But *intelligent* and *competent* mean different things to different people. Select one of the words and write an essay in which you define what the word means to you. As you think about your topic, remember that it can be useful to define something by what it is not, by comparisons.

The Myth of the Matriarch

Gloria Naylor

Best known for her novels, Gloria Naylor was born in Queens, a borough of New York City, and received her first library card at the age of four. After graduating from Brooklyn College and earning a master's degree at Yale, she began her career as a writer. Her first novel, The Women of Brewster Place, *was published in 1982 and received the American Book Award for best first novel. Her most recent,* Bailey's Café, *rounds off what Naylor calls her "novel quartet." A winner of the National Book Award for her fiction, Naylor is also noted for editing* Children of the Night: The Best Short Stories by Black Writers, 1967 to the Present *(1996). The essay that follows was published in* Life *in the spring of 1988. The neighborhood she grew up in and her travels have given Naylor lots of opportunity to observe both the myth and the reality of the matriarch.*

What to Look For   When you think of the term *paragraph,* you probably imagine a fairly large chunk of prose that illustrates and develops a particular point that's stated or implied as a topic sentence. But paragraphs serve other functions as well, as Naylor's essay shows. Her essay is complex, which makes the need for clear transitions between paragraphs important, but providing a transition from one major part of the essay to another is more difficult. Naylor does it by using a short paragraph in which she poses a question that she then answers in the paragraphs that follow.

1   The strong black woman. All my life I've seen her. In books she is Faulkner's impervious Dilsey, using her huge dark arms to hold together the crumbling spirits and household of the Compsons. In the movies she is the quintessential Mammy, chasing after Scarlett O'Hara with forgotten sunbonnets and shrill tongue-lashings about etiquette. On television she is Sapphire of *Amos 'n Andy* or a dozen variations of her—henpecking black men, herding white children, protecting her brood from the onslaughts of the world. She is the supreme matriarch—alone, self-sufficient and liking it that way. I've seen how this female image has permeated the American consciousness to the point of influencing everything from the selling of pancakes to the structuring of welfare benefits. But the strangest thing is that when I walked around my neighborhood or went into the homes of family and friends, this matriarch was nowhere to be found.

2   I know the statistics: They say that when my grandmother was born at the turn of the century as few as 10 percent of black households were headed by females; when I was born at mid-century it had crept to 17 percent; and now it is almost 60 percent. No longer a widow or a divorcée as in times past, the single woman with children today probably has never married—and increasingly she is

getting younger. By the time she is 18, one out of every four black unmarried women has become a mother.

3   But it is a long leap from a matrifocal home, where the father is absent, to a matriarchal one, in which the females take total charge from the males. Though I have known black women heading households in different parts of the country and in different social circumstances—poor, working class or professional—none of them has gloried in the conditions that left them with the emotional and financial responsibility for their families. Often they had to take domestic work because of the flexible hours or stay in menial factory or office jobs because of the steady pay. And leaving the job was only to go home to the other job of raising children alone. These women understood the importance of input from black men in sustaining their families. Their advice and, sometimes, financial assistance were sought and accepted. But if such were not forthcoming, she would continue to deal with her situation alone.

4   This is a far cry from the heartwarming image of the two-fisted black woman I watched striding across the public imagination. A myth always arises to serve a need. And so it must be asked, what is it in the relationship of black women to American society that has called for them to be seen as independent Amazons?

5   The black woman was brought to America for the same reason as the black man—to provide slave labor. But she had what seemed to be contradictory roles: She did the woman's work of bearing children and keeping house while doing a man's work at the side of the black male in the fields. She worked regardless of the advanced stages of pregnancy. In the 19th century the ideal of the true woman was one of piety, purity, domesticity and submissiveness; the female lived as a wife sheltered at home or went abroad as a virgin doing good works. But if the prevailing belief was that the natural state of women was one of frailty, how could the black female be explained? Out in the fields laboring with their muscled bodies and during rest periods suckling infants at their breasts, the slave women had to be seen as different from white women. They were stronger creatures: they didn't feel pain in childbirth; they didn't have tear ducts. Ironically, one of the arguments for enslaving blacks in the first place was that as a race they were inferior to whites—but black women, well, they were a little *more* than women.

6   The need to view slavery as benign accounted for the larger-than-life mammy of the plantation legends. As a house servant, she

was always pictured in close proximity to her white masters because there was nothing about her that was threatening to white ideas about black women. Her unstinting devotion assuaged any worries that slaves were discontented or harbored any potential for revolt. Her very dark skin belied any suspicions of past interracial liaisons, while her obesity and advanced age removed any sexual threat. Earth mother, nursemaid and cook, the mammy existed without a history or a future.

7   In reality, slave women in the house or the field were part of a kinship network and with their men tried to hold together their own precarious families. Marriages between slaves were not legally recognized, but this did not stop them from entering into living arrangements and acting as husbands and wives. After emancipation a deluge of black couples registered their unions under the law, and ex-slaves were known to travel hundreds of miles in search of lost partners and children.

8   No longer bound, but hardly equal citizens, black men and women had access to only the most menial jobs in society, the largest number being reserved solely for female domestics. Richard Wright wrote a terribly funny and satirical short story about the situation, "Man of All Work." His protagonist is unable to find a job to support his family and save his house from foreclosure, so he puts on his wife's clothes and secures a position as a housekeeper. "Don't stop me. I've found a solution to our problem. I'm an army-trained cook. I can clean a house as good as anybody. Get my point? I put on your dress. I looked in the mirror. I can pass. I want that job."

9   Pushed to the economic forefront of her home, the 19th century mammy became 20th century Sapphire. Fiery, younger, more aggressive, she just couldn't wait to take the lead away from the man of the house. Whatever he did was never enough. Not that he wanted to do anything, of course, except hang out on street corners, gamble and run around with women. From vaudeville of the 1880s to the advent of *Amos 'n Andy,* it was easier to make black men the brunt of jokes than to address the inequities that kept decent employment from those who wanted to work. Society had not failed black women—their men had.

10   The truth is that throughout our history black women could depend upon their men even when they were unemployed or underemployed. But in the impoverished inner cities today we are seeing the rise of the *unemployable.* These young men are not equipped to take responsibility for themselves, much less the children they

are creating. And with the increasing youth of unwed mothers, we have grandmothers and grandfathers in their early thirties. How can a grandmother give her daughter's family the traditional wisdom and support when she herself has barely lived? And on the other side of town, where the professional black woman is heading a household, usually because she is divorced, the lack of a traditional kinship network—the core community of parents, uncles, aunts— makes her especially alone.

11   What is surprising to me is that the myth of the matriarch lives on—even among black women. I've talked to so many who believe that they are supposed to be superhuman and bear up under all things. When they don't, they all too readily look for the fault within themselves. Somehow they failed their history. But it is a grave mistake for black women to believe that they have a natural ability to be stronger than other women. Fifty-seven percent of black homes being headed by females is not natural. A 40 percent pregnancy rate among our young girls is not natural. It is heart-breaking. The myth of the matriarch robs a woman caught in such circumstances of her individuality and her humanity. She should feel that she has the *right* at least to break down—once the kids are put to bed—and do something so simple as cry.

Organization and Ideas

1. Paragraphs 1–3 introduce the essay. In what ways do they set the stage for what follows?

2. Paragraph 3 introduces the concepts of matrifocal and kinship relationships, and Naylor refers to these concepts again in paragraphs 7 and 10. What is her point?

3. Naylor states that "A myth always arises to serve a need" (paragraph 4). Reread paragraphs 5–9 and explain the needs served by the myth of the matriarch.

4. How does Naylor's description of the present situation relate to the idea of the myth of the matriarch?

5. The essay concludes with the negative effects of the myth. What are they? Given those negative effects and the history of the myth explained in paragraphs 4–9, what is Naylor's thesis?

Technique and Style

1. The essay opens with allusions to fiction and television shows. How would you update them?

2. Paragraphs 2 and 11 introduce statistics into the essay. What do they contribute?

3. Naylor describes the role of black women in the days of slavery and the attitudes of whites toward them. Explain whether you find her tone more objective than subjective or the opposite.

4. How would you describe Naylor's audience?

5. What myth or myths have been applied to you? In what ways are they myths?

Suggestions for Writing

Journal

1. Test your own experience against Naylor's myth of the strong black woman. Does the myth exist or not? Write a journal entry in which you describe what you discovered.

2. In what ways have you been affected by a myth? List those that may apply to you, choose one, and write down your response to it.

Essay

1. The myth of the matriarch is just one of the many myths in our culture that have given rise to stereotypes similar to the mammies and Sapphires that Naylor points out. These stereotypes show up frequently in popular culture—in films, books, television shows—thus furthering the myth. Mull over recent movies or television shows you've seen or popular fiction you've read. Once you've focused on a myth, search your memory for other examples of it and for how it may show up in real life. Your paper may turn out like Naylor's, defining the myth and showing its harmful and false side, or you may prefer a simpler route, exploring only the myth. Suggested myths:
   the hero
   the "Wild West"
   the supermom
   the adorable child
   the nightmare slasher
   the happy homemaker

2. Consider the terms associated with the United States. We think of our nation as "land of the free," "home of the brave," "one nation indivisible," and so on. Make a list of all the phrases you can think of associated with the United States and then select one for the topic of an essay in which you explore whether the phrase is accurate, myth, or somewhere in between.

Where Nothing Says Everything

Suzanne Berne

*When not teaching at Harvard University, Suzanne Berne writes both
nonfiction and fiction.* A Crime in the Neighborhood, *her first novel,
was called "remarkable" by the* New York Times Book Review, *and
it went on to be chosen as a* Times *"Notable Book." In 1999, it received the United Kingdom's Orange Prize, a singular honor. To be
eligible, a novel must be written by a woman and written in English,
for the prize "aims to celebrate novels of excellence, originality and
accessibility, and to promote women writers to as wide a range of
male and female readers as possible." Berne's latest novel is* A Perfect
Relationship *(2001). When not working on fiction and teaching,
Berne contributes to the travel section of the* New York Times, *where
this essay appeared on April 21, 2002.*

What to Look For   Berne has a difficult job in trying to define
Ground Zero, as so many readers have vivid images of both the disaster and the site. As you read, notice how she uses description, contrast, narration, example, and cause and effect to define her subject.

1   On a cold, damp March morning, I visited Manhattan's financial
district, a place I'd never been, to pay my respects at what used to
be the World Trade Center. Many other people had chosen to do
the same that day, despite the raw wind and spits of rain, and so
the first thing I noticed when I arrived on the corner of Vesey and
Church Streets was a crowd.

2   Standing on the sidewalk, pressed against aluminum police barri-
cades, wearing scarves that flapped into their faces and woolen hats
pulled over their ears, were people apparently from everywhere.
Germans, Italians, Japanese. An elegant-looking Norwegian family
in matching shearling coats. People from Ohio and California and
Maine. Children, middle-age couples, older people. Many of them
were clutching cameras and video recorders, and they were all
craning to see across the street, where there was nothing to see.

3   At least, nothing is what it first looked like, the space that is now
ground zero. But once your eyes adjust to what you are looking

at, "nothing" becomes something much more potent, which is absence.

4   But to the out-of-towner, ground zero looks at first simply like a construction site. All the familiar details are there: the wooden scaffolding; the cranes, the bulldozers and forklifts; the trailers and construction workers in hard hats; even the dust. There is the pound of jackhammers, the steady beep-beep-beep of trucks backing up, the roar of heavy machinery.

5   So much busyness is reassuring, and it is possible to stand looking at the cranes and trucks and feel that mild curiosity and hopefulness so often inspired by construction sites.

6   Then gradually your eyes do adjust, exactly as if you have stepped from a dark theater into a bright afternoon, because what becomes most striking about this scene is the light itself.

7   Ground zero is a great bowl of light, an emptiness that seems weirdly spacious and grand, like a vast plaza amid the dense tangle of streets in lower Manhattan. Light reflecting off the Hudson River vaults into the site, soaking everything—especially on an overcast morning—with a watery glow. This is the moment when absence begins to assume a material form, when what is not there becomes visible.

8   Suddenly you notice the periphery, the skyscraper shrouded in black plastic, the boarded windows, the steel skeleton of the shattered Winter Garden. Suddenly there are the broken steps and cracked masonry in front of Brooks Brothers. Suddenly there are the firefighters, the waiting ambulance on the other side of the pit, the police on every corner. Suddenly there is the enormous cross made of two rusted girders.

9   And suddenly, very suddenly, there is the little cemetery attached to St. Paul's Chapel, with tulips coming up, the chapel and grounds miraculously undamaged except for a few plastic-sheathed gravestones. The iron fence is almost invisible beneath a welter of dried pine wreaths, banners, ribbons, laminated poems and prayers and photographs, swags of paper cranes, withered flowers, baseball hats, rosary beads, teddy bears. And flags, flags everywhere, little American flags fluttering in the breeze, flags on posters drawn by Brownie troops, flags on T-shirts, flags on hats, flags streaming by, tied to the handles of baby strollers.

10   It takes quite a while to see all of this; it takes even longer to come up with something to say about it.

11   An elderly man standing next to me had been staring fixedly across the street for some time. Finally he touched his son's elbow and said: "I watched those towers being built. I saw this place when they weren't there." Then he stopped, clearly struggling with, what for him, was a double negative, recalling an absence before there was an absence. His son, waiting patiently, took a few photographs. "Let's get out of here," the man said at last.

12   Again and again I heard people say, "It's unbelievable." And then they would turn to each other, dissatisfied. They wanted to say something more expressive, more meaningful. But it is unbelievable, to stare at so much devastation, and know it for devastation, and yet recognize that it does not look like the devastation one has imagined.

13   Like me, perhaps, the people around me had in mind images from television and newspaper pictures: the collapsing buildings, the running office workers, the black plume of smoke against a bright blue sky. Like me, they were probably trying to superimpose those terrible images onto the industrious emptiness right in front of them. The difficulty of this kind of mental revision is measured, I believe, by the brisk trade in World Trade Center photograph booklets at tables set up on street corners.

14   Determined to understand better what I was looking at, I decided to get a ticket for the viewing platform beside St. Paul's. This proved no easy task, as no one seemed to be able to direct me to South Street Seaport, where the tickets are distributed. Various police officers whom I asked for directions, waved me vaguely toward the East River, differing degrees of boredom and resignation on their faces. Or perhaps it was a kind of incredulousness. Somewhere around the American Stock Exchange, I asked a security guard for help and he frowned at me, saying, "You want tickets to the disaster?"

15   Finally I found myself in line at a cheerfully painted kiosk, watching a young juggler try to entertain the crowd. He kept dropping the four red balls he was attempting to juggle, and having to chase after them. It was noon; the next available viewing was at 4 p.m.

16   Back I walked, up Fulton Street, the smell of fish in the air, to wander again around St. Paul's. A deli on Vesey Street advertised a view of the World Trade Center from its second-floor dining area. I went in and ordered a pastrami sandwich, uncomfortably aware

that many people before me had come to that same deli for pastrami sandwiches who would never come there again. But I was here to see what I could, so I carried my sandwich upstairs and sat down beside one of the big plate-glass windows.

17   And there, at last, I got my ticket to the disaster.

18   I could see not just into the pit now, but also its access ramp, which trucks had been traveling up and down since I had arrived that morning. Gathered along the ramp were firefighters in their black helmets and black coats. Slowly they lined up, and it became clear that this was an honor guard, and that someone's remains were being carried up the ramp toward the open door of an ambulance.

19   Everyone in the dining room stopped eating. Several people stood up, whether out of respect or to see better, I don't know. For a moment, everything paused.

20   Then the day flowed back into itself. Soon I was outside once more, joining the tide of people washing around the site. Later, as I huddled with a little crowd on the viewing platform, watching people scrawl their names or write "God Bless America" on the plywood walls, it occurred to me that a form of repopulation was taking effect, with so many visitors to this place, thousands of visitors, all of us coming to see the wide emptiness where so many were lost. And by the act of our visiting—whether we are motivated by curiosity or horror or reverence or grief, or by something confusing that combines them all—that space fills up again.

Organization and Ideas

1. The essay is organized by the time of the day, from the morning to the late afternoon. Why might Berne have chosen that organization and how effective is it?

2. Arguably the most important newspaper in the United States, the *New York Times* has a very broad and general readership. Even so, writers often have specific readers in mind. To whom is Berne's essay addressed?

3. To what extent would you call Berne's account objective? Subjective? What evidence can you find to support your view?

4. Reread the conclusion, paragraphs 18–20. What does it imply about the site? What is the essay's thesis?

5. What kind of effect do you think Berne is trying to have on the reader? Does it work? Why or why not?

Technique and Style

1. Berne uses the pronoun *you* in the essay. Reread the piece, keeping track of where the word occurs. Who is the *you*?
2. Look up the word *paradox* in an unabridged dictionary. Where do you find examples of it in Berne's essay? How effective are they?
3. Take another look at the essay's title. To what extent is it appropriate?
4. Paragraphs 3, 10, and 17 function as transitions. Choose one and explain whether it succeeds.
5. Look up the word *understatement* in an unabridged dictionary or dictionary of literary terms. To what extent does it describe Berne's tone?

Suggestions for Writing

Journal

1. Explain why you would or would not have visited the site of the World Trade Center.
2. Berne uses the word *absence* in paragraphs 3, 7, and 11. What does her use of the word contribute to the essay as a whole?

Essay

1. Think of the times when you have made a visit to an important place. When did you go? What did you do? Who else was there? What effect did it have on you? Write an essay in which you define the meaning of such a visit. Suggestions, a
    cemetery
    historic site
    tourist attraction
    museum
    house you grew up in
2. It's almost impossible to avoid the emotional impact of 9/11. Think about your reactions at that time or now in retrospect, and list the emotions you felt—shock, horror, anger, despair, incredulity, and so on. Choose one of the words as the subject of an essay in which you define the word, using 9/11 as a starting point but also examples from your own experience, including what you have seen or read.

ADDITIONAL WRITING ASSIGNMENTS

Using Definition

1. Define an abstract term: morality, honor, courage, humility, friendship.
2. Define your taste in: music, art, film, books, television, friends.
3. Define the qualities you most admire in a person: parent, teacher, religious leader, sibling, political figure.
4. Define an article of clothing that operates as a symbol: jeans, baseball hat, tee shirt, bandanna, athletic shoes.

Evaluating the Essays

1. The essays by Henry Han Xi Lau and William Raspberry deal with identifiable groups and the conflicts both within and outside of them. Lau defines his group in terms of "ghettoness," and Raspberry defines young black children in terms of what it means to be a "man." Which conflict is the more difficult and why? Use both essays to back up your opinion.
2. Diane Ackerman and Suzanne Berne rely heavily on description and observation to define their subjects and bring them to life. Which one does the better job? Cite examples and quote material from both essays to prove your point.
3. Gloria Naylor and William Raspberry focus on race and both write as African Americans. Of the two, which one makes the more compelling argument? Again, quote from both essays to provide evidence for your choice.
4. Look up *symbol* in a dictionary of literary terms and then consider the essays by Henry Han Xi Lau and Suzanne Berne. Lau's hair, walk, clothing, and accessories are all symbols of his membership in the Kung Fu Crew (as is the name of the crew itself). Berne, however, concentrates on the site of the World Trade Center as symbol. Reread the essays, noting the larger meanings of what the symbols represent. Which author uses symbolism more effectively? What evidence supports your opinion?

On Using
Example

A ny time you encounter *for instance, such as,* or *for example,* you know what will follow: an **example** that explains and supports the generalization. Used with general statements, examples fill in the gaps. If you are writing on the subject of violent crime and want to show that the facts contradict what many people believe, you might write "Many people believe most crime is violent and that crime is increasing." Then you might continue by citing statistics as examples that show the rate of crime peaked in the seventies but then ceased to rise in the eighties and actually fell in the nineties. You would have supported the idea that crime rates have fallen, but you would still need to provide evidence for the idea that many people believe the opposite. Readers also need to know what evidence supports your claim that crime, to many people, means violent crime. That evidence is apt to come in the form of an example, an illustration that clarifies or develops a point. The most basic building block of all, examples pin down generalizations, supporting them with specifics.

To use examples well, you first need to know when to use them, then which ones to select, and finally, how to incorporate them. If you read actively, responding to the words on the page as you would to a person talking to you, odds are you will spot where examples are needed. On reading the sentence above about crime, you might think to yourself, "Hey, wait a minute! How about that violent crime statement?" Often it helps to read your own work belligerently, ready to shoot down any generalization with a "Says who?" The response to "Says who?" will vary according to your audience. A sociology paper will call for statistics; a personal narrative will draw on your own experience. Other good sources are the experiences of others and those of authorities whose work you can quote. The skill here is to match the example not only to the generalization it supports but also to the readers to whom it is addressed.

After you have found good examples, you need to sequence them logically, while at the same time you avoid overusing terms such as "for example." Where you use multiple examples, you can use **transitions** that signal addition (*and, also, again, besides, moreover, next, finally,* etc.); where you use examples that compare, opt for transitions that indicate a turn (*but, yet, however, instead, in contrast,* etc.). Occasionally you may find yourself introducing an example that serves as a concession, calling for *of course, certainly,* or *granted.* Other times you may want a transition that indicates result—*therefore, thus, as a result, so.* More obvious are transitions setting up a summary, as in *finally, in conclusion, hence,* or *in brief.* Less obvious and, therefore, apt to be more effective are transitions that don't call attention to themselves, such as the repetition of a key word from the previous sentence or the use of a personal or demonstrative pronoun. If you use pronouns, however, make sure that what they refer to is clear. The demonstrative pronoun *this,* for instance, should usually be followed by a noun, as in *this sentence* or *this idea.* A *this* standing by itself may force your reader to go back to the previous sentence to understand exactly what it refers to.

Audience and Purpose

In general, the less familiar your audience is with your subject, the more important it is to have examples, and lots of them. If you find yourself writing about a sport, for instance, you would do well to think about what your audience may or may not know about it. If the sport is ice hockey and your readers are your classmates most of whom live in Mississippi, you'll know that most of them won't know much about your topic, so you will have to use lots of examples. And if you are arguing that ice hockey is an underrated sport, you can draw on your readers' experience with more familiar games such as basketball. You might use the example of the pace of a basketball game to make the point that ice hockey is even faster, so fast that at times the crowd can't even see the puck.

If your readers are relatively familiar with your topic, then your job is to make that familiarity come to life and shape it to your purpose. If you are writing an essay that explores the various levels of anxiety experienced by a first-year college student, you will probably cite a number of instances. You might start with the example of registering by telephone and the mild concern that the machine on the other end of the line will send your course requests to electronic heaven, then the fear of not finding the right classroom and turning up, if at all, late for class; next the uneasiness that occurs with the first look at the course syllabus, followed by the apprehension over the speed of a lecture; and then you might end with the sheer terror of the first test. If you provide enough examples, at least one is bound to remind a reader of a similar response.

The examples get harder to come by if your subject is a controversial or sensitive one. On familiar topics such as abortion, capital punishment, and prayer in public schools, your readers are not only apt to have opinions but very set ones, so set that you might do well to steer clear of the topic. Even less touchy subjects are difficult to write about because you have to be sensitive to views that differ from yours so that you don't alienate those readers. When dealing with a topic on which there has been much debate, it often helps to list the opposing arguments so you can find examples to support your points and to defeat the opposite ones.

Now and then, you may also find yourself writing an essay that tackles a subject that isn't controversial but still requires some caution on your part. You might, for example, want to write about what you find to be our culture's "throwaway" mentality and how it is adversely affecting the environment. When you start listing the more obvious throwaway items you can think of, you find you have fast-food wrappings and boxes, ballpoint pens, paper napkins and towels, and plastic coverings for CDs, all items your readers probably use and throw away without thinking. Your problem then becomes one of educating your readers without insulting or blaming them, which isn't easy. Recognizing the problem, however, is halfway to solving it, and you'll read essays in this chapter that do just that.

Types of Examples

Examples generally fall into two categories, extended and multiple. An essay that rests its assertion on only one example is relatively rare, but you will run across one now and then. When you do, the example often takes the form of a narrative in support of the author's thesis. To show that a minimum-wage job can be a fulfilling one (or a demeaning one—take your pick), you might support your thesis by telling about a typical day on the job. While you are relying on only one example, you will have developed it in considerable depth, and you probably will have included a sentence or two to indicate that other experiences may contradict yours, so your readers will accept your extended example as valid.

Far more frequent, however, are multiple examples. They add clarity, support, and emphasis, and save you from having to make the kind of disclaimer mentioned above. Sometimes the examples will be drawn from your own experience and the experiences of others, but often you will find you want more generalized sources, so you consult books, magazines, interviews, reports, and so on. You may well find that examples drawn from outside sources give your essay a more objective, reasoned **tone.** If you think of that term as similar to tone of voice, you will realize that it means the writer's attitude toward the subject and audience. Examples drawn from personal experience are apt to create an informal, conversational tone; those drawn from outside sources often provide a cooler, more formal tone. No matter where you find your examples, however, you can present them with some variety, summarizing some, quoting others.

Examples not only illustrate generalizations, they expand and develop them. After you have written a draft of an essay, you may find it useful to double-check each of your examples by asking several questions: How does the example support the generalization? Is the source of the example clear? How does it connect to the readers' experiences? If the example is an extended one, is it sufficiently developed so that it can support the thesis by itself? Then you might think about the examples as a whole: Do they draw on a variety of sources? Do they incorporate both summary and quotation?

Details

In presenting an example, the writer uses many of the same techniques that come into play in description. Descriptive details can come from unlikely places, such as the pushers and products Michiko Kakutani cites as examples to support her claim that advertising has saturated our lives.

> The dead, including Marilyn Monroe (Chanel No. 5), Gene Kelly (Gap khakis) and Fred Astaire (Dirt Devil vacuum cleaners), have been hired as pitchmen, and so have New Delhi paraplegics, who now hawk Coca-Cola under bright red-and-white umbrellas. Even bananas have been colonized as billboard space, with stickers promoting the video release of "Space Jam" and the "Got Milk?" campaign turning up on the fruit. (130)

Drawing on the familiar and unfamiliar, Kakutani's examples catch our attention.

As with description, details are used to make the abstract concrete. If you were writing about an abstract principle such as freedom, for example, you might find yourself writing about one kind of freedom that you particularly value, the freedom that your parents allowed you to make mistakes. You would probably provide a number of examples, and each one might be in the form of a short narrative, but the effectiveness of those narratives will lie in the details you use. Your parents might not have wanted you to go out with a particular person, for instance, but merely stated their reasons and left the decision up to you. You decided not to take their advice, and the result was a "disaster." Spell out the details so that the reader concludes it was a disaster, and you will have made your point effectively.

Organization and Ideas

Whether an essay is developed by multiple examples or a single extended example, it has a major assertion. In your first draft, you may want to state your thesis in one sentence and in an obvious place, such as the end of your introduction. When you revise, however, you may want to play with the placement of the thesis, delaying it until the conclusion. If that's where you decide you want it, check to make sure that everything that precedes the conclusion leads up to it and that the reader has a clear focus on your subject all the way.

You might also try weaving your thesis into the introduction in a subtle way, taking the thesis apart so that it is in bits and pieces, each in its own sentence. If you try that idea, check to make sure that someone reading your introduction will come up with a thesis that closely matches the one-sentence assertion you had in your first draft.

Delaying your thesis or weaving it into your introduction are subtle ways of treating your major assertion. If you are worried that they are so subtle that the reader may miss your point, consider getting some mileage out of a title. An imaginative title can serve several purposes: arouse the reader's curiosity, set the tone, highlight the subject, reveal the essay's organization, or pave the way for the thesis. Good titles serve more than one purpose.

When examples are used as the primary mode for an essay, they are usually arranged in chronological or dramatic order, moving from what came first and ending with what came last or beginning with the least dramatic and finishing with the most. To decide which example is the most dramatic, all you need to do is ask some obvious questions: Which is the most important? Which is most likely to affect the reader? Which carries the most impact? You'll probably come up with the same answer for each question. That's the example you should use to cap your essay, the one that all the others should lead up to.

Although all the essays in this chapter have a thesis developed by examples, the examples themselves often cross over into other categories. You will discover that is also the case with your own writing. You may well find yourself using an example that is also a narrative, or, to put it more precisely, a narrative that functions as an example. Other patterns of organization such as a description, an analysis of causal relationships, a comparison, a definition, or an analysis of a process can also serve as examples. The function—to support and develop an assertion—is more important than the label.

Useful Terms

Example An illustration that supports a generalization, usually an assertion, by providing evidence that develops or clarifies it.

Tone A writer's attitude toward the subject and the audience. An author's tone can be contemplative, intense, tongue-in-cheek, aloof, matter of fact—as many kinds as there are tones of voice.

Transition A word, phrase, sentence, or paragraph that carries the reader smoothly from point A to point B. Some transitions, such as time markers (*first, next,* and the like) are obvious; others are more subtle, such as a repeated word or phrase or a synonym for a key term.

POINTERS FOR USING EXAMPLE

Exploring the Topic

1. What examples can you think of to illustrate your topic? Are all of them from your own experience? What examples can you find from other sources?

2. **Are your examples pertinent and representative?** Do they fit? Do they illustrate?

3. **Are your examples of equal weight?** Which are relatively unimportant?

4. **How familiar is your audience with each of your examples?**

5. **Which examples best lend themselves to your topic?** In what order would they best be presented?

6. **What point do you want to make?** Do your examples all support that point? Do they lead the reader to your major assertion?

7. **What is your purpose behind your point?** Is your primary aim to express your own feelings, to inform, to persuade, or to entertain?

Drafting the Paper

1. **Know your reader.** It may be that your audience knows little about your subject or that the reader simply hasn't thought much about it; on the other hand, maybe the reader knows a great deal and holds a definite opinion. Once you have made an informed guess about your audience's attitude toward your topic and thesis, reexamine your examples in light of that information. Some may have to be explained in greater detail than others, and the more familiar ones will need to be presented in a new or different light. Use the techniques you would employ in writing descriptive papers.

2. **Know your purpose.** Self-expressive papers are often difficult to write because you are so close to being your own audience. If you are writing with this aim in mind, try making yourself conscious of the personality you project as a writer. Jot down the characteristics you wish to convey about yourself and refer to this list as you revise your paper. While this is a highly self-conscious way to revise, when it is done well, the result appears natural. Also double-check your examples, making sure that you present them in sufficient detail to communicate fully to your audience. That warning serves as well for informative and persuasive papers. Again, use description to make your examples effective: use sensory detail, compare the unfamiliar to the familiar, be concrete. If you are

(Continued)

writing a persuasive paper, use these techniques to appeal to emotions.

3. **Consider extended example.** If an essay rests on one example, choose and develop that illustration with great care. Make sure your example represents its class and that you provide all relevant information. Make as many connections as you can between your example and the class it represents. During revision, you may eliminate some of these references, but at first it's best to have too many. If you are writing a persuasive paper, you don't want to be guilty of a lapse in logic.

4. **Consider multiple examples.** Most essays rely on multiple examples to support their points; nevertheless, some examples will be more developed than others. Figure out which examples are particularly striking and develop them, reserving the others for mere mention. To lend breadth and credibility to your point, consider citing statistics, quotations, authorities, and the experience of others. Comment on what you take from other sources in order to make it more your own.

5. **Arrange your examples effectively.** Most essays move from the less dramatic, less important to the most, but examples can also be arranged chronologically or in terms of frequency (from least to most frequent). Like the essay itself, each paragraph should be developed around a central assertion, either stated or implied. In longer papers, groups of paragraphs will support a unifying statement. These statements guide the reader and prevent the paper from turning into a mere list.

6. **Make a point.** Examples so obviously need to lead up to something that it's not hard to make a point. But your point may not be an assertion. Test your thesis by asking whether your point carries any information. If it does, it's an assertion. Say you come up with, "We live in a world of time-saving technology." You can think of lots of examples and even narrow down the "we" to "anyone who cooks today." The setting is obviously the kitchen, but is the revised thesis an assertion? Given the information test, it fails. Your audience knows what you are supposedly informing them about. But if you revise and come up with "Electronic gizmos have turned the kitchen into a laboratory," you've given the topic a fresher look, one that does contain information.

Sweatin' for Nothin'

Michael Barlow

Unlike many students at the University of New Orleans, Michael Barlow went straight on to college after graduating from high school. As his essay implies, he is not a fitness freak, although he is engaged in a number of college activities. An education major concentrating in teaching English at the secondary level, he may soon turn up in the classroom on the other side of the desk. No matter what he does, he will try not to emulate Mimi.

What to Look For   Starting and ending an essay are often the most difficult parts of writing. One technique that works well is the one Barlow uses. You'll see that he sets up a framework by first setting out the image of the hamster in the cage and then, in his conclusion, returning to it. The effect is a sense of closure. You can use the same technique by ending your essay with a reference to an idea you bring out in your introduction.

1   During spring break, I visited my family in Fort Worth. It was a pleasant visit, but my, how things have changed. My mother has purchased a stairmaster and joined a fitness club. My father now jogs at 6:00 every morning, and my sister is contemplating aerobics as one of her first electives when she goes off to college this August. This was not the group of people I last saw in January. These were not the laid-back complacent folks I've known so well. This was not *my* family.

2   One night around 2 a.m., after partying with some friends from high school, I was lying in bed watching Mimi, my pet hamster, crank out revolutions on an exercise wheel. I should have gone to sleep but I was captivated. The creaking of the wheel made me think of the strenuous exercise that seems to have plagued everyone at 301 Lake Country Drive. What was it? What was going on? So I asked myself whether or not Mimi knew that sprinting in a metal cylinder wouldn't get her out of the cage. She probably didn't know—her brain is smaller than a kernel of corn.

115

3   But what about humans? What about my family? I see millions of Americans, like my family, in Spandex outfits and gel-cushioned shoes trying to get out of their cages. Something is wrong with the fitness mania that has swept the Western World, and from watching Mimi I know what it is. Entropy.

4   Entropy is the measure of the amount of energy unavailable for useful work in a system—metaphorically speaking, it is a measure of waste. In our throwaway society, we waste energy at a maddening pace. Coal is lit to make a fire, which produces a lot of carbon dioxide, while heating a small amount of water to make steam, which produces electricity, which lights an incandescent bulb in a room in a house where nobody's home. Basic waste.

5   Exercise mania has crippled our culture. It is no coincidence that we are running out of cheap and available energy while at the same time polluting the air, land, and sea with our waste. According to the laws of physics, entropy diminishes in a closed system, meaning that eventually everything will be reduced to an amorphous, undifferentiated blob. The universe is a closed system. There are some parallels to a hamster cage, and Mimi creates entropy at a noisy rate.

6   What did we do for exercise in those past centuries when people did not act like captive hamsters? If a person chopped down wood or ran a long way, it was because he or she needed fuel or wanted to get somewhere. Now we do such things to fit into new pants or to develop our biceps. We have treadmills, rowing machines, stairmasters, stationary bikes, Nordic Tracks, butt busters, and wall climbers, and we labor at them while going nowhere. Absolutely nowhere! We do work that is beyond useless; we do work that takes energy and casts it to the wind like lint. And we don't even enjoy the work. Look at people in a health club. See anybody smiling?

7   There is nothing magical about fitness machines. We can get the exact same result by climbing up stairs in our homes or offices. Take a look at any set of stairs in any building. Anybody in Spandex headed up or down? No. People ride elevators all day, then drive to their fitness centers where they pay to walk up steps.

8   When I was looking at Mimi, I was thinking of Richard Simmons, the King of Entropy, who wants everybody to exercise all the time and has made insane amounts of money saying so. Simmons says that he has raised his metabolism so high that he can eat more

without gaining weight. Working out to pig out—an entropy double whammy.

9   I have a solution for such gratuitous narcissism and I think Simmons might find a tearful video in it. Let people on the machines create useable energy as they burn off their flabby thighs and excess baggage. Hook up engines and cams and drive shafts that will rotate turbines and generate electricity. Let exercisers light the health club itself. Let them air condition it. Let the clubs store excess energy and sell it to nearby shop owners at low rates.

10   Better yet, create health clubs whose sole purpose is the generation of energy. Pipe the energy into housing projects. Have energy nights where singles get together to pedal, chat, and swap phone numbers. Build a giant pony wheel that operates a flour mill, a rock crusher, a draw bridge, a BMW repair shop. Have the poles protrude from the wheel with spots for a couple hundred joggers to push the wheel around. Install magazine racks on the poles. Have calorie collections and wattage wars. Make it "cool" to sweat for the betterment of mankind, not just for yourself.

11   We cannot afford much more entropy. If we forget that, we might as well be rodents in cages, running into the night. Just like Mimi.

Organization and Ideas

1. The essay has a problem–solution structure. In your own words, what does Barlow describe as the problem?

2. Paragraphs 5–7 give examples of kinds of exercise. What distinctions does Barlow draw among them?

3. The solution appears in paragraphs 9–10 and is a humorous one. Summarize it.

4. What do you find to be the main subject of the essay? Exercise? Fads? Waste? Entropy? American culture? What reasons can you find for your choice?

5. To what extent, if any, do you agree with Barlow's thesis?

Technique and Style

1. Look up *analogy* in an unabridged dictionary. What analogy does Barlow draw? What does the analogy contribute to the essay?

2. Paragraph 4 defines *entropy*. How necessary is that definition? What does it add to the essay?

3. What does the essay gain with the example of Richard Simmons?
4. Imagine you are one of the people filling up the fitness club. Would you be offended by this essay? Why or why not?
5. The person behind the words always comes through in an essay, sometimes more clearly than others. Explain why you would or would not want Michael Barlow as a classmate or friend.

Suggestions for Writing

Journal

1. Take a few minutes to write down what you think about the exercise craze or to record your reaction to a television commercial advertising an exercise product.
2. How does exercise make you feel? Write about why you do or do not enjoy exercising.

Essay

1. Try your own hand at a problem–solution essay, giving detailed examples of both the problem and the solution. Like Barlow, you may want your tone to be humorous, sugarcoating a serious point. As for the problem, you're apt to be surrounded with choices:

   getting enough hours into the day
   scraping tuition together
   keeping up with schoolwork
   deciding which pleasure to indulge
   sorting out family loyalties

   Illustrate the problem by using examples. You may find examples for the solution harder to come by, in which case, like Barlow, you may want to propose something fantastic.

2. If you responded to the first suggestion for a journal entry, then you are already on your way to a rough draft. Think of all the ways people participate in America's fitness craze. What do they do? How do they do it? What do they get out of it? What are its hazards? Benefits? To what extent are you involved? Write an essay in which you explore what you think about the subject, providing examples to support your thesis.

Stop Ordering Me Around

Stacey Wilkins

Like many students, Stacey Wilkins works in a restaurant waiting on tables, a job that helps her pay off a student loan but one that also extracts a price of its own, as her essay points out. The essay appeared in the January 4, 1993, issue of Newsweek *in a regular feature, the "My Turn" column. A person who wants to be treated with respect, Wilkins also apparently values her privacy, for the only identification that appears at the end of the essay is the note, "Wilkins lives in Connecticut." Her forum, however, is a public one, and the readers of* Newsweek *are her ideal audience in that as educated, middle-class Americans, they are more likely to patronize the kind of restaurant where Wilkins works than the local fast-food place.*

What to Look For   The narrative that opens Wilkins' essay serves as the primary example in the essay, and one that sets the essay's tone as well. As you read the essay, try to hear it so that you can identify her tone more exactly. At times, the tone may strike you as angry, hurt, bitter, sarcastic, and any number of other variations. How would you characterize it?

1   I had just sat an extra hour and a half waiting for some country-club tennis buddies to finish a pizza. They came in 15 minutes after the restaurant closed—they hadn't wanted to cut short their tennis match. The owner complied and agreed to turn the oven back on and make them a pizza. The cook had long since gone home.

2   The customers had no problem demanding service after I explained that the restaurant had closed. They had no problem sitting there until well after 11 o'clock to recount the highlights of their tennis game (the restaurant closed at 9:30 p.m.). And, most important, they had no problem making me the brunt of their cruel little post-tennis match. What fun it was to harass the pathetic little waitress. "Oh, it's just so nice sitting here like this," one man said. After getting no response, he continued: "Boy, I guess you want us to leave." I was ready to explode in anger. "I am not going to respond to your comments," I said, and walked away.

3   He was geared up for a fight. The red flag had been waved. The man approached me and asked about dessert. A regular customer, he had never made a practice of ordering dessert before. You know, the '90s low-fat thing. But that night he enjoyed the power. He felt strong, I felt violated.

4   Three dollars and 20 cents later, I went home. Their tip was my payment for this emotional rape. As I drove, tears streamed down my face. Why was I crying? I had been harassed before. Ten years of waitressing should have inured me to this all-too-common situation. But this was a watershed: the culmination of a decade of abuse.

5   I am now at the breaking point. I can't take being the public's punching bag. People seem to think abuse is included in the price of an entree. All sense of decency and manners is checked with their coats at the door. They see themselves in a position far superior to mine. They are the kings. I am the peasant.

6   I would like them to be the peasants. I am a strong advocate of compulsory restaurant service in the United States. What a great comeuppance it would be for the oppressors to have to work a double shift—slinging drinks, cleaning up after kids and getting pissed off that a party of 10 tied up one of their tables for three hours and left a bad tip. Best of all, I would like to see that rude man with tomato sauce on his tennis shorts.

7   Eating in a restaurant is about more than eating food. It is an opportunity to take your frustrations out on the waiter. It is a chance to feel better than the person serving your food. People think there is nothing wrong with rudeness or sexual harassment if it is inflicted on a waiter.

8   Customers have no problem with ignoring the wait staff when they go to take an order. Or they won't answer when the waiter comes to the table laden with hot plates asking who gets what meal. My personal pet peeve is when they make a waiter take a separate trip for each item. "Oh, I'll take another Coke." The waiter asks, "Would anyone else like one?" No response. Inevitably when he comes back to the table someone will say, "I'll have a Coke, too." And so on and so on.

9   I find it odd because no matter what an insolent cad someone might be, they generally make an effort to cover it up in public. The majority of people practice common etiquette. Most individuals won't openly cut in line or talk throughout a movie. People are cognizant of acceptable behavior and adhere to the strictures it de-

mands. That common code of decency does not apply while eating out.

10   Food-service positions are the last bastion of accepted prejudice. People go into a restaurant and openly torment the waiter, leave a small tip and don't think twice about it. Friends allow companions to be rude and don't say a word. The friends of this man did not once tell him to stop taunting me. They remained silent.

11   It doesn't cross their minds that someone has just been rotten to another human being. I have yet to hear someone stick up for the waitress, to insist a person stop being so cruel. This is because people don't think anything wrong has occurred.

12   However, if this man had shouted obscenities at another patron about her ethnicity, say, it would have rightly been deemed unacceptable. Why don't people understand that bad manners are just as unacceptable in a restaurant? Why do they think they have license to mistreat restaurant personnel?

13   I believe it is because food-service workers are relegated to such a low position on the social stratum. Customers have the power. Food-service employees have none. Thus we are easy targets for any angry person's pent-up frustrations. What better sparring partner than one who can't fight back? Most waiters won't respond for fear of losing their jobs. Consequently, we are the designated gripe-catchers of society, along with similar service workers.

14   If people stepped down from their spurious pedestals, they might see how wrong they are. We have dreams and aspirations just like everyone else. Our wages finance those dreams. Even an insulting 10 percent tip helps us to move toward a goal, pay the rent, feed the kids.

15   I'm using my earnings to pay off an encumbering graduate-school debt. Our bus girl is financing her education at the University of Pennsylvania. My manager is saving for her first baby. Another waitress is living on her earnings while she pursues an acting career. The dishwasher sends his pay back to his children in Ecuador.

16   Our dreams are no less valid than those of someone who holds a prestigious job at a large corporation. A restaurant's flexible working hours appeal to many people who dislike the regimen of a 9-to-5 day. Our employment doesn't give someone the right to treat us as nonentities. I deserve respect whether I remain a waitress or move on to a different career. And so do the thousands of waiters and waitresses who make your dining experience a pleasant one.

Organization and Ideas

1. How does the opening narrative set the scene? Where else in the essay do you find references to that narrative? Do they unify the essay or distract you? Why?
2. At what point in the essay does the author move from the particular to the general? Which gets the most emphasis?
3. Reexamine the essay as one that poses a problem and a solution. What is the problem? The solution?
4. To what extent does Wilkins' experience coincide with your own? That of your friends?
5. Where do you find Wilkins' thesis? Explain whether you find that placement effective.

Technique and Style

1. How would you characterize the author's tone?
2. Does the opening narrative enlist your sympathies? Why or why not?
3. Some readers may find the essay's aim is more expressive than expository or persuasive, that the author is more concerned with venting her feelings than explaining the problem or persuading her readers to resolve it. Make a case for your interpretation of the author's aim.
4. In paragraph 2, Wilkins repeats variations on "they had no problem." Explain whether you find the repetition effective.
5. At various times in the essay, Wilkins uses words that suggest she is really writing about issues of power and class, as in her use of "peasant" (paragraphs 5 and 6) and "low position on the social stratum" (paragraph 13). What other examples can you find? Would the essay be stronger or weaker if these issues were discussed more openly?

Suggestions for Writing

Journal

1. We live in a service society, yet as Wilkins points out, sometimes we demand too much of those who provide the services. Record a few examples of rudeness that you have observed.
2. Write an entry recording your reaction to Wilkins' essay. Do you think her complaints are justified?

Essay

1. More than likely you have or have had a job similar to Wilkins', if not waiting on tables then some other low-paying job that is also low on the totem pole of status. Like Wilkins, you may have found you were

(or are) not treated with respect. On the other hand, your experience may be quite the opposite. Write an essay in which you use examples from your own experience or the experiences of others to explain how you were (or are) treated on your job. You will want to narrow your subject so that you can cover it thoroughly in three to five pages, so you might focus on a specific category of people:

customers
coworkers
supervisor(s)

Another way to approach the topic would be to choose an example from each of those categories, but if you select that route, make sure your examples are representative.

2. Wilkins raises the issues of power and class in her essay (see paragraphs 5, 6, and 13), but as Americans we like to think we live in a classless society. Think about the idea of class and write an essay in which you test the validity of the claim of classlessness. Make sure you define what you mean by class, and use examples from the news and any other sources to support your thesis.

A Black Fan of Country Music Finally Tells All

Lena Williams

Lena Williams started her career in journalism as a reporter for a radio station while she was a student at Howard University. After earning her BA at Howard, she entered the Columbia University Graduate School of Journalism, from which she received an MSc. She worked as a reporter while she was an intern at the Washington Post, *then as an associate editor at* Black Sports Magazine, *and has been on the staff of the* New York Times *since 1974, first as a clerk, then trainee, and now senior writer. She has written on civil rights, lifestyles, metropolitan news, and sports, winning various publishing awards along the way. An article she originally wrote for the* Times *in 1997 grew to the point where it is now a book,* It's the Little Things: The Everyday Interactions That Get under the Skin of Blacks and Whites *(2000). The essay that follows appeared on Sunday, June 19, 1994, in the* Times' *"Arts and Leisure" section's coverage of "Pop Music." The column was titled "Pop View."*

What to Look For At times, you may find yourself writing an essay on a subject that you're somewhat embarrassed about, which is
the position Lena Williams found herself in when she wrote the essay that follows. In that case, you'll need to make a decision about
your tone, the attitude you take toward your subject and your audience. Williams, as you will see, takes an unapologetic stance, almost
daring her readers to challenge her. Yet the overall tone of the essay
is not antagonistic because she takes the edge off of her "challenge"
with humor and personal narrative, techniques that you can incorporate into your own writing.

1   I heard that Reba McEntire's new album, "Read My Mind," shot to
No. 5 on the Billboard chart the first weekend of its release.

2   Well, she got my $11.95.

3   I'm a 40-something black woman who spent her youth in
Washington, lip-syncing to the Supremes and slow dancing to the
Temptations. Now I often come home to my Manhattan apartment
and put on Vince Gill, Randy Travis or Reba. Consider me a fan of
country music. So there. Deal with it.

4   For most of my adult life, I was a closet country music fan. I'd
hide my Waylon Jennings and Willie Nelson albums between the
dusty, psychedelic rock. I'd listen to Dolly Parton on my earphones,
singing along softly, afraid my neighbors might mistake my imitation twang for a cry for help. I'd enter a music store, looking over
my shoulder in search of familiar faces and flip through the rhythm-
and-blues section for about five minutes before sneaking off to the
country aisle where I'd surreptitiously grab a Travis Tritt tape off the
rack and make a beeline for the shortest cashier's line.

5   Just when I'd reached for my American Express card, I'd spot a
tall, dark, handsome type in an Armani suit standing behind me
with a puzzled look. What's he going to think? "The sister seems
down, but what's she doing with that Dwight Yoakum CD?"

6   So now I'm publicly coming out of the closet and proclaiming
my affection for country perennials like Ms. McEntire.

7   When I told a friend I was preparing this confessional, he offered
a word of caution: "No self-respecting black person would ever admit to that in public."

8   I thought about his comment. As a child growing up in the 1950's, in a predominantly black community, I wasn't allowed to play country-and-western music in my house. Blacks weren't supposed to like country—or classical for that matter—but that's another story. Blacks' contribution to American music was in jazz, blues and funk. Country music was dismissed as poor white folks' blues and associated with regions of the nation that symbolized prejudice and racial bigotry. Even mainstream white America viewed country as lower class and less desirable, often poking fun at its twangy chords and bellyaching sentiments.

9   But I was always a cowgirl at heart. I liked country's wild side; its down-home, aw-shucks musicians with the yodel in their voices and the angst in their lyrics. I saw an honesty in country and its universal tales of love lost and found. Besides, the South didn't have a monopoly on racial hatred, and country artists, like everybody else, were stealing black music, so why should I hold it against country?

10   And while snickering at country, white America also demonstrated a similar cultural backwardness toward black music, be it gospel, ragtime or the blues. So I allowed country to enter my heart and my mind, in spite of its faults. Indeed, when prodded, some blacks who rejected country conceded that there was a spirituality that resounded in the music and that in its heartfelt sentiment, country was a lot like blues. Yet they could never bring themselves to spend hard-earned dollars on Hank Williams Jr.

11   The 1980's saw country (western was dropped, much to my chagrin) become mainstream. Suddenly there was country at the Copa and at Town Hall. WYNY-FM radio in New York now claims the largest audience of any country station, with more than one million listeners. Dolly Parton and Kenny Rogers became movie stars. Garth Brooks became an American phenomenon.

12   Wall Street investment bankers bought cowboy boots and hats and learned to do the two-step. And black and white artists like Patti LaBelle and Lyle Lovett and Natalie Cole and Ms. McEntire now sing duets and clearly admire one another's music.

13   Perhaps the nation's acceptance of country has something to do with an evolutionary change in the music. Country has got edge. It has acquired an attitude. Womens' voices have been given strength. Oh, the hardship and misery is still there. But the stuff about "standing by your man" has changed to a more assertive posture.

14   In "I Won't Stand in Line," a song on Ms. McEntire's new album, she makes it clear to a skirt-chasing lover that "I'd do almost anything just to make you mine, but I won't stand in line." That line alone makes me think of Aretha Franklin's "Respect."

15   One other thing: I don't like sad songs. I've cried enough for a lifetime. Country makes me laugh, always has. Maybe because it never took itself so seriously. Think about it. "Drop-Kick Me, Jesus, Through the Goal Posts of Life." "A Boy Named Sue."

16   Ms. McEntire serves up a humorous touch in "Why Haven't I Heard From You." "That thing they call the telephone/ Now there's one on every corner, in the back of every bar/ You can get one in your briefcase, on a plane or in your car/ So tell me why haven't I heard from you, darlin', honey, what is your excuse?" Call it Everywoman's lament.

17   Well it's off my chest; and it feels good.

18   I will no longer make excuses for my musical tastes. Not when millions are being made by performers exhorting listeners to "put your hands in the air and wave 'em like you just don't care."

19   Compare that with the haunting refrain of Ms. McEntire's "I Think His Name Was John," a song about a woman, a one-night stand and AIDS: "She lays all alone and cries herself to sleep/ 'Cause she let a stranger kill her hopes and her dreams/ And in the end when she was barely hanging on/ All she could say is she thinks his name was John."

Organization and Ideas

1. What paragraph or paragraphs introduce the essay?
2. Paragraphs 4 and 5 detail a short narrative. What is Williams' point?
3. Paragraphs 8–12 sketch the evolution of country-and-western music. Trace the chronology and the changes in attitude toward the genre.
4. The essay ends with a comparison in paragraphs 18 and 19, one that Williams doesn't spell out. What is it? How does it relate to her thesis?
5. Williams maintains that since the 1980s, country music has "become mainstream" (paragraph 11). How accurate is that assertion?

Technique and Style

1. Paragraphs 2 and 17 consist of one sentence each. What effect does Williams achieve with a one-sentence paragraph?
2. Is the essay addressed primarily to a black or white audience or both? What evidence can you find to support your view?

3. Although the essay expresses Williams' personal opinion and is subjective, she achieves a balance between the personal and the general. How does she do that?
4. Williams supports her thesis with examples from popular music, both country-western and black. Explain whether you find her examples sufficient evidence for her thesis.
5. Analyze the effectiveness of the essay's title. What other titles can you think of? Which is the more effective and why?

Suggestions for Writing

Journal

1. Taste in music, as in most everything else, is apt to be idiosyncratic. Think of a band or song or type of music that represents your particular taste and explain why you like it, using examples to support your ideas.
2. Think of a time when you were embarrassed and describe it in such a way that you remove the embarrassment. You might want to use the same techniques that Williams uses—confronting the issue and then modulating your tone. You may want to turn this entry into a full essay.

Essay

1. If you look back on your tastes, you will probably find that they change over time. Perhaps a type of music that you liked some years ago you would now have a hard time listening to. Or perhaps you were disappointed in a film you recently saw again or a book that you reread, one that had impressed you in the past and belonged to a particular genre such as horror films or adventure stories. You might start by drawing up two columns—then and now—and jotting down examples representing your earlier tastes and your present ones. Like Williams, you may want to write about how your taste has evolved or explain why you like what you like. For a general category, you might think about
     music
     food
     films
     books
     heroes
     sports
2. Williams' essay is an assertive defense of her taste in music. Write an essay in which you evaluate the essay's effectiveness. You might start

by asking yourself questions such as, "Does she present enough evidence?" "Are her examples apt?" "Does she provide enough background for her explanations?"

The Joy of Starvation

James Gorman

If you had paged through some old copies of Discover, *you might have found James Gorman's column "Lighter Elements." As his column's title suggests, he often takes an amusing look at science, if not an irreverent one. Many of the essays he wrote for* Discover *have been reprinted in his* Man with No Endorphins: and Other Reflections on Science *(1989). Since that time, Gorman has taken a more serious tone in* Ocean Enough and Time: Discovering the Waters Around Antarctica *(1995), funded by the National Science Foundation, and as a contributor to* Digging Dinosaurs: The Search That Unraveled the Mystery of Baby Dinosaurs *(1996). Gorman is a frequent contributor to the* New York Times Magazine, *and the essay that follows was published in the* Times' *supplement, the* Good Health Magazine *in 1989. Reading his essay, you'll see that he has returned to what* Publisher's Weekly *calls his "finely tuned sense of the ridiculous."*

What to Look For   You might think it's hard to come up with examples, but Gorman has a different problem—controlling the large number of examples he cites. You'll see he does it by grouping them together and by varying what amounts to a list of examples with a few extended ones.

1   Recently—in the space of a few days, it seemed to me—apples, grapes and all manner of produce grown by means of photosynthesis, as well as all meats derived (directly or indirectly) from animals, have been declared unsafe. It was while I was reeling from this news that I changed my position on censorship. Muzzle the health press! That's what I said to myself. Of course, I say this sort of thing all the time. But usually I shush myself, the way I do when I have a

really grotesque thought, like "What's so bad about Donald Trump, anyway?" or "Let's have roast pork tonight. With gravy!"

2   But this time was different. I started thinking about the old days, when it was the dishes you had to use detergent on, not the food. I decided that muzzling the health press was a good idea after all. I don't take this position lightly. I'm aware that in short order all defenders of the First Amendment, from journalists to poets to the American Civil Liberties Union to the fellow who was running for President who belonged to the A.C.L.U. (what was his name?), will be after me. And all the people I don't want as friends—Donald Trump, Tipper Gore, George Bush with those awful pork rinds—will be on my side. But look, you can't cry "Fire!" in a crowded theater, so why should you be allowed to shout "Triglycerides!" in a barbecue joint? Besides, I firmly believe my plan will actually improve the health of the American people.

3   Before we take up the details, we need to step back in time for a moment and consider the practice of giving electric shocks to dogs. (Bear with me. I don't throw these things in without reason.) This was a classic, controlled, scientific experiment. Dogs in harnesses from which they could not escape were given electric shocks. Then they were put into a box containing a barrier in the middle. They were given shocks again, but this time all they had to do to escape was jump the barrier. Fresh, unshocked dogs did so. But, to quote *The Psychology of Being Human* (a text that apparently does not take a rigid position on the old Homo sapiens/Canis familiaris dichotomy), "the dogs that had been given the inescapable shock treatment howled at first and then sat passively, taking the shock."

4   The condition is called "learned helplessness," probably because the dogs had learned that they were helpless. Human beings achieve this state by reading the health news. You read that saturated fats are bad. O.K., you say, I'll eat broccoli. Well, depending on where you get it, it might have parathion residues, which might cause cancer. ZAP! Eggs, then? Sorry. With eggs we're talking cholesterol *and* salmonella; if you don't die of a heart attack you throw up. ZAP! Chicken? No, sir (or ma'am). Hormones, heptachlor and more salmonella. ZAP! again.

5   And so on. Trout? P.C.B.'s. Milk? Maybe barium carbonate, maybe dioxin. Corn meal? Aflatoxin. Peanut butter? Or lean beef? Or grapes? More aflatoxin. And antibiotics. And cyanide. ZAP! ZAP! ZAP! ZAP! ZAP! ZAP!

6   What to do? Well, I suppose everybody's heard what happened to Marc Kranz. No? I'll admit that I don't know how reliable this information is—it comes from one of those Elvis's-Baby-Bit-My-Dog newspapers (they know what news is)—but it *could* have happened. The story is that Mr. Kranz, of Leipzig, East Germany, whom the *Weekly World News* charitably described as a "health nut," gradually cut different foods out of his diet as he heard news about the bad effects of each one. Meat went first, then poultry, then dairy products. Eventually he stopped drinking tap water and eating fruits and vegetables. He got skinnier and skinner until he not only resembled a skeleton, he was one.

7   That's one approach; it's what happens if you insist on trying to avoid being zapped and refuse to learn helplessness. You sit in your room and starve to death. A more popular option is to give up, like a shock-savvy dog, and howl a bit while you eat whatever passes in front of you. Sirloin, whipped cream, a little deep-fried parathion—what's the difference?

8   Plus, I'll bet that in the United States we have an even greater variety of food alarms than they do in Leipzig, and a free press to boot. Consequently, the American public is now equally divided between helpless, fat, atherosclerotic pizza gobblers and suspicious, jumpy, very thin people (you know—the ones with those eyes) who prowl the supermarket aisles as if J. Edgar Hoover were alive and being injected into chickens. (Now there's a story for the *Weekly World News.*)

9   Something has got to be done. I know complete suppression of the news is out of the question. For one thing, I was told that if I tried to call for the outright abolition of the *Good Health Magazine* in the very pages of the *Good Health Magazine,* it wouldn't be beef brisket that would do me in. And since I know a lot of journalists, and have occasionally practiced the trade myself (I never did get it right), I know that nobody wants to give up a byline just to save a couple of hundred million people.

10   So how about a compromise? Let's just limit the number of scares. That way, we won't feel so helpless. My suggestion is one a month. Maybe everybody who writes about health and food could get together and agree on what will be the awful food news for each month. I know this would mean giving up scoops (news, not ice cream), and it would probably smack of state Communism, as well as decrease revenues for the media. But it could save lives. So how about it, folks? One a month? Two? Would you consider three . . . ?

Organization and Ideas

1. Gorman organizes his essay by a pattern of problem and solution. What is the problem? Solution?
2. In paragraphs 3 and 4, Gorman compares the experiment with dogs to the behavior of health-conscious humans. How effective is the comparison?
3. While Gorman's essay is a satire, it's not as easy to pinpoint his subject. What is he satirizing: science, "health nuts," American consumers, what?
4. To what extent are you concerned about the hidden "dangers" of food?
5. Are those "dangers" exaggerated by the media? Is Gorman's satire still relevant?

Technique and Style

1. How would you describe Gorman's tone, his attitude toward his subject?
2. What sort of person does Gorman seem to be? How would you describe him?
3. In paragraph 3, Gorman uses a number of parentheses. What function do they serve?
4. Gorman achieves a scatter shot of examples in paragraph 5 with short questions and answers. How effective is it?
5. Marc Krantz, as Gorman points out, is a dubious example. How does he make it work?

Suggestions for Writing

Journal

1. Use your journal to explain what foods you avoid and why.
2. The people Gorman refers to in paragraph 2 were familiar names in 1989, but now the examples seem a bit dated. Explain how would you update them and the reasons behind your choices.

Essay

1. Gorman writes about how scientific discoveries are reducing what we should eat to the ridiculous, a general example of overkill. The same principle of overkill operates in many areas. Think, for instance, of what appears frequently on television, in magazines, in conversation, that irritates you: particular ads, warnings, overexposed celebrities and sports figures, clichés, images. Choose one to write an essay that explores the overexposure and how it affects you.

2. In 2003, American obesity was a lead story in almost every newspaper and magazine, along with explanations of its causes and hazards and proposals for solutions. Reexamine the subject at present to determine the extent to which it is still a problem. The result can be an expository essay on the topic or an argumentative one in which you take a stand on the issue.

Bananas for Rent

Michiko Kakutani

Anyone who reads the book reviews in the New York Times *is familiar with Michiko Kakutani's by-line, for she's the lead reviewer for the newspaper, covering both fiction and nonfiction. As you might suspect, that sort of extensive analytical reading makes her an astute critic of the contemporary scene, so it's only fitting that she also contributes to the column "Culture Zone" in the* New York Times Magazine, *a column in which Ms. Kakutani takes a tough view of popular culture. Her wide range of interests is reflected in her book* Poet at the Piano: Portraits of Writers, Filmmakers, and Other Artists at Work *(1988). In 1998, Ms. Kakutani was awarded the Pulitzer Prize for Criticism. Her essay "Bananas for Rent" was a "Culture Zone" piece published on November 9, 1997.*

What to Look For   If you are writing about the contemporary scene and using examples to back up your points, you may find that some of your readers may not be familiar with the examples you use. One way out of that bind is to use lots. That is what Kakutani does in her essay, so be on the lookout for multiple examples as you read. It's easiest to think up multiple examples when you are making notes for an essay. If you were writing about blue jeans, for instance, you might be tempted to just put Levi's, but at that point, it's also easy to think of other brand names as well—Guess, Gap, Gloria Vanderbilt, and the like.

1   They are as pervasive as roaches, as persuasive as the weather, as popular as Princess Diana. They adorn our clothes, our luggage, our sneakers and our hats. They are ubiquitous on television, un-

avoidable in magazines and inevitable on the Internet. The average American, it is estimated, is pelted by some 3,000 advertising messages a day, some 38,000 TV commercials a year.

2   Not so long ago, it was only race cars, tennis stars and sports stadiums that were lacquered head-to-toe with ads. Nowadays, school buses and trucks rent out advertising space by the foot. There are entire towns that have signed exclusive deals with Coke or Pepsi. The dead, including Marilyn Monroe (Chanel No. 5), Gene Kelly (Gap khakis) and Fred Astaire (Dirt Devil vacuum cleaners), have been hired as pitchmen, and so have New Delhi paraplegics, who now hawk Coca-Cola under bright red-and-white umbrellas. Even bananas have been colonized as billboard space, with stickers promoting the video release of "Space Jam" and the "Got Milk?" campaign turning up on the fruit.

3   As the scholar James Twitchell observes, advertising has become "our cultural literacy—it's what we know." Twitchell, author of a book called *Adcult USA* and a professor at the University of Florida, says his students share no common culture of books or history; what they share is a knowledge of commercials. When he questions them at random about concepts from "The Dictionary of Cultural Literacy," he says he is likely to draw a blank. When, however, he recites a commercial jingle, his students "instantaneously know it, and they're exultant," he says. "They actually think Benetton ads are profound. To them, advertising is high culture."

4   Schoolchildren around the country avidly collect Absolut ads, and college students decorate their walls with poster-size reproductions of ads that are available from a four-year-old company called Beyond the Wall. Forget Monet and Van Gogh. Think Nike, BMW and Calvin Klein. As Brian Gordon, one of the company's founders, sees it, kids regard ads as "a form of self-expression." In today's "short-attention society," he reasons, ads are something people can relate to: they provide "insights into current culture," and they provide them in 30 seconds or less.

5   No doubt this is why entire "Seinfeld" episodes have been built around products like Pez and Junior Mints. The popularity of Nick at Nite's vintage commercials, Rosie O'Donnell's peppy renditions of old jingles, the almost nightly commercial spoofs by Letterman and Leno—all are testaments to the prominent role advertising has assumed in our lives. A whole school of fiction known as Kmart realism has grown up around the use of brand names, while a host of well-known songs (from Nirvana's "Smells Like Teen Spirit" to

Oasis' "Shakermaker") satirize old commercials. It used to be that advertisers would appropriate a hit song (like the Beatles' "Revolution") to promote a product; nowadays, the advertising clout of a company like Volkswagen has the power to turn a song (even an old song like "Da Da Da," by the now defunct German band Trio) into a hit.

6   So what does advertising's takeover of American culture mean? It's not just that the world has increasingly come to resemble the Home Shopping Network. It's that advertising's ethos of spin—which makes selling a means *and* an end—has thoroughly infected everything from politics (think of Clinton's "permanent campaign") to TV shows like "Entertainment Tonight" that try to pass off publicity as information. It's that advertising's attention-grabbing hype has become, in our information-glutted age, the modus operandi of the world at large. "Advertising is the most pervasive form of propaganda in human history," says the scholar Mark Crispin Miller. "It's reflected in every esthetic form today."

7   Miller points out that just as commercials have appropriated techniques that once belonged to avant-garde film—cross-cutting, jump cuts, hand-held camera shots—so have mainstream movies and TV shows begun to ape the look and shape of ads, replacing character and story with razzle-dazzle special effects. For that matter, more and more film makers, including Howard Zieff, Michael Bay, Adrian Lyne and Simon West, got their starts in advertising.

8   Advertising has a more insidious effect as well. Advertisers scouting TV shows and magazines are inclined to select those vehicles likely to provide a congenial (and therefore accessible or upbeat) backdrop for their products, while a public that has grown up in a petri dish of ads has grown impatient with any art that defies the easy-access, quick-study esthetic of commercials—that is, anything that's difficult or ambiguous. "People have become less capable of tolerating any kind of darkness or sadness," Miller says. "I think it ultimately has to do with advertising, with a vision of life as a shopping trip."

9   There are occasional signs of a backlash against advertising—the Vancouver-based Media Foundation uses ad parodies to fight rampant consumerism—but advertising implacably forges ahead like one of those indestructible sci-fi monsters, nonchalantly co-opting the very techniques used against it. Just as it has co-opted rock-and-roll, alienation (a Pontiac commercial features an animated version of Munch's painting "The Scream") and Dadaist jokes (an ad cam-

paign for Kohler featured interpretations of bidets and faucets by contemporary artists), so it has now co-opted irony, parody and satire.

10 The end result of advertising's ability to disguise itself as entertainment and entertainment's willingness to adopt the hard-sell methods of advertising is a blurring of the lines between art and commerce. Even as this makes us increasingly oblivious to advertising's agenda (to sell us stuff), it also makes us increasingly cynical about everything else—ready to dismiss it, unthinkingly, as junk or fluff or spin, just another pitch lobbed out by that gigantic machine called contemporary culture.

Organization and Ideas

1. Kakutani's opening sentence announces qualities that unify the essay that follows. What paragraph or paragraphs focus on ads as "pervasive"? As "persuasive"? As "popular"?

2. Which paragraphs emphasize the effect of ads? What effect do they have?

3. Reread the first and last paragraphs. What is the thesis of the essay? What evidence can you cite to back up your opinion?

4. To what extent do you agree with Kakutani's thesis?

5. Kakutani maintains that advertising "disguise[s] itself as entertainment" (paragraph 10). How accurate do you find that assertion?

Technique and Style

1. Kakutani violates a principle of usage in her first paragraph in that the pronoun "they" has no antecedent. What effect does she achieve by not initially specifying to whom the "they" refers?

2. Ads and the culture within which they exist come in for much negative criticism in this essay. How would you characterize Kakutani's tone— negative, reasoned, thoughtful, strident, what?

3. Describe what you perceive to be Kakutani's persona. What evidence can you find to support your view?

4. In a handbook of grammar and usage, look up the uses of the dash. You'll note that Kakutani uses dashes frequently, as in paragraphs 3, and 5–10. What other punctuation could she have used? What reasons can you think of for her choice of the dash?

5. Kakutani uses three similes in her first sentence. Choose one of them and make up three or four of your own. Which do you prefer and why?

Suggestions for Writing

Journal

1. Anyone who watches television learns to hate certain ads. Take a minute to write down the ads you dislike the most and then, for each, put down the reasons. You'll end up with the working notes for an essay.

2. Kakutani states that thanks to ads we are becoming "increasingly cynical about everything else—ready to dismiss it, unthinkingly, as junk or fluff or spin, just another pitch lobbed out by that gigantic machine called contemporary culture" (paragraph 10). Write an entry in which you agree or disagree with Kakutani's statement, citing examples to support your views.

Essay

1. Whether or not you agree with Kakutani, there's no arguing about the prevalence of advertisements. To test out Kakutani's points or simply to analyze advertisements on your own, flip through a popular magazine noting various categories of advertisements—cars, liquor, clothes, perfumes, and the like. Choosing a group of ads for a type of product, examine it as though it were a window into our culture. What do you see? What does it say about our concerns? Fears? Attention span? Tastes? Use your notes to write an essay that illustrates its points through multiple examples. If advertising doesn't seem to be a worthwhile subject, then choose another topic that you can use as a way to examine popular culture. Here are some suggestions:

   television shows
   films
   books
   styles
   fads
   franchises

2. What television ads do you remember and like? Make a short list (it only needs to make sense to you), and then select one to explain why you like it.

ADDITIONAL WRITING ASSIGNMENTS

●●

Using Example

What does it mean to be a "good" employee, student, parent, friend, citizen, co-worker, leader?

What is your idea of "perfect" days, classes, celebrations, vacations, meals?

What is your favorite television show, kind of music, fattening food, sport, pastime? Draw upon examples to support your thesis.

What should an entering freshman know about registration, the faculty, courses, majors, extracurricular activities? Use examples to support your thesis.

Evaluating the Essays

1. Michael Barlow and James Gorman both write about "crazes," though their subjects are different, and both use humor. Reread both essays to determine which of the two you like better. Write an essay in which you make a case for your opinion, drawing examples from both of the essays.

2. The idea of persona, the person behind the *I* in an essay, comes through very clearly in the essays by Stacey Wilkins and Lena Williams. Reread the essays, noting as you read the various characteristics of each person. Of the two, which would you prefer to know and why? Use examples from the essays as evidence for your thesis.

3. Michiko Kakutani and Stacey Wilkins are both angry, Kakutani about advertising and Wilkins about tipping. Given that one essay is personal and the other general, which of the two writers makes the more logical argument? Quote both to prove your point.

4. You can read the essays by Michiko Kakutani and James Gorman as attacks on American values, though which values are being attacked is debatable—consumerism, commercialism, conformity, capitalism. Reread the essays noting what the writers are attacking. Which essay is the more effective and why? Again, use evidence from both to support your view.

On Using
Division and
Classification

5

The next time you shop in a supermarket or clean out a closet, think about how you are doing it and you will understand the workings of **division and classification.** "How often do I wear those shoes?" and "I never did like that sweater" imply that dividing items according to how frequently you wear them would be a good principle for sorting out your closet. Supermarkets, however, do the sorting for you. Goods are divided according to shared characteristics—all dairy products in one section, meat in another, and so on—and then items are placed in those categories. The process looks easy, but if you have ever tried to find soy sauce, you know the pitfalls: Is it with the spices? Sauces? Gourmet foods? Health foods? Ethnic products?

To divide a subject and then classify examples into the categories or classes that resulted from division you must be able to examine a subject from several angles, work out the ways in which it can be divided, and then discern similarities and differences among the examples you want to classify. A huge topic such as animals invites a long list of ways they can be divided: wild animals, work animals, pets; ones that swim, run, crawl; ones you have owned, seen, or read about. These groups imply principles for division—by degree of domesticity, by manner of locomotion, by degree of familiarity. Division and classification often help define each other in that having divided your subjects, you may find that once you start classifying, you have to stop and redefine your principle of division. If your division of animals is based on locomotion, for instance, where do you put the flying squirrel?

Division and classification is often used at the paragraph level. If your essay argues that a particular television commercial for a toilet cleaner insults women, you might want to introduce the essay by enumerating other advertisements in that general category—household products— that you also find insulting to women.

From Julius Caesar's "Gaul is divided into three parts" to a 10-year-old's "animal, vegetable, or mineral," classification and division has had a long and useful history. And, of course, it has a useful present as well. In each of the essays in this chapter, you will see that the system of division and classification supports a thesis, though the essays use their theses for different purposes: to entertain, to explain, to argue.

Audience and Purpose

Knowing who your readers are and what effect you want to have on them will help you devise your system of classification and sharpen your thesis. Imagine that you are writing an essay for a newsletter put out by a health club or by students in a physical education program and that your subject is the benefits of garlic. You would know that your readers are interested in the positive effects of herbs, but you would also know that their noses may well wrinkle at the mere mention of garlic. Given the negative associations your audience may have, you would do well to begin with the unpleasant connotation, thus starting with what your readers already know, connecting your subject with their experience, and immediately addressing their first and probably negative ideas about your subject. After that, you might move quickly to the many good uses to which garlic can be put, categorizing them according to the herb's different effects. Thus you would inform your readers and at the same time argue for garlic's positive qualities and the idea that it should do more than flavor a spaghetti sauce.

To explain, however, is the more obvious use of division and classification. You may well find that when you start off on a topic that lends itself to this pattern of organization, you need to define some of your terms. Writing about the ways in which a one-year-old can both annoy and delight you, for instance, you may want to define what you mean by your central terms. In so doing, you have a chance to link the definitions to your audience's experiences, so that even if some of your readers have never spent much time around a baby, they can still appreciate your points. For *annoy*, you might define your reaction as similar to hearing a car alarm going off in the middle of the night, and for *delight*, you might remind your readers of how they felt when opening an unexpected but perfect present. Both definitions help explain while at the same time drawing on common experiences.

Should you tackle that same topic with a humorous tone, you will not only be informing your audience but entertaining them as well. But humor comes in many forms, evoking everything from belly laughs to giggles to knowing smiles. To produce those responses, you may find yourself using exaggeration (also known as **hyperbole**), or **irony,** or **sarcasm** or a combination of all three, and more. Your title can tip off your readers to your tone: "Baby Destructo" (exaggeration); "Little Baby, Big Problem" (irony); "The Joys of Parenthood" (sarcasm).

System of Classification

To work effectively, a system of classification must be complete and logical. The system that governs how goods are arranged in a supermarket needs to be broad enough to cover everything a supermarket might sell, and it needs to make sense. Can openers should be with kitchen implements, not with vegetables; cans of peas should be with other canned goods, not with milk.

So, too, when you are writing an essay all your examples should be in the correct category. If you were thinking of the subject of campaign spending in the recent presidential election and, in particular, who contributed what to which political party, you would first concentrate on the Republicans and the Democrats, ignoring the campaigns of the minor political groups (the money they raised being minor in comparison). Then you would sort out the kinds of contributions—small donations from private citizens, large ones from individuals, money from PACs, from corporations, and the like—made to each of those two political parties. At that point, you would find you had so much material that you would be better off narrowing your subject, but no matter what you did, you wouldn't mix in intangible gifts such as a volunteer's time or tangible ones such as the "free" donuts handed out to the campaign workers.

More likely, however, as you think about your topic and work on your draft, you will find your classifications are not watertight. Yet you can account for the occasional leak by explaining it or by adjusting your system of division. In the example of campaign contributions, for instance, it would be impossible to put an accurate price tag on the time spent by volunteers or on the goods and services donated to the two political parties, though it's reasonable to assume that the dollar figure would be high. And that's all you need to say. You've explained why you have omitted those kinds of contributions. Adjusting the system of division, the other alternative, so that it included every conceivable kind of donation isn't a reasonable solution as it would make an already large topic even larger, impossibly so.

Other Patterns of Organization

Earlier in this chapter, you read about what definition can add to classification and division, but description, narration, and example are useful as well. The essay on political contributions, for instance, might open with a brief narrative recounting your having been besieged by a telephone caller who was trying to raise money for a particular candidate. And if that narrative described your having discovered the plea by listening to the caller's recorded message talking to your answering machine, then you could also underscore your point that raising money for campaigns has reached absurd heights (or depths).

Examples are also essential to classification, usually in the form of multiple illustrations. Your practice in using examples in other papers will help you here, for as you know, you can select examples from your own experience or that of others or both. Outside sources such as evidence drawn from books and magazines are also helpful, showing your reader that you have looked beyond your personal experience. When using examples, however, you need think through the most effective way to sequence them, which will often be according to dramatic effect—moving from least to most dramatic—or in chronological order.

Organization and Ideas

Some writers begin their essays by first dividing the subject into their system of classification, then moving on to focus on one of the classes. Say you chose as a topic the electronic objects we often take for granted. You might have found yourself making notes that include a huge list. Thinking through that list you might have noticed that you can divide it into machines that can be controlled with a remote device and those that cannot. In one category are items such as microwaves, answering machines, and computers, and in the other you've lumped together CD players, television sets, VCRs.

You sketch out notes that may look like this:

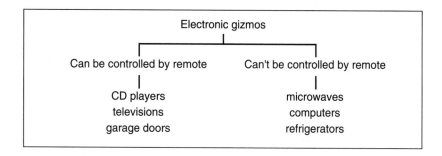

The more you think about it, the longer the list for remote-controlled objects becomes, so instead of writing about both categories, you stick to one, speculating upon a world with the ultimate universal remote.

On the other hand, you may find your central question so intriguing that you want to get right to it, in which case you wouldn't need to discuss the division at all; instead, you can leap straight into presenting the category of remote-controlled objects, illustrating it with multiple examples.

Perhaps the greatest trap in writing an essay that uses division and classification is that your means don't add up to an end, that what you have is a string of examples that don't lead anywhere. All your examples are well developed, yes, but they don't support an assertion. It's the cardinal sin—an essay without a thesis.

If you find yourself headed in that direction, one solution is to answer your own questions. In the course of thinking about your subject, you may well have come up with a solid, focused, central question, such as "What kind of life will the American consumer have in a remote-controlled world?" Your one-sentence answer to that question can be your thesis.

Often it helps to think of writing as a sort of silent dialogue with yourself. Reading a sentence in your draft and thinking about it, you find that thought leads to another sentence, and so on till you've filled up a number of pages. By the time you have stopped, you may realize that your first draft could more accurately be called a discovery draft, for in the course of writing it, you have found out what you want to say. Sum it up in one sentence that has a debatable point and you have your thesis.

If you are using division or classification to develop only one part of your paper, then where you place it depends on where you think it would be most effective. But if your essay, like most of those in this chapter, is structured primarily by division and classification, then you would do best to use a straightforward pattern of organization, devoting the body of the paper to developing the category or categories involved. Your reader can then follow your reasoning and understand how it supports your thesis. For the sake of clarity—readers can sometimes get lost in a tangle of examples—you may opt for an explicit thesis in an obvious place, such as at the end of your introduction.

Useful Terms

Division and classification Methods of examining a subject. Division involves the process of separating, first dividing the subject into groups so that they can be sorted out—classified—into categories; classification focuses on shared characteristics, sorting items into categories that share a similar feature.

Hyperbole Obvious overstatement, exaggeration.

Irony A statement or action in which the intended meaning or occurrence is the opposite of the surface one.

Sarcasm A caustic or sneering remark or tone that is usually ironic as well.

POINTERS FOR USING DIVISION AND CLASSIFICATION

Exploring the Topic

1. **How can your topic be divided?** What divisions apply? Of those you list, which one is the best suited?

2. **What examples can you think of?** What characteristics do your examples have in common? Which do you have the most to say about?

3. **Are your categories for classification appropriate?** Are the categories parallel? Do they overlap? Do you need to make any adjustments?

(Continued)

4. **Do your examples fit your categories?** Are you sure the examples have enough in common? Are they obvious? Which are not?
5. **What is your principle for classification?** Have you applied it consistently to each category?
6. **Are your categories complete?** Do they cover the topic? Do they contain enough examples?
7. **How can your categories be sequenced?** From simple to complex? Least to most important? Least to most effective?
8. **What is your point?** What assertion are you making? Does your system of classification support it? Are your examples appropriate?
9. **What is your purpose?** Are you primarily making your point to express your feelings, to inform, to persuade, or to entertain?

Drafting the Paper

1. **Know your reader.** Where does your reader stand in relation to your system of classification? Is the reader part of it? If so, how? If the reader is not part of your system, is he or she on your side, say a fellow student looking at teachers? What does your audience know about your topic? About your system of classification? What does the reader not know? Your audience might be biased toward or against your subject and classification system. How can you best foster or combat the bias?
2. **Know your purpose.** If your primary purpose is to express your feelings, make sure that you are not just writing to yourself and that you are not treading on the toes of your audience. Similarly, if you are writing to persuade, make sure you are not convincing only yourself. Check to see that you are using material that may convince someone who disagrees with you or who, at the least, is either sitting on the fence or hasn't given the matter much thought. Writing to inform is probably the easiest here, for though your subject may be familiar, your system of classification is probably new. On the other hand, writing to entertain is difficult and requires a deft use of persona.
3. **Set up your system of classification early in the paper.** You may find that a definition is in order or that some background

information is necessary, but make your system clear and bring it out early.

4. **Explain the principle behind the system.** To give your system credibility, you need to provide an explanation for your means of selection. The explanation can be brief—a phrase or two—but it should be there.

5. **Select appropriate examples.** Perhaps you can best illustrate a class by one extended example, or maybe it would be better to pile on examples. If your examples are apt to be unfamiliar to your audience, make sure you give enough detail so that they are explained by their contexts.

6. **Make a point.** Remember that what you have to say about your subject is infinitely more interesting than the subject itself. So, too, your major assertion is more important than your system of classification: it is what your system of classification adds up to. It's easy, in writing this kind of paper, to mistake the means for the end, so make sure that you use classification to support an overall assertion.

The New York Walk: Survival of the Fiercest

Caryn James

Division and classification plays a small part in Caryn James' essay, but it's a crucial one, for misreading the kind of man who hassles women on a city street can have serious consequences. Central to James' essay is the initial division between "a harmless gesture and a threat" (paragraph 13). Faced with either, most women adopt the "'don't mess with me glare" that James finds natural. As the essay explains, James lives in New York City. Her essay was, appropriately, published in the New York Times, *October 17, 1993.*

> **What to Look For**   As you write, you'll probably discover that you use a number of patterns of organization. James, for example, begins and ends with narration and description, and the body of her essay incorporates division and classification, example, process, cause and effect, and comparison and contrast. The mixture of modes may make the essay hard to classify, but it also gives it variety.

1   I know better than to talk back to guys who hassle women on the street. But on one weird August afternoon, I was caught in pedestrian gridlock in Times Square and the humidity turned my common sense to mush. A young man so average-looking he belonged in a Nike commercial planted himself on the sidewalk in front of me, purposely blocking my path, and offered some not-poetic variation on "Hey, baby."

2   What I did next was something no short, slight, sane person should ever do: I stamped my little foot and snapped at him in unprintable terms to get out of my way, right now! And while I was wondering why I had chosen a response that was both ineffectual *and* ridiculous, the street hassler smiled, stepped aside and said in a good-natured, singsong voice, "You're gonna learn to love me."

3   Humor is a desirable quality in a man, but this remark did not make him a person to take home. He was visibly affected by some

chemical or other, so I made sure to stay behind him as he woozed his way toward traffic. A basic rule of navigating the New York sidewalks, like driving anyplace, is that it's safer to be behind the drunk driver or drug-addled walker than in front of him.

4   And I didn't want him to see that my deliberately off-putting scowl was turning into a laugh.

5   For an instant I had almost lost the protective covering, the "don't mess with me" glare, that so many of us wear on crowded urban streets. Then I remembered that danger is real—the humor made him seem harmless, but his swaying toward an intersection suggested someone seriously out of control—and that walking in the city is a precise defensive maneuver.

6   This is especially, though not exclusively, true for women. Men are hassled, too, but physical size and social conditioning have made women more likely to be picked on. Walking can become an exhausting series of paralyzing questions. Should you slow down for the guy who seems, quite obviously, about to ask for directions? (I tried it once and was asked to join a theater group.) When is someone being innocently friendly, and when is he sidling up to get a better grip on your wallet or purse? When is a comment an invisible weapon, and when is it just a remark?

7   What's more, 30 years of raised feminist consciousness has taught us all that when men yell out to women on the street, whether to comment on a smile or issue a crude invitation, no compliment is involved. The average street hassler is not a fussy type, and while he may keep an eye out for a 17-year-old with no thighs, he will happily go after whoever crosses his line of vision: your mother, your granny, your self.

8   So most women have mastered the New York Walk for avoiding unpleasant encounters: eyes ahead but with good peripheral vision, bag clutched to your side, a purposeful stride and an unfriendly look. If someone talks to you, think of him as an obscene phone caller. Hang up. Do not acknowledge that he exists. In a big city, this is as necessary as locking your doors, and only a naïf would think otherwise.

9   Most of the time, this survival strategy doesn't bother me. I've always thought that my chilly, don't-talk-to-strangers New England upbringing has given me a Darwinian advantage; I've been naturally selected for this urban life. Ignoring strangers who talk to me

in Times Square—people to whom I have not, after all, been properly introduced—makes me feel right at home.

10   I could have evolved differently. My sister transplanted herself to Virginia, and while walking with her there on a civilized cobblestoned street once, I was shocked to hear her say: "You know, you don't have to grab your bag like that. You're not in New York anymore."

11   At moments like that, it's easy to wonder about the psychic cost of living in a city where such guardedness becomes second nature. Is it even possible, when you step into your house or office, to drop the hostile mask quite so easily or thoroughly as you imagine you can?

12   What residue of snarling distrust must build up over the years, so slowly you'd never notice it accumulating? Those are finally moot questions for someone like me, for whom New York will always be tinged with Holly Golightly glamour. Assuming a defensive posture while walking down the street seems a reasonable trade-off for the advantages of living here. Just as a matter of personal preference. I'd rather be hassled outside the Metropolitan Museum or Tiffany's than on a farm or in the 'burbs. (Don't say it doesn't happen.)

13   Maybe the best one can do is to savor those rare episodes during which it is easy to tell the difference between a harmless gesture and a threat. On another summer day, by a fluke in the law of averages, I happened to be the only person walking by a real-life cliché: a scaffold full of construction workers having lunch at a site on Broadway. As I passed, glare in place and prepared for anything, they started to sing a cheerful version of an oldies song: "There she goes, a-walkin' down the street/Singin' doo-wah-diddy-diddy-dum-diddy-do."

14   Hours later as I left my office, several blocks away, I passed a man who gave a big surprised wave. "Hey, I know you!" he said with a friendly smile of recognition as he passed by. "We sang to you!" I almost said hello.

Organization and Ideas

1. Paragraph 6 briefly describes various categories of men who approach women on the street. What are they?
2. Paragraph 7 tells the reader that "no compliment is involved." What is?
3. The essay ends with an example of "a harmless gesture" (paragraph 13). What is James' reaction?

4. Think about the division that James makes, her glare and its "psychic cost" (paragraph 11), and in your own words, state the thesis.
5. Does James' experience ring true compared to your own? How so?

Technique and Style

1. Though the essay is certainly a literate one, James includes a number of words that best fit the category of slang. What, if anything, do they add to the essay?
2. What evidence can you find to disprove the idea that the essay deals only with the hassling of women?
3. How would you describe James' tone?
4. Where in the essay does James use process? Cause and effect?
5. Explain whether you find James' mixing of modes adds or detracts from the essay.

Suggestions for Writing

Journal

1. Have you ever been followed, or whistled or yelled at, on the street? Write a paragraph or two about how it made you feel.
2. Describe your behavior when you walk along a crowded street. What do you do or not do? Why?

Essay

1. We interact with strangers in many different ways according to many different circumstances. The next time you find yourself in one of those situations, note how people act. Think about how various people behave and what categories they can be placed into. Then, when you draft your paper, make your categories come alive through description, narration, and example. Likely spots to observe behavior:
   traffic jams
   elevators
   lines (at a bank, supermarket, movie, cafeteria)
   train stations or airports
2. Think about the times when you were appreciated for something you do not value, and other times when you were not appreciated for something you do value. Perhaps you were praised for winning a prize or sports event that you didn't think much of, yet another time you didn't win though you performed better. Take those two categories

and jot down examples for each. The result will guide you as you write an essay using division and classification. Choose one of those times and write an essay in which you use it as an example, devoting most of the essay to an analysis of its meaning.

Always, Always, Always

Bill Rohde

The essay that follows was written for a class required for students who intended to teach English. Focusing on both writing and the teaching of writing, the course asked students to analyze their own writing habits, including elements in the writing process that gave them problems. No matter what their stage of experience, most writers hit at least one question that sends them to the nearest handbook. The assignment here asked the class to choose one matter of grammar or usage that sent them in search of answers, then to research what the handbooks had to say, and to write an essay explaining both the question and the answers. Since the students were prospective English teachers, they were to use the Modern Language Association's (more familiarly known as the MLA) system of documentation and their audience was the class itself. Bill Rohde questioned the necessity of using a comma before the last item in a series.

What to Look For   Bill Rohde takes an inherently dry subject—the serial comma—and uses it to satirize composition teachers and classify students. As you read the essay, try to imagine the person behind the prose. Also keep in mind that Rohde creates a distinct personality for the narrator of the essay without ever using the first-person *I*.

1   A student inquiring about the "correctness" of the serial comma finds conflicting advice in her *Harbrace,* her teacher's *MLA Style Manual,* and the library's *Washington Post Deskbook on Style.* *Harbrace* tells her she may write either

The air was raw, dank, and gray.

or

The air was raw, dank and gray.

Ever accommodating, the tiny, red handbook considers the comma before the conjunction "optional" unless there is "danger of misreading" (132). *The MLA Style Manual,* with its Bible-black cover, neither acknowledges ambivalence nor allows for options. "Commas are required between items in a series," it clearly states in Section 2.2.4., after which it provides a typically lighthearted sample sentence:

The experience demanded blood, sweat, and tears. (46)

The paperback *Post Deskbook,* so user-friendly it suggests right in the title the handiest place to keep it, advises the student to "omit commas where possible," as before the conjunction in a series (126–27). Apparently written on deadline, the book offers sample sentence fragments:

red, white, green and blue; 1, 2 or 3 (127)

2   What should you, the composition teacher, tell this puzzled student when she approaches with her problem? Tell her she must always use the serial comma—no ifs, ands, or buts about it. Regardless of whether you believe this to be true, you must sound convincing. If the student appears satisfied with your response and thanks you, you may go back to grading papers. If, however, she wrinkles her nose or bites her lip in a display of doubt, then you may safely label her a problem student and select one of the following tailor-made responses.

3   *The struggling student* appreciates any burden a teacher can remove. You should explain to her that out of sympathy for her plight—so much to keep track of when writing—you have just given her one of the few hard-and-fast rules in existence. Tell her to concern herself with apostrophes or sentence fragments, and not with whether the absence of a serial comma might lead to a misreading.

4   *The easily intimidated student* (often ESL) should have accepted your unequivocal answer, but perhaps you do not (yet) strike her as an authority figure. Go for the throat. Say, "Obey the MLA. It is

the Bible (or Koran or Bhagavad-Gita) of the discourse community to which you seek entry. Expect blood, sweat, and tears if you do not use the serial comma."

5   *The skeptic* needs an overpowering, multifarious theory to be convinced, so pull out Jane Walpole's *A Writer's Guide* and read the following:

> [A]ll commas indicate an up-pause in the voice contour, and this up-pause occurs after *each* series item up to the final one. Listen to your voice as you read this sentence:
>
> *Medical science has overcome tuberculosis, typhoid, small pox, and polio in the last hundred years.*
>
> Only *polio,* the final series item, lacks an up-pause; and where there is an up-pause, there should be a comma. The "comma and" combination before the final item also tells your readers that the series is about to close, thus reducing any chance of their misreading your sentence. (95)

While that's still soaking in, drop the names of linguists who have stated that writing is silent speech and reading is listening. Then tell her that omitting the serial comma represents an arrogant, foolish, and futile attempt to sever the natural link between speech and text.

6   Show *the visually oriented student,* possibly an artist, how

> Chagall, Picasso, and Dali

are nicely balanced, but

> Chagall, Picasso and Dali

are not.

7   Tell *the metaphor-happy student* that commas are like dividers between ketchup, mustard, and mayonnaise; fences between dogs, cats, and chickens; or borders between Israel, Syria, and Lebanon. Without them, messes result. (Dodge the fact that messes may result even if they are present.)

8   If the student is *a journalism major* who cites the *Deskbook* as proof of the serial comma's obsolescence, point out that her entire profession is rapidly approaching obsolescence. Add that

editors who attempt to speed up reading by eliminating commas in fact slow down comprehension by removing helpful visual cues.

9   One hopes that reading, seeing, and hearing so many strong arguments in favor of the serial comma has so utterly convinced you of its usefulness that every student from here on in will accept your rock-solid, airtight edict without question.

Works Cited

Achtert, Walter S., and Joseph Gibaldi. The MLA Style Manual. New York: MLA, 1985.

Hodges, John C., et al. Harbrace College Handbook. New York: Harcourt, 1990.

Walpole, Jane. A Writer's Guide. Englewood Cliffs: Prentice, 1980.

Webb, Robert A. The Washington Post Deskbook on Style. New York: McGraw, 1978.

Organization and Ideas

1. At what point in the essay does Rohde use division? What does he divide and into what groups?
2. Rohde begins his classification in paragraph 3 and ends it with paragraph 8. What reasons can you infer for the order in which he presents his categories?
3. Where in the essay do you find Rohde's thesis? How effective is that placement?
4. On the surface, Rohde's thesis is explicit, but what is his implied thesis?
5. In what ways is the essay a satire on education?

Technique and Style

1. How would you describe Rohde's tone? His persona? What does his research on the topic contribute to his persona?
2. Who is the *you* in the essay? How effective do you find the direct address?
3. Note the use of parentheses in paragraph 4. Check out what your handbook says about parentheses. To what extent does Rohde's use fit the handbook's explanation?

4. A writer's choice of pronoun has become an issue ever since the once generic *he* lost its general nature and gained a specific gender connotation. What is Rohde's solution? Explain why you do or do not find his choice of pronoun effective.

5. The point of documentation is to provide specific and relevant references in an unobtrusive manner. Evaluate how well Rohde uses his research and how well he documents it.

Suggestions for Writing

Journal

1. Write out your response to Rohde's persona. Would you like to have him as your teacher? Would you like to have him in your class?

2. Commas give many writers fits. Thinking about your own writing, jot down the kinds of problems you have with commas. When you've finished, reread what you have written. Do you find a pattern?

Essay

1. Given that people's personalities range over a continuum with extremes at either end, the extremes can be good subjects for an essay that uses division and classification. Think about virtually any activity people are involved in and identify the behavior that represents the two extremes, thus dividing the subject. Then choose one of those groups and consider the categories your choice can be classified into. Here are some suggestions:

   drivers
   readers
   writers
   teachers
   professional athletes

2. Think about the various kinds of teachers you have had and have heard about. What categories can they be sorted into? Write an essay in which you explain those categories, giving examples for each.

The Search for Human Life in the Maze of Retail Stores

Michelle Higgins

Michelle Higgins is a reporter for the Wall Street Journal *who covers personal finance. She joined the paper as an intern for the popular* Friday Weekend Journal *in 1999 and quickly moved up to reporter. At* Weekend Journal, *Ms. Higgins authored a weekly travel column, "Takeoffs & Landings" and wrote cover stories on everything from the online travel business to theme park vacations. In April 2002, Ms. Higgins began writing for the newspaper's new "Personal Journal" section. Featured as the "Cranky Consumer," her recent stories have included consumer issues concerning everything from online banking to 401(k)s to summer camp. The review that follows was published in the May 6, 2003, issue of the* Wall Street Journal.

What to Look For   A report on retail stores that critiques their ability to help shoppers find what they are looking for could be very dull indeed, but Michelle Higgins keeps it from being so. As you read, look for the ways she keeps her reader's interest.

1   When Jonathan Gordon went shopping at a Macy's in New Jersey for a vacuum cleaner recently, he couldn't find anyone to answer his questions. After a 10-minute search, he solved his problem by standing in the aisle and shouting, "Is there anybody here who can help me?"

2   Finally, a staffer appeared—who couldn't tell him anything he couldn't already read on the box.

3   Attention, shoppers: It is getting even tougher to get help in the aisles. The nation's third-largest discount retailer, **Kmart,** is expected to come out of bankruptcy Tuesday, and retailers overall are anticipating a postwar sales boost. But many are still in retrenching mode. In January, **Toys "R" Us** cut 700 positions in 400 stores. The next month, **Circuit City** eliminated 4.8% of its work force, including an average of three salespeople per store. Overall last year, the

number of employees in retail fell for the first time in a decade, according to the Bureau of Labor Statistics.

4   All this comes on top of a major effort in recent years by retailers to build ever-more-colossal shops—while simultaneously redesigning them to encourage people to serve themselves instead of getting help from the staff.

5   To see just how tough it is out there, we recently went shopping at six retailers. They included two big discounters Kmart and **Wal-Mart Stores,** the home-improvement giants **Lowe's** and **Home Depot**—and what is often the lion's den of retail: sprawling, kid-packed toy stores.

6   We picked stores in six different cities and visited them all on a Saturday between the busy hours of one and five. At each place we tried to find an employee who would help us locate two items we knew the store stocked. To see how much staff knew about their merchandise, we also asked for help with a specific task; for example, we asked at the toy stores for gift suggestions for a smart 10-year-old boy—but nothing too nerdy.

7   Our experience varied widely. At **KB Toys,** we were out the door in eight minutes with our three purchases: A Furreal Friend robotic cat, Shrinky Dinks and a basketball-player action figure. But at Wal-Mart, it took us 30 minutes and conversations with 10 people—and still, we left without finding one of the three things we wanted (a fondue pot) because the staff didn't know where they were.

8   KB Toys stores, of course, are small in comparison to warehouse-style Wal-Marts. But the staff was among the most helpful: One person even offered to carry our purchases for us while we kept shopping.

9   The retail business, struggling through its worst slump in years, can ill afford to be alienating shoppers. The pace of annual sales growth has tumbled from a high of 6.7% four years ago to just 2.9% last year. The outlook continues to look grim. The month of March was the weakest for U.S. retailers since 1995, according to a survey by Bank of Tokyo-Mitsubishi Ltd.

10   "In the past year, customer service has absolutely become dreadful," says Judson Rees of Brand Marketing, a company that dispatches "mystery shoppers" to test service at stores and restaurants. In a survey of shoppers, he said, more than three-quarters reported that it's "common" to see salespeople ignoring customers this year, up from 39% last year.

11   It turns out there are a few ways to beat the system. Though we passed over it the first time, for example, Lowe's has buzzers in its stores to summon a staffer. Toys "R" Us has phones scattered around that you can pick up and ask for help.

12   We got off to a rocky start at a Toys "R" Us in Colma, California, when we asked where to find a Furreal Friend robotic cat. "It's right there," the staffer told us—pointing about 30 yards away and wagging his finger. "Right there! Right there!"

13   But later, the same guy warmed up and complimented us on our toys. While we had his attention, we asked where to find Shrinky Dinks. He consulted his walkie-talkie and announced: "The Imaginarium. Follow me." We were done shopping in 21 minutes.

14   A Toys "R" Us official said the first salesman should have been more polite.

15   The Lowe's we visited had a people-greeter at the front door, who deflected our question about a squirrel-proof birdfeeder to a customer-service desk that was already swarming with impatient shoppers. But after being directed to the right department, a staffer there told us Lowe's doesn't sell them—even though we later noticed that he was standing right in front of one. (Admittedly, it was on a very high shelf.)

16   After that, service picked up. Another employee got off a forklift and gave us detailed help after we asked for advice on closet organizers. He even drew us a sketch.

17   At a nearby Home Depot, we shopped for the same items and got efficient service. A cashier who was clocking out for the day even hung around to assist us.

18   Wal-Mart, Lowe's and Kmart said they are focusing on improving service.

19   Service was mixed at a Kmart in New York City. We asked the first employee we saw, a woman with an armful of clothes, for help finding a foot spa. She asked, "What is that?" before pointing us to the right department. There we asked another guy for help— who simply grunted and started walking away from us. We followed, on the chance that he intended us to, and he led us to the foot spas.

20   A third staffer helped us find cleaning products to take out a ketchup stain. "This one has a brush, so you can, shhh, shhh," he said, making a helpful brushing motion. We took it and said thanks. "You're welcome, sweetie," was the reply.

Store	Time	People We Talked To	Snafu	Comment
Home Depot *Secaucus, N.J.*	We spent 30 minutes in the store.	Four, counting a cashier who was clocking out for the day but hung around to help us.	"You wanna do it my way? Or you wanna do it your way?" one smarty-pants staffer asked us when we were looking for a closet organizer.	Knowledgeable staff. Mr. Smarty-Pants ended up telling us everything we needed to organize our closet—including the size of the drill bit.
Lowe's *North Bergen, N.J.*	40 minutes (the longest).	Five, including a greeter who reminded us of our cute grand-mother.	We found the squirrel-proof bird feeder (but first, a staffer tried to tell us the store didn't carry it).	Mixed service. One staffer botched the bird feeder. But another walked us right to the bag-o-rags we needed.
Kmart *New York*	29 minutes.	Seven, including a guy who just walked away when we asked about foot spas. We followed (and he led us to the right place).	We had to ask three people before we found a fondue set.	People helped us find everything—but we had to ask a bunch of differ-ent people to find some things.
Wal-Mart *Panorama City, Calif.*	30 minutes.	Ten—the most of any store we visited.	No one we asked knew what a fondue set was.	Most staffers just pointed us to a department in-stead of walking us over. Wal-Mart says we should have been escorted.

Store	Time	People We Talked To	Snafu	Comment
Toys "R" Us *Colma, Calif.*	21 minutes.	Two. One seemed annoyed at first, but later chatted us up about the gray robotic cat we bought.	We got the hard sell at checkout when the cashier asked us if we wanted batteries with that.	The Shrinky Dinks box was opened—so a staffer sat right down on the floor and made sure we got a complete set.
KB Toys *Daly City, Calif.*	Eight minutes— the fastest exit.	Two. Tied for the least number of people we needed to ask.	One didn't know what Shrinky Dinks were—but asked someone who did.	Helpful and courteous. One employee offered to carry our items to the counter while we finished shopping.

Organization and Ideas

1. Outline the system of division and classification in a drawing similar to the one on page 142.
2. In paragraph 6, Higgins outlines her methodology behind her system and examples. How trustworthy is it?
3. Higgins uses a framing device, beginning and ending the piece with narratives. In what ways are they similar? Different?
4. Higgins is careful to point out the stores' problems as well as those of the shopper. In what ways are the two sets of problems related?
5. How necessary and helpful is the chart that concludes the piece?

Technique and Style

1. What is Higgins' primary purpose: to entertain, inform, persuade? Some combination of the three?
2. Higgins writes under the title of the Cranky Consumer. How apt is the title?
3. What devices and techniques does Higgins use to keep the piece from being dry?
4. In what ways is the selection an appropriate article for the *Wall Street Journal*?
5. How appropriate is the article's title?

Suggestions for Writing

Journal

1. Higgins uses a lot of examples in her article. Which do you find the most interesting and why?
2. In a way, the article seems to stop instead of end. Write a concluding paragraph for it.

Essay

1. Write your own division and classification essay, using retail stores as a general subject. One of two ways to divide the topic is to think about the people you would see in them, dividing the general "people in retail stores" into

   shoppers
   sales personnel
   cashiers

Of if you'd prefer a more abstract system, you can use the general "large retail stores" and divide it into

efficiency

convenience

variety of merchandise

Choose one of these divisions or your own and consider the possible classifications. While you do not need to begin with a thesis, one will probably evolve as you write about your topic.

2. One of the arguments against the megastores such as the ones Higgins writes about is that they undercut and in many cases destroy the smaller "Mom and Pop" stores. Think about the kinds of stores that fall into the "Mom and Pop" category and write an essay that describes them. Your thesis can be linked to their value to the community or lack of it. You may well come up with your own thesis as you work on the subject.

The Plot Against People

Russell Baker

Russell Baker is best known for his light tone, one that many readers have enjoyed during the 36 years he was a regular columnist for the New York Times. *Winner of two Pulitzer Prizes, one for biography and another for commentary, Baker is the author of several collections of essays and autobiographical books—*Growing Up *(1982),* The Good Times *(1989),* There's a Country in My Cellar *(1991)— and the editor of* The Norton Book of Light Verse *(1986) and* Russell Baker's Book of American Humor *(1993). The essay that follows typifies the humorous side of Baker's style, for he has discovered the principles behind the continuing battle between humans and inanimate objects. He discusses these principles as he neatly divides things into three categories and then places objects into his classifications.*

What to Look For   Transitions between paragraphs can be wooden, so obvious that they leap off the page to say "Look at me! I'm a transition." The more effective variety is subtle, and one way to bring that about is to pick up a key word from the previous sentence and repeat it in the first sentence of the paragraph that follows. After you've read Baker's essay, go back over it searching for his transitions between paragraphs.

1   Inanimate objects are classified into three major categories—those that don't work, those that break down and those that get lost.

2   The goal of all inanimate objects is to resist man and ultimately to defeat him, and the three major classifications are based on the method each object uses to achieve its purpose. As a general rule, any object capable of breaking down at the moment when it is most needed will do so. The automobile is typical of the category.

3   With the cunning typical of its breed, the automobile never breaks down while entering a filling station with a large staff of idle mechanics. It waits until it reaches a downtown intersection in the middle of the rush hour, or until it is fully loaded with family and luggage on the Ohio Turnpike.

4   Thus it creates maximum misery, inconvenience, frustration and irritability among its human cargo, thereby reducing its owner's life span.

5   Washing machines, garbage disposals, lawn mowers, light bulbs, automatic laundry dryers, water pipes, furnaces, electrical fuses, television tubes, hose nozzles, tape recorders, slide projectors—all are in league with the automobile to take their turn at breaking down whenever life threatens to flow smoothly for their human enemies.

6   Many inanimate objects, of course, find it extremely difficult to break down. Pliers, for example, and gloves and keys are almost totally incapable of breaking down. Therefore, they have had to evolve a different technique for resisting man.

7   They get lost. Science has still not solved the mystery of how they do it, and no man has ever caught one of them in the act of getting lost. The most plausible theory is that they have developed a secret method of locomotion which they are able to conceal the instant a human eye falls upon them.

8   It is not uncommon for a pair of pliers to climb all the way from the cellar to the attic in its single-minded determination to raise its owner's blood pressure. Keys have been known to burrow three

feet under mattresses. Women's purses, despite their great weight, frequently travel through six or seven rooms to find a hiding space under a couch.

9   Scientists have been struck by the fact that things that break down virtually never get lost, while things that get lost hardly ever break down.

10   A furnace, for example, will invariably break down at the depth of the first winter cold wave, but it will never get lost. A woman's purse, which after all does have some inherent capacity for breaking down, hardly ever does; it almost invariably chooses to get lost.

11   Some persons believe this constitutes evidence that inanimate objects are not entirely hostile to man, and that a negotiated peace is possible. After all, they point out, a furnace could infuriate a man even more thoroughly by getting lost than by breaking down, just as a glove could upset him far more by breaking down than by getting lost.

12   Not everyone agrees, however, that this indicates a conciliatory attitude among inanimate objects. Many say it merely proves that furnaces, gloves and pliers are incredibly stupid.

13   The third class of objects—those that don't work—is the most curious of all. These include such objects as barometers, car clocks, cigarette lighters, flashlights, and toy train locomotives. It is inaccurate, of course, to say that they never work. They work once, usually for the first few hours after being brought home, and then quit. Thereafter, they never work again.

14   In fact, it is widely assumed that they are built for the purpose of not working. Some people have reached advanced ages without ever seeing some of these objects—barometers, for example—in working order.

15   Science is utterly baffled by the entire category. There are many theories about it. The most interesting holds that the things that don't work have attained the highest state possible for an inanimate object, the state to which things that break down and things that get lost can still only aspire.

16   They have truly defeated man by conditioning him never to expect anything of them, and in return they have given man the only peace he receives from inanimate society. He does not expect his barometer to work, his electric locomotive to run, his cigarette

lighter to light or his flashlight to illuminate, and when they don't, it does not raise his blood pressure.

17   He cannot attain that peace with furnaces and keys and cars and women's purses as long as he demands that they work for their keep.

Organization and Ideas

1. Paragraphs 3–6 explain the first category. What effects does the automobile achieve by breaking down? How do those effects support Baker's contention about "the goal of all inanimate objects"? What other examples does Baker put into his first category? What example does not fit?
2. Paragraphs 7–12 present the second classification. What causes, reasons, or motives are attributed to the examples in this group?
3. Paragraphs 13–16 describe the third group. What are its qualities? Why might Baker have chosen to list it last? What principle of organization can you discern beneath Baker's ordering of the three groups?
4. Consider how each group frustrates and defeats people together with the first sentence of paragraph 2. Combine this information into a sentence that states the author's thesis.
5. To what extent does Baker use the absurd in his essay? How is it appropriate?

Technique and Style

1. In part, the essay's humor arises from Baker's use of anthropomorphism, attributing human qualities to inanimate objects. How effectively does he use the technique?
2. Baker has a keen eye for the absurd, as illustrated by paragraph 10. What other examples can you find? What does this technique contribute to the essay?
3. Baker's stance, tone, and line of reasoning, while patently tongue-in-cheek, are also mock-scientific. Where can you find examples of Baker's explicit or implied "scientific" trappings?
4. The essay's transitions are carefully wrought. What links paragraph 3 to paragraph 2? Paragraph 7 to paragraph 6? Paragraph 10 to paragraph 9? Paragraph 12 to paragraph 11?
5. How an essay achieves unity is a more subtle thing. What links paragraph 8 to paragraph 6? Paragraph 9 to paragraphs 3–6? Paragraph 16 to paragraph 2? Paragraph 17 to paragraphs 10–12 and paragraphs 3–5?

Suggestions for Writing

Journal

1. Describe a fight you have had with an inanimate object.
2. Of all the inanimate objects that can frustrate you, which one tops the list and why?

Essay

1. Write your own "plot" essay, imagining something else plotting against people. Like Baker, you can take a "scientific" stance or you may prefer your own humorous tone. Suggestions:
   clothes
   food
   pets
   the weather
   plants
   traffic
2. It's no news that we live in a highly technological society; it's also no news that at times that technology is frustrating. You may, for instance, have a number of objects that display the time—VCR, clock, stove, answering machine—but when the electricity goes off, getting them back in sync is a challenge. Choose a category and write an essay in which you explore whether or not that particular group of technological advances is good, bad, or somewhere in between.

Desert Religions

Richard Rodriguez

The son of Mexican immigrants, Richard Rodriguez did not learn English until he went to school but he learned it well. He holds a BA from Stanford University and a PhD in English literature from the University of California at Berkeley. He is best known, however, for his writing, particularly his memoirs: Hunger of Memory *(1982),* Days of Obligation: An Argument with My Mexican Father *(1992), and* Brown: The Last Discovery of America *(2002). A contributing editor at* Harper's *and the* Los Angeles Times, *Rodriguez has been called the "best American essayist" by the* Village Voice. *You might have heard his own voice on* The News Hour with Jim Lehrer *where he is a regular contributor. The essay reprinted here first was aired on that show on July 8, 2002.*

What to Look For   When you think about placing items in categories, you are analyzing their shared characteristics, their similarities. That's exactly what Rodriguez does, so as you read, look for the ways he tracks what the three "desert religions" have in common.

1   The Catholic priest is under arrest, accused of raping altar boys. The Muslim shouts out the name of Allah as the jetliner plows into the skyscraper. The Jewish settler's biblical claim to build on the West Bank is supported by fundamentalist Protestants who dream of the last days.

2   These have been months of shame and violence among the three great desert religions—Judaism, Christianity, and Islam—the religions to which most Americans adhere. These desert religions are sister religions in fact, but more commonly they have been brother religions, united and divided by a masculine sense of faith. Mullahs, priests, rabbis—the business of religion was traditionally the males. It was the male's task to understand how God exists in our lives.

3   Judaism gave Christianity and Islam a notion both astonishing and radical, the notion that God acts in history. The desert religions became, in response to this idea, activist religions, ennobled at times by a sense of holy purpose, but also filled with a violence fed by the assumption that God is on my side and not yours. The history of the desert religions oft repeated by old men to boys, got told through stories of battles and crusades, sultans and emperors.

4   But within the three great desert faiths there was a feminine impulse, less strong but ever present, the tradition of absorption rather than assertion, assertive rather than authority, of play rather than dogmatic servitude. Think of the delicate poetry of the song of songs or the delicacy of the celebration of the maternal represented by the Renaissance Madonna or the architectural lines of the medieval mosques of Spain, light as music. And yet the louder, more

persistent tradition has been male, concerned with power and blood and dogmatic points.

5   Now on the evening news, diplomats come and go speaking of [everything from] truces and terrorists to the price of oil. In truth, we are watching a religious war, Muslim versus Jew—a war disguised by the language of diplomacy. In decades and centuries past there have been Holocausts and crusades and violence as fierce among the leaders of a single religion, for example, Catholics contending with Protestant and Eastern Orthodox over heresies and questions of authority. Yahweh, God, Allah—the desert Deity rarely expressed a feminine aspect as in Hinduism.

6   The men who interpreted the bible or Koran rarely allowed themselves a sense of unknowing or paradox as in Buddhism. And not coincidentally I know many Americans who are turning away from the desert religions or are seeking to moderate the mass unity of the desert religions by turning to the contemplative physics of yoga and the play of the Zen koan.

7   Meanwhile, in my own Catholic Church, there is the squalor of sexual scandal—men forcing themselves on boys. One hears conservative Catholics who speak of ridding the seminaries and the rectors of homosexuals. As one gay Catholic, a single man in this vast world, I tell you pedophilia is no more an expression of homosexuality than rape is an expression of heterosexuality. Pedophilia and rape are assertions of power. Polls indicate that a majority of American Catholics are more forgiving of the fallen priests than they are forgiving of the bishops and cardinals who have treated us like children, with their secret meetings and their clutch on power, apologizing but assuming no penance.

8   Polls indicate also that Catholics continue to go to church. We go to church because of the sacramental consolation our religion gives. All of us now in our churches and synagogues and mosques, what knowledge unites us now in this terrible season? Are we watching the male face of the desert religion merely reassert itself? Or are we watching the collapse of the tradition and the birth of—what?

9   I think of the women of America who have become priests and rabbis. I think of the women of Afghanistan who came to the school door the first morning after the Taliban had disappeared. I think of Mother Teresa whose name will be remembered long after we have forgotten the names of the cardinals in their silk robes. I think that

we may be at the beginning of a feminine moment in the history of the desert religions, even while the tanks rumble and the priest is arrested and the girl, unblinking, straps explosives onto her body.

Organization and Ideas

1. Rodriguez divides desert religions into three groups and then traces the masculine and feminine impulses within them. How valid is his view of the masculine principle?
2. Paragraph 4 examines the feminine principle in the three religions. What other examples can you think of?
3. The essay was aired in 2002. To what extent, if any, is it dated?
4. In paragraph 8 Rodriguez speculates on why people still attend places of worship. What questions does he pose? What is his answer to those questions? How can you state it as a thesis?
5. Reread the first and last paragraphs. In what ways do they frame the essay?

Technique and Style

1. In paragraph 4, Rodriguez defines what he means by the feminine impulse. How adequate is his definition?
2. The essay was written for television. What evidence can you find to show that Rodriguez shaped his prose to be heard instead of read?
3. Where in the essay does Rodriguez bring in his own experience? What does he achieve by doing so?
4. The details that Rodriguez uses, particularly those in paragraphs 1 and 9, are tied to the events of 2001 and 2002, times removed from that at which you are reading his essay. To what extent are those details still effective?
5. How would you describe the essay's overall tone: Pessimistic? Optimistic? Somewhere in between? What evidence supports your view?

Suggestions for Writing

Journal

1. Think of your own religion or a religion you know well. Use your journal to write down examples of the masculine impulse.
2. Reread the essay, paying particular attention to Rodriguez's idea of the feminine impulse. To what extent does it apply to your religion or one that you know well?

Essay

1. Reread the essay, noting how Rodriguez defines the masculine and feminine impulses and the examples he uses to illustrate his definitions. Think about those impulses and consider how they operate in other areas or within other groups. If, for example, you were analyzing theme parks, you might think of all the kinds of rides, and then sort them into categories according to gender. Roller coasters would probably be masculine, ferris wheels feminine, and so on. Pick one of the suggestions below or one of your own and write an essay in which you analyze how masculine and feminine characteristics operate:

   musicians
   writers
   comics
   sports
   food

2. The terms *masculine* and *feminine* are very broad, encompassing a wide variety of behavior. Arnold Schwarzenegger and Jay Leno would both be called masculine, though they are very different. Choose one of the terms and write an essay in which you analyze the variations within the general category.

ADDITIONAL WRITING ASSIGNMENTS

Using Division and Classification

1. Consider the types of locomotion associated with sports: skateboard, Roller Blades, surfboard, skis, snowshoes.
2. Consider what ads tell us about products and ourselves: cars, lingerie, liquor, beer, men's cologne, men's underwear.
3. Consider the ideal house pet: dog, cat, gerbil, snake, exotic animal, guinea pig.
4. Consider the ideal vehicle: SUV, pickup, sedan, convertible, sports car.

Evaluating the Essays

1. The concept of the feminine plays a large role in the essays by Richard Rodriguez and Caryn James. How does each author define it? How important is it to the writer's main point? How valid is the author's use of the concept? Write an essay in which you analyze the writers' use of the concept together with your own view of it. Use evidence from both essays to support your opinion.
2. The selections by Michelle Higgins and Russell Baker use very clear patterns of division and classification. Trace the organization of each essay to determine its structure. Granted that Baker's essay is humorous and Higgins' is serious, both rely on clear distinctions to maintain their tones and support their theses. Which does so more effectively?
3. Reread "Always, Always, Always" and "The Plot Against People," considering the essays as satires. What is being satirized? How? Of the two writers, which is the more successful and why? Use quotations from both essays to back up your opinion.
4. Division and classification can be a predictable and dull kind of organization, but often is saved from that trap by the thesis it supports and the writer's style. Choose among the five essays in this chapter to argue for the one that makes the best use of the pattern. Draw upon the other essays as evidence to prove your point.

On Using
Comparison and Contrast

6

What's the difference?" gets at the heart of **comparison and contrast,** and it is a question that can fit into any context. In college, it often turns up in the form of essay questions; in day-to-day life, it implies the process behind most decisions: "What shall I wear?" "Which movie will I see?" "Should I change jobs?" All these questions involve choices that draw on comparison and contrast. Like description, narration, example, and classification, comparison and contrast forces you to observe, but here you are looking for similarities and differences. In a way, comparison and contrast is the simplest and most analytical form of division and classification in that you are examining only two categories, or perhaps only one example from each of the two categories. "Which sounds better, tapes or records?" compares two categories; "Which sounds better, compact discs or records?" compares two items in the same category.

No matter what you select, however, you need to be sure that the comparison is fair. Deciding where to go out to dinner often depends on how much you are willing to spend, so comparing a fast-food place to an elegant French restaurant doesn't have much of a point unless you want to treat the comparison humorously. If neither is worth the money, however, you have a serious assertion to work from, but you have to work carefully.

Sometimes the similarities will not be readily apparent. Imagine that Michael Jordan decided to run for president of the United States and you decided to write a paper on his campaign; you might well wonder how he connected his basketball days with serving in public office. But as you think about what playing on a professional basketball team has in common with his experience serving in the United States Senate, similarities begin to emerge: both positions require teamwork and leadership; both depend on the ability to make quick decisions based on complex situations; both call for stamina and training, including what could be called homework. A cynic might add that both involve fancy footwork and the ability to dodge the opposition, but if you want to keep to a serious tone and carry the comparison further, you'd also realize that both jobs call for many public appearances and the ability to be at ease in front of cameras, to be a public figure, if not a celebrity.

There the similarity ends. One position is relatively short-lived and pays millions. The other is at least a six-year term and not nearly so well remunerated. And no matter how seriously you take basketball, it is essentially a game, a sport, whereas the other may well affect every citizen in the United States and potentially—as economic and foreign policies are involved—citizens elsewhere as well.

Essays that depend primarily on other modes, such as description, narration, and definition, often use comparison and contrast to heighten a difference or clarify a point, but the pieces in this section rely on comparison and contrast as their main principle of organization, even though their purposes differ.

Audience and Purpose

Often you may want only to inform your reader; that gives you at least three possible theses:

> *x* is better or worse than *y*.
> *x* has a lot in common with *y*, though not obviously so.
> *x* is quite different from *y*, though superficially similar.

If, for instance, your college is primarily residential, you might be interested in how it differs from a nonresidential institution. Assuming that your classmates are your audience, they might be surprised to find that on the average, students at nonresidential campuses are quite different. Compared to those at residential institutions, they are older, work more hours at jobs, miss more classes, carry fewer hours, attend fewer sports events, participate in fewer on-campus activities, and take longer to earn a degree.

You could easily turn what started out as an informative essay into an argumentative one if in the course of writing, you decide that living on a campus that is primarily residential has some drawbacks that may not be apparent at first. A dorm room may not be half as pleasant as an apartment off campus, and eating in the cafeteria can be monotonous. On the other hand, living on campus makes it easier to form solid friendships, and classes don't have to be over at the bell—the discussion can continue without the pressure of having to race off for a job downtown. As you come up with more and more information, you are able to assess the pros and cons and, therefore, to construct a strong argument in favor of the side you believe is best.

Comparison can also be used to entertain your readers. A seemingly simple job such as washing the dog can be as much of a challenge as performing major surgery. At least at hospitals, you don't have to catch the patient first.

Analogy

One useful form of comparison is **analogy,** for it can emphasize a point or illuminate an idea. If you are writing about an abstraction, for example, you can make it more familiar by using an analogy to make it concrete and, therefore, more understandable. An intangible word such as *rumor* becomes more distinct, more memorable, if you write of it as cancer. Or, if you are explaining a process, analogy can often make the unfamiliar familiar; many a tennis instructor has said, "Hold your racquet as though you are shaking hands with a person."

An analogy is an extended **metaphor,** in which a primary term is equated with another quite dissimilar term. The process of writing, for example, is a far cry from making music, but if you think of all the elements of the writing process—coming up with a topic and ideas about it, planning how to organize what you want to say, working on drafts, editing as you go along—then you can see how you can extend the description into a metaphor. You, the writer, are the leader of the orchestra. Organizing your ideas for an essay is rather like getting all the members of the orchestra to play the same tune. Can't find quite the right word? That's similar to having a musician missing from the string section. Wonder if that comma is in the right place? One of the horns skipped a note. Tone not quite what you want it to be? Some of the musicians are flat. Once you have a solid draft, however, it's as though rehearsal is over and the piece is ready for an audience.

So in exposition, analogy clarifies—because by making x analogous to y, you bring all the associations of y to bear on x. If you were to compare the differences in the style of two television newscasters, you might find that one delivers the news in a rush, like a machine gun firing, while the other is more like a single-shot target rifle. The machine gun person fires rapid lines and barely pauses for breath, a sharp contrast to the target rifle person, who hesitates between sentences as though to reload an idea before aiming it at the viewers.

To use analogy well, however, you have to use it cautiously. Often writers use it sparingly, working one into a sentence or paragraph instead of using it as the basic structure for an entire essay. Five pages of the ship of state can make you and your readers seasick.

Method of Comparison

Comparison and contrast essays group information so that the comparison is made by **blocks** or **point by point** or by a combination of the two. If you were to write an essay explaining the differences between an American feast, such as Thanksgiving, and a Chinese one, here is what the two major types of organization would look like in outline form:

Type	**Structure**	**Content**
Block	Paragraph 1	Introduction
	Block A, paragraphs 2–4	American culture
	Point 1	Preparation
	Point 2	Courses & types of food
	Point 3	Manners
	Block B, paragraphs 5–7	Chinese culture
	Point 1	Preparation
	Point 2	Courses & types of food
	Point 3	Manners
	Paragraph 8	Conclusion
Point by point	Paragraph 1	Introduction
	Point 1, paragraph 2	Preparation
		Chinese
		American
	Point 2, paragraph 3	Courses & types of food
		Chinese
		American

And so on. As you can see, sticking rigorously to one type of organization can become boring or predictable, so writers often mix the two.

In this chapter you'll find essays organized by block, point by point, and by a combination of the two. Outlining an essay readily reveals which type of organization the writer uses. In your own writing, you might first try what comes easiest; then, in a later draft, you might mix the organization a bit and see what you find most effective. Fortunately word processing makes such changes easy, but if you don't have a word processor, try writing each paragraph on a separate piece of paper. Shuffling them around is then a simple task, though you'll have to supply some transitions after you decide on the best sequence for your paragraphs.

Other Modes

A close look at any of the essays that follow will show how you can use other modes, such as description, narration, and cause and effect, to help flesh out the comparison and contrast. A brief narrative or anecdote is often a good way to begin an essay as it usually sets a conversational tone and establishes a link between writer and reader. Examples can clarify your points and description can make them memorable, while exploring why the differences or similarities exist or what effect they may have will lead you into pondering cause-and-effect relationships.

Organization and Ideas

The one-sentence thesis placed at the end of an introductory paragraph certainly informs your readers of your subject and stance, but you might find your paper more effective if you treat your thesis more subtly, trying it out in different forms and positions. While some of the essays in this chapter save their major assertion until last, others combine ideas from various points in the essay to form a thesis. And, of course, not all theses are explicit, but if you want to imply it, you have to be sure your implication is clear or the reader may miss the point.

Although some writers begin the writing process with a thesis clearly set out, many find that it is easier to write their way into one. As a result, you may find that the last paragraph in your draft will make a very good introductory one, for by the time you write it, you have refined your thesis. At that point, you'll find writing a new introduction isn't the task it was to begin with; you already know where you ended up and how you got there.

Useful Terms

Analogy An analogy examines a subject by comparing it point by point to something seemingly unlike but more commonplace and less complex. An analogy is also an extended metaphor.

Block comparison A comparison of *x* to *y* by grouping all that is to be compared under *x* and then following with the same information under *y*.

Comparison and contrast An examination of two or more subjects by exploring their similarities and differences. Similarities and differences are usually developed through literal and logical comparisons within like categories.

Metaphor An implied but direct comparison in which the primary term is made more vivid by associating it with a quite dissimilar term. "Life is a bed of roses" is a familiar metaphor.

Point by point A comparison that examines one or more points by stating the point, then comparing subject *x* to subject *y*, and then continuing to the next point.

POINTERS FOR COMPARISON AND CONTRAST

Exploring the Topic

1. **What are the similarities?** What characteristics do your two subjects share? Are the two so similar that you have little to distinguish them? If so, try another subject; if not, pare down your list of similarities to the most important ones.

2. **What are the differences?** In what ways are your two subjects different? Are they so different that they have little in common? If so, make sure you can handle a humorous tone or try another subject; if not, pare down your list of differences to the most important ones.

3. **Should you emphasize similarities or differences?** Which pattern of organization best fits your material? Block? Point by point? A combination of the two?

4. **What examples will work best?** If your reader isn't familiar with your topic, what examples might be familiar? What examples will make clear what may be unfamiliar?

5. **What metaphor does your subject suggest?** Given the metaphor and your subject, what characteristics match? How can the metaphor be extended into an analogy? How can you outline the analogy as an equation? What equals what?

6. **What other modes are appropriate?** What modes can you draw on to help support your comparison and the organization of the essay? Do you need to define? Where can you use description? narration? example? Do any of your comparisons involve cause and effect?

7. **What is your point? your purpose?** Do you want to entertain, inform, persuade? Given your point as a tentative thesis, should you spell it out in the essay or imply it? If you are writing to inform, what information do you want to present? If you are writing to persuade, what do you want your reader to believe or do?

8. **What persona do you want to create?** Is it best for you to be a part of the comparison and contrast or to be an observer? Do you have a strongly held conviction about your subject? Do you want it to show? Does your persona fit your audience, purpose, and material?

Drafting the Paper

1. **Know your reader.** Use your first paragraph to set out your major terms and your general focus and to prepare the reader for the pattern of organization and tone that will follow. Reexamine your list of similarities and differences to see which ones may be unfamiliar to your reader. Jot down an illustration or brief description by each characteristic that the reader may not be familiar with. If your reader is part of the group you are examining, tread carefully, and if your teacher may have a bias about your topic, try to figure out what the bias is so you can counter it. Reread your paper from the perspective of the reader

(Continued)

who is biased so that you can check your diction as well as
your choice of examples and assertions.

2. **Know your purpose.** If you are writing to persuade, keep in
mind the reader's possible bias or neutral view and see how
you can use your persona as well as logical and emotional appeals to get the reader on your side. Informative papers run the
risk of telling readers something they already know, so use description, detail, example, and diction to present your information in a new light. If your paper's main purpose is to entertain,
these techniques become even more crucial. Try adding allitera-
tion, allusions, paradox, and puns to the other techniques you
draw on.

3. **If you use an analogy, double-check it.** Make sure your analogy is an extended metaphor, not a statement of fact. See what
you want to emphasize. Also make sure the placement is effective by trying out the analogy in different positions. Perhaps it
works best as a framing device or standing alone in a sentence
or paragraph.

4. **Use other modes to support your comparison.** Description
and example are probably the most obvious modes to use, but
consider narration, cause and effect, definition, and analogy as
well. Perhaps a short narrative would add interest to your paper, or perhaps cause and effect enters into your comparisons.
Definition may be vital to your thesis, and analogy may help
clarify or expand a point.

5. **Check your pattern of organization.** If you are using block
comparison, make sure you have introduced your two subjects
and that your conclusion brings them back together. In the body
of the paper, make sure that what you cover for one, you also
cover for the other. In point-by-point comparison, check to see
that your points are clearly set out. You may want to use both
types of organization, though one will probably predominate.

6. **Make a point.** Perhaps you want to use your comparison to
make a comment on the way we live, perhaps to clarify two
items that people easily confuse, perhaps to argue that one
thing is better than the other. Whatever your point, check it to
make sure it is an assertion, not a mere fact. Whether your purpose is to inform or to persuade, take a stand and make sure
that your thesis clearly implies or states it.

Living on Tokyo Time

Lynnika Butler

During the five years Lynnika Butler spent in Japan, she taught English, worked as a coordinator for international relations, and volunteered as an interpreter—experience that made her an astute observer of how the Japanese treat time. That experience, together with her BA in English and Spanish, may have also contributed to her decision to pursue a graduate degree in linguistics, and she is now enrolled at the University of Arizona. Her goal is "to use what I am learning about the science of language to help communities who are trying to preserve or revitalize their native languages." Butler's essay was first published in the Salt Journal, *fall, 2001, and then reprinted in* Utne*'s January-February 2003 issue.*

What to Look For   The concept of time is a slippery one, but Butler explains it clearly. As you read her essay, be aware of how she leads into it and then explains how the two cultures view it.

1   It's fair to say that Japanese people are unbelievably busy. Working 10 hours a day, and often coming in on days off, they rarely take a vacation of more than three or four days. A straight week is a hedonistic luxury. Students have less than a month for summer vacation, and even then they have all kinds of assignments to do.

2   Watching people live like this, with almost no time for themselves, makes an American like me wonder why more of them don't throw themselves under subway trains. But I seem to have far more anxiety about free time than my Japanese friends do—even though, compared to them, I have much more of it. Why doesn't this cradle-to-grave, manic scheduling bother them?

3   A lot of Westerners make the glib assumption that Japanese people are simply submissive, unoriginal, or masochistic enough to put up with such a punishing system. I don't think that's it. In Japan, time is measured in the same hours and minutes and days as anywhere else, but it is experienced as a fundamentally different phenomenon. In the West, we save time, spend time, invest time, even kill time—all of which implies that it belongs to us in the first place.

179

We might find ourselves obliged to trade huge chunks of our time for a steady salary, but most of us resent this as something stolen from us, and we take it for granted that our spare hours are none of our teachers' or bosses' business.

4   The Japanese grow up with a sense of time as a communal resource, like the company motor pool. If you get permission, you can borrow a little for your own use, but the main priority is to serve the institution—in this case, society as a whole. Club activities, overtime, drinks with the boss, and invitations to the boring weddings of people you hardly know are not seen as intruding on your free time—they are the *shikata ga nai* (nothing you can do about it) duties that turn the wheels of society. "Free" time (*hima*) is something that only comes into existence when these obligations have all been fulfilled. This is nicely borne out by an expression my boss uses whenever he leaves work a little early: *chotto hima morau* ("I'm going to receive a little free time").

5   Though I can't pretend I like living on a Japanese schedule, I try hard not to make judgments. *Oku ga fukai*—things are more complicated than they appear. The Japanese sacrifice their private time to society, but in return they get national health insurance, a wonderful train system, sushi, the two thousand temples of Kyoto, and traditional culture so rich that every back-water village seems to have its own unique festivals, seasonal dishes, legends, and even dialect. All of which are invaluable social goods that I would not trade for a lifetime of free hours.

Organization and Ideas

1. Butler opens by stating that the Japanese are "busy." How effective are the examples that support her statement?
2. In paragraph 2, Butler poses a question. What is the answer?
3. Sum up the Japanese attitude toward time. What is the American one?
4. Of the two views of time, which does Butler prefer and why?
5. Butler says that Americans treat time as though "it belongs to us" (paragraph 3). How accurate do you find that statement?

Technique and Style

1. Butler states a paradox in paragraph 2. How effective is it?
2. The essay opens with a description of Japanese "busyness" and follows it with a paragraph that gives Butler's reaction to it. To what extent is her response similar to the reader's?

3. Think about the simile Butler uses in paragraph 4. How effective is it?
4. Butler occasionally uses a Japanese term that she then translates. What does her use of the Japanese add to the essay?
5. Reread the last paragraph. Given your sense of what a conclusion should do, how effective is it?

Suggestions for Writing

Journal

1. To what extent do you share the American sense of time being a personal possession?
2. How difficult would it be for you to adapt to the Japanese sense of time? Explain.

Essay

1. You can use Butler's essay as a model for your own, one in which you compare and contrast two groups' attitudes toward something. Think, for instance, of the difference between how you and your parents view vacations. For your own topic, consider first two different groups and then think your way into their attitudes toward *x*, with *x* standing for what they differ about. Suggestions for different categories:

   generations
   regions, for example, North and South
   city and country residents
   males and females
   teachers and students

2. Butler contrasts the various intrusions on what Americans would think of as their free time to what Japanese see as "duties that turn the wheels of society" (paragraph 4). Think about your own sense of obligation and those things you do and do not feel a sense of duty towards. Write an essay in which you define your sense of duty by contrasting examples of where it does and does not apply.

PLAYING HOUSE

Denise Leight

A student at Middlesex County College in Edison, New Jersey, Denise Leight wrote "Playing House" in response to Daniel Zimmerman's research assignment for his English class. The essay was then published in the Spring 2001 issue of "Becoming Writers," one of the English Department's three journals. The collection, according to its editors, "celebrates the achievements of our students, who worked hard over the past semester to translate the insights and responses of full and busy lives into the well-crafted and thoughtfully imagined essays reprinted here. As writers we know it is never easy to find the words and form that most accurately communicates what we know, and the finished piece almost never emerges in the shape we originally imagined it. But it is in the struggle to express ourselves that our thoughts become fully ours, and the battle is always a richly rewarding process." "Becoming Writers" is an appropriate title for such a collection.

What to Look For   As you read Denise Leight's essay, figure out if she is explaining her subject or arguing for a specific position or something in between.

1   More and more couples today live together or "play house" before taking the matrimonial plunge. Living together before marriage has become so popular that approximately half the couples in America participate in this activity (Gorrell 16). Some couples choose to live together to test their compatibility and possibly avoid an unsuccessful marriage. With the number of marriages ending in divorce these days, it sounds reasonable that many couples want to give marriage a trial run before making any formal commitment. But do the chances of a successful marriage actually improve by cohabiting?

2   "Cohabitation isn't marriage," says sociology professor Linda Waite of the University of Chicago (qtd. in Jabusch 14). Married and cohabiting couples do not have the same characteristics. According to Professor Waite, cohabiting couples lack both specialization and

commitment in their relationships (Jabusch 14). Unwed cohabitants generally live more financially and emotionally independent of one another to allow themselves the freedom to leave. This often results in less monogamous, short-term relationships.

3   Married couples specialize—while one partner might take over the cooking, the other might specialize in cleaning. They pool their money, time, and other resources, creating a higher quality lifestyle. Unmarried couples find it much harder to trust each other financially without the legal bond and, therefore, do not move quickly to pool those resources. While marriage does not ensure monogamy, married couples have more invested in their relationship and think longer before acting on their impulses and stepping outside of the relationship. Unmarried couples do not operate as a partnership, says Waite: "they are being two separate people—it is trading off freedom and low levels of commitment for fewer benefits than you get from commitment" (qtd. in Jabusch 15).

4   Many singles believe that by practicing marriage they will receive the commitment they desire. With this in mind, they move in together intending to tie the knot eventually. Time passes and the couple rarely talks seriously about finalizing the commitment. And so, they often end up cohabiting for a few years until eventually someone gets tired of waiting and leaves. Cohabitation can suppress the development of a higher level of commitment.

5   Sometimes, one or both of the people involved become complacent in the relationship, and without any pressure to move forward, they won't. As social psychologist Dr. Julia Hare puts it, "Why would you go to the store to buy some milk with the cow standing in the living room?" (qtd. in "Why . . . Marriage?" 53). Certainly, to call a marriage successful, it must actually take place.

6   A study conducted by an assistant professor of human development and family studies at Pennsylvania State University, Catherine Cohan, Ph.D., found that those who had lived together before marriage "displayed more negative and fewer positive problem solving and support behaviors than couples that had not cohabitated prior to marriage" (Gorrell 16). For example, if one partner of a cohabiting couple diagnosed a particular topic as a problem, the other would express more negative behaviors such as forcefulness and attempts to control. Women who had lived with their partners before marriage generally exhibited more verbal aggressiveness than those in the couples without premarital cohabitation.

7   One cannot ignore the possibility that cohabitants as a group may have certain distinguishable characteristics that make them more likely to divorce. The type of people who would choose to cohabit before marriage may simply be less willing to put the full amount of effort required into a relationship. However, a recent study determined that "the cohabitor selectivity reflected in four sociodemographic variables—parental divorce, marital status homogamy, age homogamy, and stepchildren—is unable to materially account for the cohabitation effect" (Hall and Zhao 424). In other words, the study did not show that these predisposing factors contributed greatly to the marriage dissolution of cohabiting couples.

8   Cohabiting does not necessarily equal the tragic end of a relationship, but couples who do marry after living together have higher rates of separation and divorce (Gorrell 16). The lack of commitment in such a relationship plays a large role in this scenario. If a couple wishes to have a successful marriage, they should show their commitment to each other from the beginning. If they trust each other enough not to cohabit before marriage, their marriage already has a higher probability of success.

Works Cited

"Why Are So Many Couples Living Together Before Marriage?" Jet 3 Aug. 1998: 52-55.

Gorrell, Carin. "Live-in and Learn." Psychology Today. Nov. 2000: 16.

Hall, David R., and John Z. Zhao. "Cohabitation and Divorce in Canada: Testing the Selectivity Hypothesis." Journal of Marriage & the Family 57.2 (1995): 421-27.

Jabusch, Willard F. "The Myth of Cohabitation." America 7 Oct. 2000: 14-16.

Organization and Ideas

1. Leight poses a question in paragraph 1. What is it and what is her answer?

2. What are the characteristics of a cohabiting couple? A married couple?

3. What is Leight's view of cohabitation versus marriage? What evidence supports your opinion?
4. As expected in a research paper, you find Leight cites evidence throughout. Is it sufficient? Why or why not?
5. What arguments or loopholes can you think of that Leight does not mention?

Technique and Style

1. In what ways is the title a pun?
2. What is the function of paragraph 7 and how necessary is it?
3. How would you describe Leight's level of diction? How appropriate is it for the assignment?
4. Think about what Leight lists as works cited. What conclusions can you draw from her list?
5. What is the essay's aim—to explain, argue, both? What evidence can you find to back up your view?

Suggestions for Writing

Journal

1. To what extent are you convinced by Leight's essay?
2. How would you describe Leight's persona, the person behind the writing? Quote from the essay to illustrate your impressions.

Essay

1. Leight's essay focuses on an important decision that many people face. Think about the decisions you have made between two choices, choose one, and write an essay in which you explain the choice and analyze whether it was the correct one. Suggestions:
   to go to college
   to take a particular job
   to pick a major
   to stand up for a friend
   to take a risk
2. Write your own version of "Playing House," researching the subject, selecting your own sources, using Leight's essay as an additional source, and arguing for your own point of view.

World and America Watching Different Wars

Danna Harman

Any newspaper would be hard-pressed to find someone as qualified to cover the war in Iraq as Danna Harman. After earning a BA in history from Harvard, she studied economics and Arabic at the University of California, Berkeley, and received an MPhil from Cambridge University in Islamic Studies. Now based in Washington DC as a feature writer for the Christian Science Monitor, *Harman has served as the paper's Africa correspondent with special assignments in Egypt, Israel, Yemen, Jordan, and Iraq. Her work has also been published in the* New Republic, *the* London Times, *the* Sunday Times, *the* Chicago Sun Times, *and* Elle. *Sent to cover the war for the* Monitor, *she was stationed in Egypt. There, she says, "I spent the whole month with the TV tuned to the local channels and went out to talk to people in the street as much as possible about what they believed was going on—and found the gap between the perceptions here and in the US of what was happening pretty amazing." You'll see what she means. Her piece was published in the* Monitor *on March 25, 2003, where she also acknowledges the assistance of special correspondent Dan Murphy in Jakarta, Indonesia, and Alexandra Marks in New York.*

What to Look For   As you read Harman's piece, keep in mind that it was written for a newspaper. The paragraphs are set to fit a news column, and the subheadings guide the reader through the story. Look for how they help.

1   CAIRO, EGYPT—The Hamouda family is gathered around the TV, sipping sugary tea and glued to the pictures of captured U.S. soldiers being interrogated by Iraqis on the popular Qatar-based satellite station Al Jazeera.

2   "What's your name?" A terrified young female POW is asked. "How old are you?" The camera moves to her feet, which are bloody and bare.

3   "Yieee!," cheers eldest son Ahmed, knocking over a fake geranium plant as he shoots up from the couch in excitement. "Show it how it is!"

4   It is not that they are happy to see suffering, says Hellmy, the father, somewhat apologetically, as the camera weaves between several bodies. "But the other side of the story needs to be told."

5   The gruesome video shown Sunday on Al Jazeera—reaching 35 million Arab-speakers worldwide, including about 20 percent of the Egyptian population—will probably never be seen by the average American TV viewer.

6   In fact, American audiences are seeing and reading about a different war than the rest of the world. The news coverage in Europe, the Middle East, and Asia, reflects and defines the widening perception gap about the motives for this war. Surveys show that an increasing number of Americans believe this is a just war, while most of the world's Arabs and Muslims see it as a war of aggression. Media coverage does not necessarily create these leanings, say analysts, but it works to cement them.

7   "The difference in coverage between the United States and the rest of the world helped contribute to the situation that we're in now," says Kim Spencer, president of WorldLink TV, a U.S. satellite channel devoted to airing foreign news. "Americans have been unable to see how they're perceived."

8   For example, most Americans, watching CNN, Fox, or the U.S. television networks, are not seeing as much coverage of injured Iraqi citizens, or being given more than a glimpse of the antiwar protests now raging in the Muslim world and beyond.

9   In the Middle East, Europe, and parts of Asia, by comparison, the rapid progress made by U.S. led troops has been played down. And many aspects of the conflict being highlighted in the U.S.—such as the large number of Iraqi troops surrendering, the cooperation between U.S.-led forces and various Gulf states, commentary on America's superior weapons technology, and the human interest angles on soldier life in the desert—are almost totally absent from coverage outside the U.S.

10 "Sure, the news we get in the Arab world is slanted," admits Hussein Amin, chair of the department of journalism and mass

communication at Cairo's American University. "In the same way the news received in the U.S. is biased."

The View from Europe

11   Some analysts note that European press ownership is less concentrated than its counterparts in the U.S. and is seen as providing more perspectives than either the Arab or American outlets. In Frankfurt, for example, readers have access to 16 different German-language newspapers—many of which present different vantage points, which makes for a more lively and varied debate.

12   European journalists also seem to ask different, more skeptical, questions of this war, often being the ones at White House and Pentagon press conferences to ask whether the invasion of Iraq has turned up any of the weapons of mass destruction that used to justify the invasion—even as their American counterparts repeatedly focus on such questions as whether Saddam Hussein is alive or dead.

13   Media watchers say the European press has tended to be more balanced than the U.S. media in dealing with the war, in part because Europe is so much closer to the Muslim world. John Schmidt, a former reporter for the *International Herald Tribune,* who has just returned from Europe, notes that in Marseille, France, 30 percent of the population is Muslim. In Berlin, the biggest minority population is the Turks.

14   "These are countries in Europe that live cheek by jowl with Islamic people, they know how deep the dislike for the West can be, they know how sensitively some of these issues have to be transmitted," says Mr. Schmidt, who is now an economics writer for the *Milwaukee Journal Sentinel.*

15   "There are really two stories unfolding here, one is the war and its progress and the second one is the progress of world opinion," says Tom Patterson, a media expert at Harvard University's Kennedy School of Government. "That second dimension is there in the American press, but it's clearly way underreported."

16   For instance, American media outlets may report on the demonstrations in other countries, particularly if there are violent clashes. But they don't devote as many resources to covering in depth the growing anti-American sentiment—even among American allies—or its implications for the future, says Professor Patterson.

Reporter or Soldier?

17   Back in his Cairo living room, the elder Mr. Hamouda flips to CNN for a moment, over cries of protest from the rest of the family. It is vaguely possible to make out U.S. troop maneuvers on a grainy green screen. In the corner there is a small photo of a middle-aged man in an Army jacket.

18   Nadia, the great-grandmother in the family, wonders aloud who CNN correspondent Walter Rogers is and what he is doing with the troops. "He is in bed with them," says an English speaking nephew, laughing at the well-worn joke, a pun on "embedding," in which the Pentagon allows journalists to report from within military units. Nadia has no idea what the boy is talking about. "Turn it back to Al Jazeera," she demands, adjusting her false teeth, "let's see those bodies again."

19   Across the globe, in Indonesia, student leader and antiwar activist Muhammad Hermawan has seen these same pictures on his local channel, which pirates Al Jazeera's signal and adds simultaneous Indonesian translation. "The more these pictures are shown, the more people will understand America's brutal aggression," he says. "People will learn, and we'll see bigger and bigger protests."

20   Interest in the war has been so high that Indonesia's TV7 began pirating Al Jazeera's signal shortly before the start of the war. The new station carries the Arab-language broadcast with simultaneous Indonesian translation. Though Al Jazeera is only shown from 10 in the evening until 11 in the morning an official at TV7 says the news department is receiving about 100 calls a day from viewers, up from "almost zero" before the U.S. invasion began.

21   The news broadcasts in Indonesia, the world's most populous Muslim nation, have been tamer than the news in the Middle East, focusing on protests against the war at home, with official statements against the war from abroad.

22   But they have also carried some stories sympathetic to U.S. soldiers, including an interview with Anecita Hudson of Alamogordo, Texas. Mrs. Hudson says her son, 23-year-old Army Specialist Joseph Hudson, was one of the prisoners of war shown on Al Jazeera. She said seeing her son captured was "like a bad dream."

23   Mrs. Hudson didn't see her son on American news outlets. She spotted him on a Filipino cable channel she subscribes to. She is originally from the Philippines.

24   The pictures of U.S. troops drew condemnation from U.S. Defense Secretary Donald Rumsfeld and other officials. "It seems to

me that showing a few pictures on the screen, not knowing who they are and being communicated by Al Jazeera, which is not a perfect instrument of communication, obviously is part of Iraqi propaganda," Mr. Rumsfeld told CBS.

25   "War is ugly by nature and we did not create these pictures—we are only there to reflect reality on the ground," says Jihad Ali Ballout, Al Jazeera's media relations head. "Truth is sometimes unpleasant and gruesome, and I feel distressed when people ask me to dress it up."

Washington Watches Al Jazeera

26   The Bush administration sees Al Jazeera—the cable news channel made famous for its airing of Osama Bin Laden tapes—as having an anti-American bias. But, since the seven-year-old Al Jazeera has grown from six to 24 hours of daily programming and reaches more than 35 million Arab speakers around the world, including 150,000 in the United States, Washington seems to be attempting to work more closely with the network.

27   The Pentagon offered Al Jazeera four choice spots for its reporters to be embedded with U.S. military units and assigned it a special media liaison officer, and both National Security Adviser Condoleezza Rice and Defense Secretary Donald Rumsfeld have given extensive interviews to Al Jazeera in recent days. Al-Arabiya and Abu Dhabi, two other 24-hour Arab-language stations, have received similar attention from the administration.

28   Al Jazeera says that it has two of its correspondents "embedded" with U.S. units—but the units in question are in Kuwait. It has no reporters with U.S. troops directly participating in the invasion.

Variety Breeds Objectivity?

29   Professor Amin in Cairo argues that while watching this war unfold in the various media outlets is a good example of how bias clearly exists on all sides, there are nonetheless positive signs that international media are collectively moving toward becoming more objective, by force of necessity.

30   "The fact that the common man has access to different sources today means that it's harder for one source to get away with showing only one side of the story. You can piece together a broader, more accurate story yourself," he says.

31   There is some awareness in the Hamouda living room that Arab broadcasters may also spread propaganda.

32   In 1967, four days after Israel had won the war against Egypt, Egyptian radio was still declaring victory, recalls Hellmy Hamouda. "I was in the Suez Canal at the time and I had seen some of the war with my own eyes," he says, "I had a hunch that radio was not telling the truth."

33   "Today, we can find the better truth by simply changing channels or going on the Internet," says Hamouda. He then flips back to Al Jazeera at the demand of grandma Nadia, "If we want to."

Organization and Ideas

1. Harman covers a lot of topics in her essay—the media, bias, anti-American sentiment, the war in Iraq, pro-Muslim sentiment. What is her primary subject and what evidence supports your view?
2. In what ways does the American media differ from that in the Middle East, Europe, and much of Asia?
3. When published, the piece was subtitled "CNN vs. Al Jazeera: Seeing is Often Believing." What evidence can you find to support that idea?
4. To what extent is Harman explaining the situation? Arguing for a particular point of view?
5. In one sentence, state Harman's thesis.

Technique and Style

1. Throughout the piece, Harman makes extensive use of sources, both with quotations and summaries. What do they contribute to the essay?
2. The Hamouda family appears in paragraphs 1–4, 17 and 18, and again in 31–33. What do they add to the piece?
3. Look again at the subheadings. To what extent do they work to guide you through the essay?
4. In what ways is Harman's essay appropriate for the *Christian Science Monitor*?
5. The story opens and closes with a narrative. What does it add?

Suggestions for Writing

Journal

1. Would you call Harman optimistic, pessimistic, something in between? Explain.

2. How do you obtain world news? To what extent do you find the source credible and why?

Essay

1. The media is often accused of bias or sensationalism but other considerations are also at work—time constraints, availability of sources, concerns of the readership, and so on. Use a recent major event to analyze the accuracy and depth of its reporting. You might compare the story as covered in two
   national daily newspapers
   national evening television news shows
   weekly news magazines
   national Sunday newspapers
   daily Web news reports
2. Choose a political news story of some importance and read about it—start to finish—in a major American newspaper and one from Great Britain, using print versions from the library or available on the Web. What differences do you note? What, if any, biases can you find? Where does the truth lie?

Two Ways to Belong in America

Bharati Mukherjee

You will find out much about Bharati Mukherjee as you read the essay that follows. What she does not say, however, is that she is the author of seven novels, two short story collections, and two nonfiction books. Her seventh novel, Desirable Daughters, *was published in 2002. Her essay also does not mention the numerous awards she has received, among them the 1988 National Book Critics' Circle Award (for her collection* The Middleman and Other Stories*) as well as Guggenheim and Canada Council grants and fellowships. Born and educated in India, Mukherjee was awarded a scholarship to the University of Iowa, where she earned an MFA in Creative Writing and a PhD in English and Comparative Literature. She now teaches at the University of California, Berkeley. Much of Mukherjee's writing focuses on the experiences of immigrants. That is also the focus of the essay that follows, one that appeared in the Op-Ed section of the* New

York Times *on September 22, 1996, a time when the U.S. Congress, along with many states, was considering bills that would severely curtail the benefits of legal immigrants.*

What to Look For   Like Mukherjee, you may at times find yourself directly affected by a proposed law or political debate and you may want to make yourself heard about it. When that happens, you will probably want to begin by explaining how the proposal affects you personally. Yet to make your point to a wider audience, you will need to broaden it so that you speak not just for yourself, but for a larger group. As you read Mukherjee's essay, look for the ways in which she does just that, moving from the particular to the general, from personal narrative to a more universal stance.

1   This is a tale of two sisters from Calcutta, Mira and Bharati, who have lived in the United States for some 35 years, but who find themselves on different sides in the current debate over the status of immigrants. I am an American citizen and she is not. I am moved that thousands of long-term residents are finally taking the oath of citizenship. She is not.

2   Mira arrived in Detroit in 1960 to study child psychology and pre-school education. I followed her a year later to study creative writing at the University of Iowa. When we left India, we were almost identical in appearance and attitude. We dressed alike, in saris; we expressed identical views on politics, social issues, love and marriage in the same Calcutta convent-school accent. We would endure our two years in America, secure our degrees, then return to India to marry the grooms of our father's choosing.

3   Instead, Mira married an Indian student in 1962 who was getting his business administration degree at Wayne State University. They soon acquired the labor certifications necessary for the green card of hassle-free residence and employment.

4   Mira still lives in Detroit, works in the Southfield, Michigan, school system, and has become nationally recognized for her contributions in the fields of pre-school education and parent-teacher relationships. After 36 years as a legal immigrant in this country, she clings passionately to her Indian citizenship and hopes to go home to India when she retires.

5   In Iowa City in 1963, I married a fellow student, an American of Canadian parentage. Because of the accident of his North Dakota birth, I bypassed labor-certification requirements and the race-related "quota" system that favored the applicant's country of origin over his or her merit. I was prepared for (and even welcomed) the emotional strain that came with marrying outside my ethnic community. In 33 years of marriage, we have lived in every part of North America. By choosing a husband who was not my father's selection, I was opting for fluidity, self-invention, blue jeans and T-shirts, and renouncing 3,000 years (at least) of caste-observant, "pure culture" marriage in the Mukherjee family. My books have often been read as unapologetic (and in some quarters overenthusiastic) texts for cultural and psychological "mongrelization." It's a word I celebrate.

6   Mira and I have stayed sisterly close by phone. In our regular Sunday morning conversations, we are unguardedly affectionate. I am her only blood relative on this continent. We expect to see each other through the looming crises of aging and ill health without being asked. Long before Vice President Gore's "Citizenship U.S.A." drive, we'd had our polite arguments over the ethics of retaining an overseas citizenship while expecting the permanent protection and economic benefits that come with living and working in America.

7   Like well-raised sisters, we never said what was really on our minds, but we probably pitied one another. She, for the lack of structure in my life, the erasure of Indianness, the absence of an unvarying daily core. I, for the narrowness of her perspective, her uninvolvement with the mythic depths or the superficial pop culture of this society. But, now, with the scapegoating of "aliens" (documented or illegal) on the increase, and the targeting of long-term legal immigrants like Mira for new scrutiny and new self-consciousness, she and I find ourselves unable to maintain the same polite discretion. We were always unacknowledged adversaries, and we are now, more than ever, sisters.

8   "I feel used," Mira raged on the phone the other night. "I feel manipulated and discarded. This is such an unfair way to treat a person who was invited to stay and work here because of her talent. My employer went to the I.N.S. and petitioned for the labor certification. For over 30 years, I've invested my creativity and professional skills into the improvement of *this* country's pre-school system. I've obeyed all the rules, I've paid my taxes, I love my work, I love my students, I love the friends I've made. How dare America now change its rules in midstream? If America wants to

make new rules curtailing benefits of legal immigrants, they should apply only to immigrants who arrive after those rules are already in place."

9   To my ears, it sounded like the description of a long-enduring, comfortable yet loveless marriage, without risk or recklessness. Have we the right to demand, and to expect, that we be loved? (That, to me, is the subtext of the arguments by immigration advocates.) My sister is an expatriate, professionally generous and creative, socially courteous and gracious, and that's as far as her Americanization can go. She is here to maintain an identity, not to transform it.

10   I asked her if she would follow the example of others who have decided to become citizens because of the anti-immigration bills in Congress. And here, she surprised me. "If America wants to play the manipulative game, I'll play it too," she snapped. "I'll become a U.S. citizen for now, then change back to Indian when I'm ready to go home. I feel some kind of irrational attachment to India that I don't to America. Until all this hysteria against legal immigrants, I was totally happy. Having my green card meant I could visit any place in the world I wanted to and then come back to a job that's satisfying and that I do very well."

11   In one family, from two sisters alike as peas in a pod, there could not be a wider divergence of immigrant experience. America spoke to me—I embraced the demotion from expatriate aristocrat to immigrant nobody, surrendering those thousands of years of "pure culture," the saris, the delightfully accented English. She retained them all. Which of us is the freak?

12   Mira's voice, I realize, is the voice not just of the immigrant South Asian community but of an immigrant community of the millions who have stayed rooted in one job, one city, one house, one ancestral culture, one cuisine, for the entirety of their productive years. She speaks for greater numbers than I possibly can. Only the fluency of her English and the anger, rather than fear, born of confidence from her education, differentiate her from the seamstresses, the domestics, the technicians, the shop owners, the millions of hard-working but effectively silenced documented immigrants as well as their less fortunate "illegal" brothers and sisters.

13   Nearly 20 years ago, when I was living in my husband's ancestral homeland of Canada, I was always well-employed but never allowed to feel part of the local Quebec or larger Canadian society. Then, through a Green Paper that invited a national referendum on the unwanted side effects of "nontraditional" immigration, the

Government officially turned against its immigrant communities, particularly those from South Asia.

14   I felt then the same sense of betrayal that Mira feels now. I will never forget the pain of that sudden turning, and the casual racist outbursts the Green Paper elicited. That sense of betrayal had its desired effect and drove me, and thousands like me, from the country.

15   Mira and I differ, however, in the ways in which we hope to interact with the country that we have chosen to live in. She is happier to live in America as expatriate Indian than as an immigrant American. I need to feel like a part of the community I have adopted (as I tried to feel in Canada as well). I need to put roots down, to vote and make the difference that I can. The price that the immigrant willingly pays, and that the exile avoids, is the trauma of self-transformation.

Organization and Ideas

1. It's possible to identify Mukherjee's introduction as her first paragraph or as paragraphs 1–5. Make a case for what you find best serves to introduce the essay.
2. Trace the essay's pattern of organization. Is it block, point by point, or a mixture of the two? If the latter, which paragraphs conform to which pattern?
3. Where in the essay does Mukherjee broaden the base of her narrative? Why might she have chosen the examples she uses?
4. The essay deals with a number of topics—the "trauma of self-transformation" (paragraph 15), the injustice of the proposed laws, the concept of citizenship, the plight of the immigrant, the question of what it means to hold a green card. What do you find to be the essay's major focus and what is Mukherjee saying about that subject?
5. Which sister made the right decision? Why?

Technique and Style

1. How would you describe Mukherjee's tone? Does it change in the course of the essay and if so, where and how?
2. Mukherjee makes extensive use of quotation marks (paragraphs 5–8 and 10–13). To what different uses does she put them? What do they add to the essay?
3. What facts do you come to know about Mukherjee's family? What do they add to the essay's point? To Mukherjee's persona?
4. *Immigrant* has many connotations. What are some of them? Where in the essay does Mukherjee allude to the word's connotations? Why does she do so?

5. Mukherjee poses a question at the end of paragraph 11. What is her implied answer? How does her answer relate to the essay's thesis?

Suggestions for Writing

Journal

1. Write a page or two that records your associations with the word *immigrant.*
2. If you were to move to another country and work there, would you be more likely to become like Mukherjee or her sister?

Essay

1. Mukherjee writes about having certain privileges. Consider what you have that can be called privileges and write an essay in which you analyze one of them—what it means to have it compared to not having it. Suggestions:
   a driver's license
   a credit card
   a voter's card
   membership in a certain group
   a green card or student visa
2. Mukherjee describes two ways of looking at a culture, from the outside looking in and from the inside looking out—perspectives all of us are used to. Write your own essay comparing the two views, drawing on your own experiences and that of others to make your point. For suggestions, think of two ways of examining a topic:
   what you thought college was going to be like and what you actually found it to be like
   what you expected from a job and what you learned

The Raven

Barry Lopez

Although Barry Lopez was born in Port Chester, New York, he spent much of his early life in southern California, and it was there where he first fell in love with landscapes in general and deserts in particular, the Mojave Desert to be precise. After returning to New York and then graduating from Notre Dame with a major in English, he became a professional photographer specializing in nature and land-scape scenes. Finding that his lens didn't get close enough to nature, he turned to writing, traveling the world to write about its wonders. His work is published regularly in journals such as Harper's Magazine *and* The Paris Review, *and his list of books is a long and distinguished one.* Of Wolves and Men *(1982) received the John Burroughs Medal for distinguished natural history writing, and* Arctic Dreams: Imagination and Desire in a Northern Landscape *(1986) won the National Book Award for Best Book of Nonfiction. His most recent book is a collection of his writings,* Vintage Lopez *(2004). Lopez's writing has often been compared to that of Henry David Thoreau. According to one interviewer, Lopez "brings an acute sense of obligation to detail and integrity with his every observance, and something that can only be described as a spiritually driven, almost Zen-like regard for non-fiction." The essay that follows appeared in* Desert Notes: Reflections in the Eye of a Raven *(1976).*

What to Look For   You'll find that Lopez's essay rides a fine line between fantasy and reality, although his point is a serious one. In that sense, you can read the piece as a sort of fable, much like those of Aesop, the sixth century Greek who wrote the still familiar tale of the tortoise and the hare, among many others. The idea of depicting animals with human traits is still much with us though the creatures have changed into the likes of the Roadrunner and Mickey Mouse.

1   I am going to have to start at the other end by telling you this: there are no crows in the desert. What appear to be crows are ravens. You must examine the crow, however, before you can understand the raven. To forget the crow completely, as some have tried to do, would be like trying to understand the one who stayed without talking to the one who left. It is important to make note of who has left the desert.

2   To begin with, the crow does nothing alone. He cannot abide silence and he is prone to stealing things, twigs and bits of straw, from the nests of his neighbors. It is a game with him. He enjoys tricks. If he cannot make up his mind the crow will take two or three wives, but this is not a game. The crow is very accommodating and he admires compulsiveness.

3   Crows will live in street trees in the residential areas of great cities. They will walk at night on the roofs of parked cars and peck at the grit; they will scrape the pinpoints of their talons across the steel and, with their necks outthrust, watch for frightened children listening in their beds.

4   Put all this to the raven: he will open his mouth as if to say something. Then he will look the other way and say nothing. Later, when you have forgotten, he will tell you he admires the crow.

5   The raven is larger than the crow and has a beard of black feathers at his throat. He is careful to kill only what he needs. Crows, on the other hand, will search out the great horned owl, kick and punch him awake, and then, for roosting too close to their nests, they will kill him. They will come out of the sky on a fat, hot afternoon and slam into the head of a dozing rabbit and go away laughing. They will tear out a whole row of planted corn and eat only a few kernels. They will defecate on scarecrows and go home and sleep with 200,000 of their friends in an atmosphere of congratulation. Again, it is only a game; this should not be taken to mean that they are evil.

6   There is however this: when too many crows come together on a roost there is a lot of shoving and noise and a white film begins to descend over the crows' eyes and they go blind. They fall from their perches and lie on the ground and starve to death. When confronted with this information, crows will look past you and warn you vacantly that it is easy to be misled.

7   The crow flies like a pigeon. The raven flies like a hawk. He is seen only at a great distance and then not very clearly. This is true of the crow too, but if you are very clever you can trap the crow. The only way to be sure what you have seen is a raven is to follow him until he dies of old age, and then examine the body.

8   Once there were many crows in the desert. I am told it was like this: you could sit back in the rocks and watch a pack of crows working over the carcass of a coyote. Some would eat, the others would try to squeeze out the vultures. The raven would never be seen. He would be at a distance, alone, perhaps eating a scorpion.

9   There was, at this time, a small alkaline water hole at the desert's edge. Its waters were bitter. No one but crows would drink there, although they drank sparingly, just one or two sips at a time. One day a raven warned someone about the dangers of drinking the bitter water and was overheard by a crow. When word of this passed

among the crows they felt insulted. They jeered and raised insulting gestures to the ravens. They bullied each other into drinking the alkaline water until they had drunk the hole dry and gone blind.

10   The crows flew into canyon walls and dove straight into the ground at forty miles an hour and broke their necks. The worst of it was their cartwheeling across the desert floor, stiff wings outstretched, beaks agape, white eyes ballooning, surprising rattlesnakes hidden under sage bushes out of the noonday sun. The snakes awoke, struck and held. The wheeling birds strew them across the desert like sprung traps.

11   When all the crows were finally dead, the desert bacteria and fungi bored into them, burrowed through bone and muscle, through aqueous humor and feathers until they had reduced the stiff limbs of soft black to blue dust.

12   After that, there were no more crows in the desert. The few who watched from a distance took it as a sign and moved away.

13   Finally there is this: one morning four ravens sat at the edge of the desert waiting for the sun to rise. They had been there all night and the dew was like beads of quicksilver on their wings. Their eyes were closed and they were as still as the cracks in the desert floor.

14   The wind came off the snow-capped peaks to the north and ruffled their breath feathers. Their talons arched in the white earth and they smoothed their wings with sleek, dark bills. At first light their bodies swelled and their eyes flashed purple. When the dew dried on their wings they lifted off from the desert floor and flew away in four directions. Crows would never have had the patience for this.

15   If you want to know more about the raven: bury yourself in the desert so that you have a commanding view of the high basalt cliffs where he lives. Let only your eyes protrude. Do not blink—the movement will alert the raven to your continued presence. Wait until a generation of ravens has passed away. Of the new generation there will be at least one bird who will find you. He will see your eyes staring up out of the desert floor. The raven is cautious, but he is thorough. He will sense your peaceful intentions. Let him have the first word. Be careful: he will tell you he knows nothing.

16   If you do not have the time for this, scour the weathered desert shacks for some sign of the raven's body. Look under old mattresses and beneath loose floorboards. Look behind the walls.

Sooner or later you will find a severed foot. It will be his and it will be well preserved.

17   Take it out in the sunlight and examine it closely. Notice that there are three fingers that face forward, and a fourth, the longest and like a thumb, that faces to the rear. The instrument will be black but no longer shiny, the back of it sheathed in armor plate and the underside padded like a wolf's foot.

18   At the end of each digit you will find a black, curved talon. You will see that the talons are not as sharp as you might have suspected. They are made to grasp and hold fast, not to puncture. They are more like the jaws of a trap than a fistful of ice picks. The subtle difference serves the raven well in the desert. He can weather a storm on a barren juniper limb; he can pick up and examine the crow's eye without breaking it.

Organization and Ideas

1. Reread paragraph 1. What does it imply about the rest of the essay? How does it set up the focus of paragraphs 2–4?
2. What does Lopez tell you about the crow? About the raven? Write down the details and the paragraphs they come from.
3. What do paragraphs 15–18 convey about the relationship between humans and ravens?
4. To come up with a thesis for the essay, first think about the crow versus the raven: which one does Lopez prefer and why? Take your answer to that question and add to it your answer to question 3. Then reduce your responses to a one-sentence assertion and that will be the thesis.
5. How successfully does Lopez mix fantasy and reality?

Technique and Style

1. To what extent does Lopez's essay fit the genre of the fable? Does it have a moral? If so, what is it?
2. How would you describe the tone of the essay?
3. To what extent does Lopez use the first person pronoun *I*? What reasons can you discover for the degree to which he uses it?
4. If you are familiar with the desert, to what extent does Lopez portray it realistically? If you are not familiar with the desert, to what extent does he make you understand what it is like?

5. Reread the essay, marking every time Lopez mentions *patience*, either directly or indirectly. What is he saying about patience? How does that point reinforce the tone of the essay?

Suggestions for Writing

Journal

1. Take a few minutes to write up your response to Lopez's essay. Do you have questions about it? To what extent did you like or dislike it and why?
2. We often discover human characteristics in animals we know well, pets in particular. Describe an animal you know well, attributing human traits to it.

Essay

1. Write your own version of a fable or semifable. Like Lopez, you may want to mix fantasy and reality, or you may want to shape your tone to the one or the other. To start off with, consider a possible subject such as two similar
    animals
    clothing styles
    foods
    game shows
    textbooks
   Once you have a topic to work with, decide on the kind of tone you want for the essay and then start to play with characteristics that you can attribute to your choices. If it's a fable that you're writing, you can be an observer, like Lopez, or remove yourself from the narrative and have the characters speak for themselves.
2. Reread Lopez's essay, noting what is fantasy and what is reality. Does he treat the two equally or is one predominant? What effect is he trying to achieve? Write an essay in which you compare his use of the two and analyze its effect.

ADDITIONAL WRITING ASSIGNMENTS
●●●●●●●●●●●●●●●●●●●●●●●●●●●●●●●●●●●●●●

Using Comparison and Contrast

1. Compare two dissimilar subjects to make a satirical point: partying vs. studying, pets vs. children, poker vs. football, bicycle vs. a car, junk food vs. cooking.

2. Compare two ways to the same goal: studying or cramming, using logic or emotion, knee-jerk or thoughtful reaction, planning fun or being spontaneous.

3. Compare two people who had a distinct influence on their fields: sports, music, film, medical research, history, politics.

4. Compare yourself to someone else: parent, celebrity, political figure, friend, sibling.

Evaluating the Essays

1. "Living on Tokyo Time" and "World and America Watching Different Wars" examine different cultures: the Japanese attitude toward time, and an Egyptian family's view of the war in Iraq. Which essay do you find the more interesting and why? Use quotations from both to make your point.

2. In a real sense, both "Playing House" and "Two Ways to Belong in America" focus on responsibility. How is it defined? What differences do you perceive? Of the two, which is closer to your definition?

3. Barry Lopez uses fantasy to set up a conflict and make a point; Danna Harman uses reality to explain a conflict and make a point. Lopez relates what might best be called a fable, and Harman explains a very real situation. Given those large differences, what similarities can you discover? To what extent, if any, do the similarities outweigh the differences?

4. Reread "Living on Tokyo Time" and "Playing House." Butler analyzes how the Japanese view time, and Leight explains how couples view marriage. List the qualities each group values or represents. Write an essay in which you explain what you discover and analyze the values involved.

On Using
Process

If you have ever been frustrated in your attempts to put together a barbecue grill or hook up a stereo system, you know the value of clear and complete directions. And if you have tried to explain how to get to a particular house or store, you also know that being able to give clear directions is not as easy as it seems. We deal with this practical, how-to kind of **process analysis** every day in recipes, user's manuals, and instruction booklets. Basic to this process is dividing the topic into the necessary steps, describing each step in sufficient detail, and then sequencing the steps so they are easy to follow. You can also help by anticipating trouble spots. If you were writing a set of directions for a barbecue grill, for example, you might start by describing the parts that must be put together so that you familiarize the reader with them and force a quick inventory. And if the plans call for 12 screws but the packaging includes 15, telling the reader that there are three extra will stave off the inevitable "I must have done it wrong" that leftover parts usually elicit.

But writing directions is only one kind of process analysis. "How does it work?" and "How did it happen?" are questions that get at other sorts of processes—the scientific and the historical. Lab reports exemplify scientific process analysis, as do the kinds of papers published in *Scientific American* or the *New England Journal of Medicine*. Like the practical, how-to process paper, the report of an experiment or explanation of a physical process clearly marks the steps in a sequence. The same is true of essays that rely on historical process, though sometimes it's harder to discern the steps. A paper that analyzes how the United States became involved in the Vietnam War, for instance, identifies the major stages of involvement and their chronology, the steps that led up to open warfare. Essays that focus on a historical process often condense time in a way that practical or scientific process analysis does not, but the chronology itself is still important.

Although process analysis is usually associated with specialized subjects—how to do *x*, how *y* works, or how *z* came about—it also finds its way into less formal prose. If you were to write about how you got interested in a hobby, for instance, you would be using process analysis, as you would if you were writing an explanatory research paper on the history of Coca-Cola. Process analysis is also useful as a means of discovery. If you were to analyze the process you go through to revise a draft of one of your papers, you might find out that you overemphasize a particular stage or leave out a step. It's easy to underrate process analysis as a way of thinking and expressing ideas, because it is often equated with the simpler forms of how-to writing.

Audience and Purpose

The concept of audience is crucial to process essays, for you must know just how familiar the reader is with the topic so you know what you need to explain and how to explain it. Familiar topics present you with a challenge, for how can you interest your readers in a subject they already know something about? The answer lies in what you have to say about that subject and how you say it. A seemingly dull topic such as making bread can be turned into an interesting paper if you start with the negative associations many readers have about the topic—air bread, that tasteless, white, compactible substance better suited to bread ball fights than human consumption—and then go on to describe how to make the kind of bread that is chewy, substantive, tasty, and worth $4.50 a loaf in a specialty food store.

Your purpose in such an essay is informative, but if you want your essay to be read by people who don't have to read it, then you need to make your approach to your subject interesting as well. A straightforward, follow steps 1–10, how-to essay will get the job done, but unless the need for the information is pressing, no one will read it. But if you relate the bread-baking process, for example, so that your reader enjoys the essay, then even the person who would never willingly enter a kitchen will probably keep reading.

If what you have to say involves a personal subject, you need to present the information in a believable way, and at the same time, adjust it to the level of the audience. The process involved in friends growing apart, for instance, can be explained in terms so personal that only the writer could appreciate it. If that were your topic, you would need to gear your description to the general reader who may have experienced something similar. That way, you would place your personal narrative into a larger, more general context.

On the other hand, if you know not only more but also more specialized information than the reader, you must be careful to make sure your audience is following every step. Sometimes a writer explores a process to inform the reader and other times to persuade, but always the writer has an assertion in mind and is trying to affect the reader. If, for example, you enjoy scuba diving and you're trying to describe the physiological effects the body is subject to when diving, you might first describe the necessary equipment and then take the reader on a dive, emphasizing the different levels of atmospheric pressure—the instant and constant need to equalize the air pressure in your ears, the initial tightness of your mask as you sink to 10 feet, the gradual "shrinking" of your wet suit as the pressure increases with the depth of the dive. Then after a quick tour of the kinds of fish, sea creatures, and coral formations you see during the dive, you would return your reader to the surface, stopping at 15 feet to release the buildup of nitrogen in the blood. The whole process may strike your reader as not worth the risk, so you would want to make sure not only that your thesis counters that opinion, but also that you describe what you see, so the attractions outweigh the hazards and momentary discomfort.

Sequence

Chronology is as crucial to process as it is to narration. In fact, it is inflexible. A list of the ingredients in the bread has to precede baking instructions; a quick safety check of the necessary equipment has to come before the dive. And then you must account for all the important steps. If time is crucial to the process, then you have to account for it also, although in a historical process essay, time is apt to be compressed or deemphasized to underscore a turning point. An essay on the Civil Rights movement, for instance, might well begin with a brief account of the slave trade, even though the body of the paper focuses on the 1950s and 1960s, culminating with the assassination of Martin Luther King in 1968. And if you were to identify King's death as the turning point in the movement, you would emphasize the chronology and character of the events leading up to and following his assassination.

Undergirding the concept of sequence, of course, is the pattern of cause and effect—in the example above, you might want to explore the effect of King's death on the Civil Rights movement. What's most important to process analysis, however, is neither cause nor effect, but the stages or steps, the chronology of events. Without a set sequence or chronology, neither cause nor effect would be clear.

Other Modes

In writing a process analysis, you will draw on the same skills you use for description, narration, definition, and example papers, for without supporting details and examples to further and describe the process, a process essay can be tedious indeed. An essay on the Civil Rights movement would probably need to draw on statistics—such as the percentage of the population held in slavery in 1860—as well as examples of protests and boycotts, and quotations from those involved, both for and against equal rights for African Americans. An essay on scuba diving may need to define some terms and bring in examples from mathematics and physiology, as well as from scientific articles on the relative health of coral reefs in the Caribbean. Incorporating references to well-known people—a Mohammed Ali or a Jacques Cousteau—or to current events or adding a narrative example or even an amusing aside can make what might otherwise be little more than a list into an interesting paper.

Transitions

To make the stages of the process clear, you will need to rely on logically placed transitions that lead the reader from one stage to the next. Most writers try to avoid depending only on obvious links, such as *first, next, next*, and instead use chronology, shifts in tense, and other indicators of time to spell out the sequence. The process itself may have clear markers that you can use as transitions. An essay explaining a historical event, for instance, will have pegs such as specific dates or actions that you can use to indicate the next stage in the sequence.

Organization and Ideas

The body of a process essay almost organizes itself because it is made up of the steps you have identified, and they must occur in a given sequence. Introductions and conclusions are trickier, as is the thesis, for you must not only set out a process but also make an assertion about it.

Your thesis should confront the reader with a point, implicit or explicit, about the process involved, and in so doing, head off the lethal response, "So what?"

Useful Terms

Chronology The time sequence involved in events; what occurred when.

Process analysis A type of analysis that examines a topic to discover the series of steps or acts that brought or will bring about a particular result. Whereas cause and effect analysis emphasizes *why*, process emphasizes *how*.

POINTERS FOR USING PROCESS

Exploring the Topic

1. **What kind of process are you presenting?** Is it a practical, "how-to" process? A historical one? A scientific one? Some mixture of types?

2. **What steps are involved?** Which are crucial? Can some be grouped together? Under what headings can they be grouped?

3. **What is the sequence of the steps?** Are you sure that each step logically follows the one before it?

4. **How familiar is your reader with your subject?** Within each step (or group of steps), what information does the reader need to know? What details can you use to make that information come alive? What examples? What connections can you make to what the reader already knows? Do you use any terms that need to be defined?

5. **Is setting or context important?** If so, what details of the setting or context do you want to emphasize?

6. **What is the point you want to make about the process?** Is your point an assertion? Will it interest the reader?

Drafting the Paper

1. **Know your reader.** Using two columns, list what your reader may know about your topic in one and what your reader may

not know in the other. If you are writing about a practical process, figure out what pitfalls your reader may be subject to. If you are writing about a historical or scientific process, make sure your diction suits your audience. Be on the lookout for events or actions that need further explanation to be understood by a general audience. If your reader is apt to have a bias against your topic, know what that bias is. If your topic is familiar, shape your first paragraph to enlist the reader's interest; if the topic is unfamiliar, use familiar images to explain it.

2. **Know your purpose.** If you are writing to inform, make sure you are presenting new information and that you are making an assertion about your topic. Don't dwell on information that the reader already knows if you can possibly avoid it. If you are writing to persuade, remember that you do not know whether your audience agrees with you. Use your persona to lend credibility to what you say, and use detail to arouse your reader's sympathies.

3. **Define your terms.** Think through the process you have chosen for your topic to make sure that your reader is familiar with all the terms associated with it. If any of those terms are technical or unusual ones, be sure you define them clearly.

4. **Present the steps in their correct sequence.** Make sure that you have accounted for all the important steps or stages in the process and that they are set out in order. If two or more steps occur at the same time, make sure you have made that clear. If time is crucial to your process, see that you have emphasized that point. If, on the other hand, the exact time at which an event occurred is less important than the event itself, make sure you have stressed the event and have subordinated the idea of time.

5. **Use details and examples.** Whether you are writing an informative or a persuasive essay, use details and examples that support your purpose. If you are explaining how to make your own ice cream, for example, draw on what the reader knows about various commercial brands and flavors to bolster the case for making your own. After all, your reader may not want to take the time and trouble to complete that process and may have to be enticed into trying it. Choose details and examples that combat your reader's negative associations.

(Continued)

6. **Double-check your transitions.** First mark your stages with obvious transitions or with numbers. After you have turned your notes into a working draft, review and revise the transitions you have used, checking to see that they exist, that they are clear, and that they are not overly repetitious or obvious. Make sure each important stage (or group of stages) is set off by a transition. See if you can indicate shifts by using verb tense or words and phrases that don't call attention to themselves as transitions.

7. **Make a point.** What you say about a subject is far more interesting than the subject itself, so even if you are writing a practical process essay, make sure you have a point. A paper on a topic such as "how to change a tire" becomes unbearable without a thesis. Given an assertion about changing a tire—"Changing my first flat was as horrible as I had expected it to be"—the paper at least has a chance.

Runner

Laura Carlson

Running has been a sport Laura Carlson has enjoyed for the past 10 years, both on her own and for her school. Now a junior at Valley City State University in Valley City, North Dakota, she wrote the essay that follows in a class taught by Noreen Braun, who reprinted the essay on a Web page devoted to what she titled as "Some Fine Student Writing from Composition I, Fall Semester, 1997." Thinking about the essay and reading it over, she comments: "I am really taken aback. I remember writing it and thinking that this is my favorite type of writing, descriptive, and that I could really do a good job on it—if I wanted to. It was really hard for me to sit down and write something with a due date. One thing I did was to basically forget that I had to do it for class, but that I had to write the essay for myself."

Stumped for a subject, Carlson thought about what she enjoyed and came up with the topic that is the title of the essay. She notes that the idea for the essay "came naturally to me. I actually went out that day to run." Thinking about that experience, she "tried to remember what it had been like; the feelings that I felt, the cold and the pictures in my mind, and I tried to incorporate them back into my writing. I think it really worked. I really just wrote about what I knew and how I really felt. Visualization was the key to my success with this essay." What worked for Laura may well work for you.

What to Look For   Not everyone knows what it feels like to run for a fairly long distance, and even those who do may not know what it's like to do that on a cold North Dakota morning. To make her experience come alive and to make it immediate, Carlson, therefore, chooses the present tense and descriptive details. The result is an essay that explains the process she goes through when she runs and makes the reader feel what Carlson feels.

1   When I wake up this morning, I can feel the chill of the air in my joints. I am almost reluctant to give up the warmth of my bed, but I know I need to. Slowly, I step out of my bed and quickly

throw on a sweatshirt and pants. Leaving my room, still tired, but slowly awakening, I yawn.

2 I stretch my tired limbs, first my arms, then my legs. Noticing a tightness in my right hip, I take a little extra time to stretch it. I am still moving slowly as if in a drugged stupor. Maybe I should just go back to bed. Before I change my mind, I hurry outside into the brisk early morning air. I take three or four breaths to acclimate myself to the cold, cold air. I can see my breath on the air in little white puffs. I want to reach out as if I could float away with the rising mist. It is still dark outside. The sun hasn't quite poked his head out to greet the day. The blue black sky is waiting to engulf me as his arms extend as far as I can see.

3 Running on an October morning is so exhilarating! I think it is only about 20 degrees this morning. I am so cold!

4 My steps are slow to start. I feel my legs tighten and restrain me, not wanting to exert the effort to propel me forward, yet I know that it is mind over matter and I am going to win this battle! I tell myself that I need to get ready for the big meet that is coming up at the end of the month. My adrenaline is pumping and my mind is whirling at a mile a minute taking in the frosty scenery that is surrounding me. The trees are covered in a fine layer of crystals forming together to make a wintry scene unlike any other I have seen yet this season. My breathing is accelerating and my pulse is beating in my ears. The biting cold is gnawing at my skin. I refuse to give into the cold of the air and the gripping of my lungs.

5 As I slowly retreat into a solid pace, my body is more aware of my feet steadily pounding on the pavement and of the crunching of the leaves and twigs as they collapse under the weight of my body. The burning in my lungs is lessening as my pace is increasing. The steady flow of traffic helps keep my mind from wandering and keeps me focused. I only have a couple of miles to go. My nose is running just as fast as my feet. I feel the slight burning as if the air were actually freezing the breath entering and exiting my nostrils.

6 I can tell by the landmarks of the city that I am closing in on my destination: home. I pass the fenced-in yard with the barking dog who chooses to torment me each time I pass. I keep running, my pace not faltering. As I come within three blocks of my house, I pick up my pace as if in a race. I am feeling winded as my stride lengthens and my breathing becomes much more shallow. I am al-

most home. The scenery is changing as the sun has finally approached the horizon. The hues of the sky are changing rapidly with the approaching daylight.

7   My house is in sight. I slow my pace to a fast walk and slowly make my way to my driveway. I take deep breaths to get used to the different pace. I am done for another day. I feel refreshed and awakened. I am now ready to continue with another day.

Organization and Ideas

1. Which paragraph or paragraphs make up the essay's introduction? What does it tell you?
2. Trace the process of the run itself. What paragraphs describe it?
3. One technique Carlson uses to avoid the stilted *first-next-then* marking of the essay's chronology is to use the progress of the sunlight. Where in the essay does she note that progress?
4. Is Carlson's thesis stated or implied? What evidence can you find to support your idea?
5. If you're a runner, how well does Carlson describe the experience? If you're not, to what extent does she convince you that running is a pleasure?

Technique and Style

1. Carlson gives the essay unity by frequently referring to the weather. What descriptive details does she use?
2. Throughout the essay, Carlson uses the first person *I.* Does she avoid overusing it or not? How can you back up your opinion?
3. In paragraph 2, Carlson personifies the sun and the sky by referring to them with the pronoun *he.* What would be lost without that personification? What is gained?
4. The first sentence of paragraph 6 uses a full colon. What other punctuation could be used? Which is the most effective and why?
5. Reread the last paragraph. How else might the essay have ended that would fit in with what has come before? Which is the more effective ending and why?

Suggestions for Writing

Journal

1. Write your own last paragraph for the essay and then, briefly, explain why you think it is better or not as good as Carlson's.

2. Briefly describe the feelings you have when you are involved in a sport, either as a spectator or a participant.

Essay

1. Like Carlson, you might start by thinking about what you enjoy. Perhaps it's a sport or a hobby, but no matter what the subject you can use Carlson's essay as a model to write your own description of the process involved. You may find it easiest to start with the process, jotting down the steps or stages. Then once you have a rough draft, you can decide on the kind of introduction and conclusion that would be most effective for the essay, and, of course, where best to put the thesis, if you want to state rather than imply it. Suggestions for a topic:

   playing a sport
   being involved with your hobby
   playing a card game
   cooking a favorite dish
   enjoying a "do nothing" day

2. Even though many people participate in sports, even more watch games on television. During play-offs and championships, watching television has almost turned into a ritual. Choose a sport you like or a television show you are addicted to and describe the process you go through to watch it.

How to Swat a Fly

Will Cuppy

Writing in the tradition of American humorists that found humor by poking fun at what is often taken seriously (too seriously, they would say), Will Cuppy's essays appeared in both newspapers and magazines. Born in Indiana, he later moved to Illinois where he earned his BA and MA degrees from the University of Chicago, while at the same time beginning his career in journalism writing for Chicago's newspapers. Most of his career, however, was spent in New York, where he became a book reviewer for the New York Herald Tribune *as well as a frequent contributor to the* New Yorker *and the* Saturday Evening Post.

The Bronx Zoo became one of Cuppy's favorite haunts, and that is where his observations of animal behavior evolved into his mock-scientific essays about humans and other creatures. How to Tell Your Friends from the Apes *(1931) gathered together many of the pieces he wrote for the* New Yorker, *and that same tone is echoed in* The Great Bustard and Other People *(1941) as well as his posthumously published* The Decline and Fall of Practically Everybody *(1950).* "How to Swat a Fly," *the essay that follows, appeared in* How to Attract the Wombat *(1949), but flies haven't changed much.*

What to Look For   Dullness is a cardinal sin for any piece of prose, and it's the main danger in essays that describe processes. These types of essays are apt to fall too easily into the first-second-third enumerating of steps (*first-next-then* is almost as deadly), and the thesis can easily slide into what is obvious instead of an assertion. Cuppy's essay dodges around being boring by using humor and by commenting on the steps he sets out, techniques you can use in your own writing.

1   Being as sound in mind and body as I am ever likely to be, I have decided to release my notes on Fly-swatting made from time to time during many years of active service at my Long Island beach cottage, Chez Cuppy. (It's the same old place I used to call Tobacco Road, but I think the new name sort of lends a tone—and, besides, it's a change.) In the belief that Fly-swatting is here to stay for awhile, DDT and other squirts to the contrary notwithstanding, I am passing on the torch in Ten Easy Lessons, as follows:

1. Get set. Be sure you're not going to fall off your chair backwards in the act of swatting. Here as elsewhere, style is everything.

2. Still, don't take too much time with the preliminaries. The Fly won't wait there forever. He has other things to do with his time.

3. Try to ascertain in some unobtrusive way whether the object you're after is actually a Fly or a nail head, such as often occurs in the woodwork of country homes. Don't go poking at the thing to see which it is. When in doubt, swat.

2   Little situations like this are bound to occur in every swatter's routine. For instance, there is a small black spot on the ceiling of my bedroom that has embarrassed me dozens of times, it looks so exactly like a Fly of some large and vicious species. If I have

crept up on it once—Oh, well! Stalking an imperfection in the paint and swinging one's heart out at a nail head are not things one likes to remember, but perhaps they have their place in the give and take of daily living. We can't be heroes to ourselves every instant.

3   4. In any case, never flirt your swatter back and forth past a Fly before swatting, expecting to get him your next time around. When you finally make up your mind to hit him, he will not be there. The Fly who hesitates is lost. He knows this and acts accordingly.

4   5. Take aim quickly but carefully. A complete miss is not good for the morale, either yours or the Fly's.

5   6. If possible, fix him with the first swat. Failure to do so may be serious. For one thing, you didn't get him. That alone is bad. Secondly, conditions will never be quite the same again, since you are now dealing with an alert and disillusioned Fly. He is never going to trust you as he did before. He will avoid you in the future.

6   That was one of the many faults of my dear Aunt Etta's swatting. She never hit her Fly the first time and she seldom came anywhere near him on repeated attempts, partly because she employed that worst of all swatting techniques, the folded newspaper, or slow motion, method. She would lunge at the Fly again and yet again with her antiquated weapon in a free-for-all that left her exhausted and the Fly in the best of health and spirits. A folded newspaper is only about 17 per cent efficient in anybody's hands, and Aunt Etta's form was nothing to boast of. Her batting average must have been something incredible. I'm glad to state that she often thought she had won. Her eyesight wasn't so good, either.

7   I assure you that Aunt Etta was one of the kindest persons I have ever known, though not so soft about Flies as my Uncle Toby, who did so much in his day to encourage the spread of typhoid fever and other diseases. There was certainly no sadistic urge in her swatting activities. She never engaged a Fly in hand-to-hand combat until after she and we children had staged a ceremonious Fly-drive with kitchen aprons and dish towels, then a second and often a third to chase the last one out the open screen door. It was only the Fly or Flies who failed to respect these rites that she tackled, and it always amazed me that there would be any such. If we thought Aunt Etta had one of her headaches, or felt a nap coming on, or couldn't stand such a racket—in which case she would tell us so in no uncertain terms—we disappeared. We vanished utterly, with the

usual gift of cookies. But Flies are not brought up that way, apparently. They cannot take a hint.

8　　The family would want me to add that Aunt Etta's house was no more Fly-ridden than any other home of the period. In fact, it was less so than most, as it was thoroughly screened. Which reminds me that she never did, to my knowledge, solve the riddle of how they got in. She was always saying there wasn't a crack where they could squeeze through. All right, then, how did the Mouse get in?

9　　7. Don't mind a little incidental breakage around the house. Aunt Etta was much too careful of her bric-a-brac. She wouldn't strike within yards of her whatnot when a Fly took sanctuary there. For the cause I would smash anything in Chez Cuppy to smithereens, except possibly my shaving mirror. I'm not having seven years of bad luck for any Fly.

10　　8. Cultivate patience. It is a beautiful thing in itself, and when you are after a Fly who will not light, you will need it. Eventually that Fly will light, and ten to one it will be in some dark, inaccessible corner, down behind the stove.

11　　The Fly who absolutely refuses to settle is a problem for advanced swatters, and not an easy one. Talk about a watched pot! Do not stalk such a Fly too openly, but try to act as though you were interested in something else altogether. This involves looking wall-eyed at the Fly while gazing fixedly in the other direction, but it can be done, with practice. It is my opinion that a Fly will not settle while you are looking straight at him with a swatter in your fist. At any rate, he won't while you are following him around the room, making passes at him. Believe me, he knows what you are up to.

12　　I would go so far as to say that a Fly knows the exact moment when you start looking for a swatter, if you should be caught without one. Edge yourself ever so casually in the general direction of a swatter, and notice what happens. Other persons who may be present will simply wonder why you are hitching your chair along in that insane fashion or tiptoeing across the room with one groping hand outstretched and a haunted look in your eyes. They won't have the faintest notion of what goes on, but the Fly will. He has already figured out his first five moves and several of yours.

13　　This does not necessarily prove that the Fly is more intelligent than you are. If such things could be measured—and they will be, some day—I have little doubt that you, gentle swatter, would be found to have a higher I.Q. than the average Fly. You may be slow on the uptake, while the Fly is unbelievably fast. His sheer brilliance in planning and executing maneuvers of every sort on the ground and in the air amounts to genius, and you have all you can do to keep from falling over your feet. You cannot make quick decisions, or, if you do, you are generally dead wrong, as everybody at the office knows but yourself. The Fly's decisions are mostly right. They have to be.

14   Yet on the whole, taking it by and large, and allowing for individual exceptions, you are smarter than the Fly. You know more than he does about more things. Above all, you possess the power of abstract reasoning, a faculty which distinguishes mankind from the merely brute creation, such as Flies. You can listen to the radio, look at television, and go to the movies. You can read mystery stories and try to guess who done it. Keep your chin up and always remember that if you are not the Fly's superior in every single respect one might mention, you are at least his equal, mentally. Since you are fighting on practically even terms, then, when you are after a Fly who will not light you must seek for a flaw in his intellectual equipment if you hope to gain the initiative, and I can help you there. The key is his imperfect memory. You can remember as far back as yesterday. The Fly cannot. He forgets. The particular Fly of whom we were speaking will be out of his dark corner in a few brief moments, and you can begin the whole show all over again.

15   *9.* Check up on yourself occasionally. Ask yourself, "Am I a better swatter than I was last year?" The correct answer is No.

16   *10.* Don't be discouraged at a few failures. I don't always get them myself, but I give them pause. It makes 'em think.

Organization and Ideas

1. Examine Cuppy's first paragraph in terms of the journalistic questions *who? where? what? when? why? how?* Which ones does the paragraph answer and how?
2. What is the relationship between paragraph 2 and point 2?
3. What is the relationship between paragraphs 6–8 and point 6?
4. What is the relationship between paragraphs 11–14 and point 8?
5. Consider Cuppy's humor together with his directions, and state the essay's thesis in your own words.

Technique and Style

1. Why does Cuppy capitalize the word *fly*? What effects does he achieve by doing it?
2. Describe Cuppy's characterization of the Fly.
3. Examine the first sentence in each of Cuppy's directions. In what way are the sentences parallel or not?
4. Describe Cuppy's tone. How would you characterize his humor?
5. From your reading of the essay, describe the sort of person that Cuppy seems to be. What sort of persona does he present?

Suggestions for Writing

Journal

1. Briefly outline the steps involved in a familiar chore—cleaning out the bathroom cabinet, washing the car, mowing the lawn, painting a room. Your outline plus a thesis can be the basis of a longer essay.
2. Think of a process you are used to (washing the car, cooking, studying, packing, playing a sport or the like) and find an analogy that fits all or part of the process. For instance, packing for a trip may be like preparing to climb Mt. Everest—you never know what you are going to need so you take almost everything.

Essay

1. Cuppy's essay deals with a common experience, and you can find your subject in the same general area. Think, for example, of various common actions, how you
   wash dishes
   study
   make a sandwich
   wait in line
   deal with boring people
   Once you have a subject, then consider the steps involved and write them down. Review the list to make sure you have them in an order that makes sense. Like Cuppy, you may want to enumerate the steps, commenting on some of them. Or like Carlson (see p. 211), you may want to use a more subtle kind of chronology.
2. Cuppy describes how to deal with a common frustrating annoyance. What has happened to you recently that might fit the same category? Perhaps you misplaced something and had to search for it or planned the perfect day only to have it go sour. Write an essay in which you describe how you dealt with the situation.

A Woman's Place

Naomi Wolf

Naomi Wolf was working on her PhD at Princeton University when she adapted her dissertation into The Beauty Myth: How Images of Beauty Are Used Against Women, *a best seller published in 1991. As the title of the book implies, Wolf is concerned with issues that affect women, an interest that runs through all of her work as she tries to redefine and revive feminism. She has explored the relation between women and politics in* Fire with Fire: The New Female Power *(1993); girls, women, and sexuality in* Promiscuities: The Secret Struggle for Womanhood *(1997); and women, childbirth, and the medical industry in* Misconceptions: Truth, Lies and the Unexpected on the Journey to Motherhood *(2001). Her essays have been published in print media as diverse as* Ms., Glamour, *the* Wall Street Journal, *and the* New Republic. *The essay below was published in the* New York Times *on May 31, 1992, and is adapted from a commencement address she gave at Scripps College, a women's college in California.*

What to Look For   Many writers steer away from beginning a sentence with the word *and* because they are afraid of creating a sentence fragment. But as long as the sentence has a subject and main verb, it can begin with *and* (or, like this one, *but* or any other conjunction) and still be an independent clause, a complete sentence, with the conjunction serving as an informal transition. To see how effective that kind of sentence can be, notice Wolf's last paragraph.

1   Even the best of revolutions can go awry when we internalize the attitudes we are fighting. The class of 1992 is graduating into a violent backlash against the advances women have made over the last 20 years. This backlash ranges from a senator using "The Exorcist" against Anita Hill, to beer commercials with the "Swedish bikini team." Today I want to give you a backlash survival kit, a four-step manual to keep the dragons from taking up residence inside your own heads.

2   My own commencement, at Yale eight years ago, was the Graduation from Hell. The speaker was Dick Cavett, rumored to have been our president's "brother" in an all-male secret society.

3   Mr. Cavett took the microphone and paled at the sight of hundreds of female about-to-be Yale graduates. "When I was an undergraduate," I recall he said, "there were no women. The women went to Vassar. At Vassar, they had nude photographs taken of the women in gym class to check their posture. One year the photos were stolen, and turned up for sale in New Haven's redlight district." His punchline? "The photos found no buyers."

4   I'll never forget that moment. There we were, silent in our black gowns, our tassels, our brand new shoes. We dared not break the silence with hisses or boos, out of respect for our families, who'd come so far; and they kept still out of concern for us. Consciously or not, Mr. Cavett was using the beauty myth aspect of the backlash: when women come too close to masculine power, someone will draw critical attention to their bodies. We might be Elis, but we still wouldn't make pornography worth buying.

5   That afternoon, several hundred men were confirmed in the power of a powerful institution. But many of the women felt the shame of the powerless: the choking on silence, the complicity, the helplessness. We were orphaned from our institution.

6   I want to give you the commencement talk that was denied to me.

7   Message No. 1 in your survival kit: redefine "becoming a woman." Today you have "become women." But that sounds odd in ordinary usage. What is usually meant by "You're a real woman now"? You "become a woman" when you menstruate for the first time, or when you lose your virginity, or when you have a child.

8   These biological definitions are very different from how we say boys become men. One "becomes a man" when he undertakes responsibility, or completes a quest. But you, too, in some ways more than your male friends graduating today, have moved into maturity through a solitary quest for the adult self.

9   We lack archetypes for the questing young woman, her trials by fire; for how one "becomes a woman" through the chrysalis of education, the difficult passage from one book, one idea to the next. Let's refuse to have our scholarship and our gender pitted against each other. In our definition, the scholar learns womanhood and the woman learns scholarship; Plato and Djuna Barnes, mediated to

their own enrichment through the eyes of the female body with its wisdoms and its gifts.

10   I say that you have already shown courage: Many of you graduate today in spite of the post-traumatic stress syndrome of acquaintance rape, which one-fourth of female students undergo. Many of you were so weakened by anorexia and bulimia that it took every ounce of your will to get your work in. You negotiated private lives through a mine field of new strains of VD and the ascending shadow of AIDS. Triumphant survivors, you have already "become women."

11   Message No. 2 breaks the ultimate taboo for women: *Ask for money in your lives.* Expect it. Own it. Learn to use it. Little girls learn a debilitating fear of money—that it's not feminine to insure we are fairly paid for honest work. Meanwhile, women make 68 cents for every male dollar and half of marriages end in divorce, after which women's income drops precipitously.

12   Never choose a profession for material reasons. But whatever field your heart decides on, for god's sake get the most specialized training in it you can and hold out hard for just compensation, parental leave and child care. Resist your assignment to the class of highly competent, grossly underpaid women who run the show while others get the cash—and the credit.

13   Claim money not out of greed, but so you can tithe to women's political organizations, shelters and educational institutions. Sexist institutions won't yield power if we are just patient long enough. The only language the status quo understands is money, votes and public embarrassment.

14   When you have equity, you have influence—as sponsors, shareholders and alumnae. Use it to open opportunities to women who deserve the chances you've had. Your B.A. does not belong to you alone, just as the earth does not belong to its present tenants alone. Your education was lent to you by women of the past, and you will give some back to living women, and to your daughters seven generations from now.

15   Message No. 3: Never cook for or sleep with anyone who routinely puts you down.

16   Message No. 4: Become goddesses of disobedience. Virginia Woolf wrote that we must slay the Angel in the House, the censor within. Young women tell me of injustices, from campus rape coverups to classroom sexism. But at the thought of confrontation,

they freeze into niceness. We are told that the worst thing we can do is cause conflict, even in the service of doing right. Antigone is imprisoned. Joan of Arc burns at the stake. And someone might call us unfeminine!

17   When I wrote a book that caused controversy, I saw how big a dragon was this paralysis by niceness. "The Beauty Myth" argues that newly rigid ideals of beauty are instruments of a backlash against feminism, designed to lower women's self-esteem for a political purpose. Many positive changes followed the debate. But all that would dwindle away when someone yelled at me—as, for instance, cosmetic surgeons did on TV, when I raised questions about silicone implants. Oh, no, I'd quail, people are mad at me!

18   Then I read something by the poet Audre Lorde. She'd been diagnosed with breast cancer. "I was going to die," she wrote, "sooner or later, whether or not I had ever spoken myself. My silences had not protected me. Your silences will not protect you. . . . What are the words you do not yet have? What are the tyrannies you swallow day by day and attempt to make your own, until you will sicken and die of them, still in silence? We have been socialized to respect fear more than our own need for language."

19   I began to ask each time: "What's the worst that could happen to me if I tell this truth?" Unlike women in other countries, our breaking silence is unlikely to have us jailed, "disappeared" or run off the road at night. Our speaking out will irritate some people, get us called bitchy or hypersensitive and disrupt some dinner parties. And then our speaking out will permit other women to speak, until laws are changed and lives are saved and the world is altered forever.

20   Next time, ask: What's the worst that will happen? Then push yourself a little further than you dare. Once you start to speak, people *will* yell at you. They *will* interrupt, put you down and suggest it's personal. And the world won't end.

21   And the speaking will get easier and easier. And you will find you have fallen in love with your own vision, which you may never have realized you had. And you will lose some friends and lovers, and realize you don't miss them. And new ones will find you and cherish you. And you will still flirt and paint your nails, dress up and party, because as I think Emma Goldman said, "If I can't dance, I don't want to be part of your revolution." And at last you'll know with surpassing certainty that only one thing is more frightening than speaking your truth. And that is not speaking.

Organization and Ideas

1. Wolf's essay could easily be retitled "How to Survive the Backlash." What is the backlash?
2. Why does Wolf include the anecdote about Dick Cavett? How is it related to the backlash?
3. What are the four steps for survival?
4. Wolf's essay gives advice and explains how to survive, but it also comments on women's place in society today. Combine those comments with her advice and the result will be the thesis.
5. The original audience for the essay was women, but it was republished for an audience that also includes men. Explain whether men would find the essay offensive. Is it antimale? Dated?.

Technique and Style

1. What saying does Wolf's title refer to? How does her title set up her essay?
2. Throughout the essay, Wolf uses allusion—Anita Hill (paragraph 1), Plato and Djuna Barnes (paragraph 9), Virginia Woolf (paragraph 16), Audre Lorde (paragraph 19), and Emma Goldman (paragraph 21). Use an encyclopedia to look up one of these allusions so that you can explain to the class how it is (or is not) appropriate.
3. To explore the effect of Wolf's repeated use of *and* in her last paragraph, try rewriting it. What is gained? Lost?
4. What can you find in the prose that suggests that "A Woman's Place" was written to be heard, not read?
5. Wolf is obviously a feminist, but think of feminism as a continuum ranging from conservative to radical. Based on this essay, what kind of feminist is Wolf? What evidence can you find for your opinion?

Suggestions for Writing

Journal

1. Choose one of Wolf's "messages" and test it out against your own experience. Do you find the advice helpful? Necessary?
2. Relate an experience in which you ran into sexism, either antimale or antifemale. You could use this entry later as the basis for an essay in which you explain how to cope with sexism.

Essay

1. All of us at one time or another have played a role we didn't believe in or didn't like. Those roles vary greatly. Think about the roles you have

had to play and how you broke out of them. Choose one and draft a paper explaining "How to Survive" or "How to Break Out." Some roles to think about:

dutiful daughter
responsible sibling
perfect husband (or wife)
brave man
happy homemaker

2. Write your own version of the essay but title it "A Student's Place" and create the advice and explanation to fit the title.

Independence Day

Dave Barry

It's a rare columnist who can lay claim to both a Pulitzer Prize and a television sit-com, but few things aren't unusual about Dave Barry. Barry was the focus of the show "Dave's World," which ran from 1993 to 1997 and was based on two of his 24 books, and in 1988, he won a Pulitzer for Commentary "for his consistently effective use of humor as a device for presenting fresh insights into serious concerns." A humor writer for the Miami Herald, *his columns are carried by over 500 newspapers. A number of those columns have been collected in his most recent book* Boogers Are My Beat *(2003), but Barry has also written two novels:* Big Trouble *(1999) and* Tricky Business *(2002). His Web site (<davebarry.com>) notes that he "lives in Miami, Florida, with his wife, Michelle, a sportswriter. He has a son, Rob, and a daughter, Sophie, neither of whom thinks he's funny." His essay "Independence Day" first appeared in* Tropic *magazine and was reprinted in* Mirth of a Nation, *Michael J. Rosen, editor.*

What to Look For   As you read Barry's essay, look for the ways he avoids using obvious markers as he takes his readers through a typical Fourth of July celebration.

1   This year, why not hold an old-fashioned Fourth of July picnic?

2   Food poisoning is one good reason. After a few hours in the sun, ordinary potato salad can develop bacteria the size of raccoons. But

don't let the threat of agonizingly painful death prevent you from celebrating the birth of our nation, just as Americans have been doing ever since that historic first July Fourth when our Founding Fathers—George Washington, Benjamin Franklin, Thomas Jefferson, Bob Dole and Tony Bennett—landed on Plymouth Rock.

3   Step one in planning your picnic is to decide on a menu. Martha Stewart has loads of innovative suggestions for unique, imaginative and tasty summer meals. So you can forget about her. "If Martha Stewart comes anywhere near my picnic, she's risking a barbecue fork to the eyeball" should be your patriotic motto. Because you're having a *traditional* Fourth of July picnic, and that means a menu of hot dogs charred into cylinders of industrial-grade carbon, and hamburgers so undercooked that when people try to eat them, they leap off the plate and frolic on the lawn like otters.

4   Dad should be in charge of the cooking, because only Dad, being a male of the masculine gender, has the mechanical "know-how" to operate a piece of technology as complex as a barbecue grill. To be truly traditional, the grill should be constructed of the following materials:

- 4 percent "rust-resistant" steel;
- 58 percent rust;
- 23 percent hardened black grill scunge from food cooked as far back as 1987 (the scunge should never be scraped off, because it is what is actually holding the grill together);
- 15 percent spiders.

5   If the grill uses charcoal as a fuel, Dad should remember to start lighting the fire early (no later than April 10) because charcoal, in accordance with federal safety regulations, is a mineral that does not burn. The spiders get a huge kick out of watching Dad attempt to ignite it; they emit hearty spider chuckles and slap themselves on all eight knees. This is why many dads prefer the modern gas grill, which ignites at the press of a button and burns with a steady, even flame until you put food on it, at which time it runs out of gas.

6   While Dad is saying traditional bad words to the barbecue grill, Mom can organize the kids for a fun activity: making old-fashioned

ice cream by hand, the way our grandparents' generation did. You'll need a hand-cranked ice-cream maker, which you can pick up at any antique store for $1,875. All you do is put in the ingredients, and start cranking! It makes no difference what specific ingredients you put in, because—I speak from bitter experience here— no matter how long you crank them, they will never, ever turn into ice cream. Scientists laugh at the very concept. "Ice cream is not formed by cranking," they point out. "Ice cream is formed by freezers." Our grandparents' generation wasted millions of man-hours trying to produce ice cream by hand; this is what caused the Great Depression.

7   When the kids get tired of trying to make ice cream (allow about twenty-five seconds for this) it's time to play some traditional July Fourth games. One of the most popular is the "sack race." All you need is a bunch of old-fashioned burlap sacks, which you can obtain from the J. Peterman catalog for $227.50 apiece. Call the kids outside, have them line up on the lawn and give each one a sack to climb into; then shout "GO!" and watch the hilarious antics begin as, one by one, the kids sneak back indoors and resume trying to locate pornography on the Internet.

8   Come nightfall, though, everybody will be drawn back outside by the sound of loud, traditional Fourth of July explosions coming from all around the neighborhood. These are caused by the fact that various dads, after consuming a number of traditionally fermented beverages, have given up on conventional charcoal-lighting products and escalated to gasoline. As the spectacular pyrotechnic show lights up the night sky, you begin to truly appreciate the patriotic meaning of the words to *The Star-Spangled Banner,* written by Francis Scott Key to commemorate the fledgling nation's first barbecue:

> *And the grill parts' red glare;*
> *Flaming spiders in air;*
> *Someone call 911;*
> *There's burning scunge in Dad's hair*

9   After the traditional visit to the hospital emergency room, it's time to gather 'round and watch Uncle Bill set off the fireworks that he purchased from a roadside stand operated by people who spend way more on tattoos than dental hygiene. As Uncle

Bill lights the firework fuse and scurries away, everybody is on pins and needles until, suddenly and dramatically, the fuse goes out. So Uncle Bill re-lights the fuse and scurries away again, and the fuse goes out again, and so on, with Uncle Bill scurrying back and forth with his Bic lighter like a deranged Olympic torchbearer until, finally, the fuse burns all the way down, and the firework, emitting a smoke puff the size of a grapefruit, makes a noise—"phut"—like a squirrel passing gas. Wow! What a fitting climax for your traditional old-fashioned July Fourth picnic!

10   Next year you'll go out for Chinese food.

Organization and Ideas

1. You could describe Barry's essay as a "how-to" guide for a traditional celebration on the Fourth of July, but his breaking down the event into steps is subtle. How does he do it?
2. It's possible to argue that the essay is organized by process (steps), chronology (time), drama (least to most effective), or some combination. Make a case for the way you read the organization.
3. How effective is Barry's last paragraph?
4. Barry's essay is obviously a satire, but of what: the Fourth of July, family gatherings, American values, the consumer culture, American sense of history, tradition, or some combination? What in the essay supports your view?
5. Take a look at the biographical information and note the reason Barry was awarded a Pulitzer Prize. In what ways does that statement apply to this essay?

Technique and Style

1. Look up *hyperbole* (pp. 140, 143). To what extent does Barry use the device? How effective is it?
2. Barry includes contemporary figures (paragraphs 2 and 3). Why might he have done that and what effect does he achieve?
3. What is the point of the fractured "facts" in paragraph 2?
4. Granted that the essay is humorous, but what kind of humor? How would you describe Barry's tone?
5. Reread the essay marking every use of *traditional*. To what extent is the repetition effective? What is Barry's point in using it?

Suggestions for Writing

Journal

1. In what ways is the title a pun?
2. What description do you find the most amusing and why? Quote from the essay to back up your view.

Essay

1. Write your own "how-to" essay on the preparations for a typical, traditional, or important time. Like Barry, you may want to remove yourself from the scene and generalize, or you may want to be part of it. Suggestions:

   Thanksgiving
   first date
   first day of classes
   looking cool
   dealing with a computer problem

2. Barry does an amusing job depicting the "typical" American family at play on a celebratory occasion. Think about the family gatherings you have attended, those of either your own family or someone else's, and write your own survivor's guide.

Inspiration? Head Down the Back Road, and Stop for the Yard Sales

Annie Proulx

As you will be able to tell from reading Annie Proulx's essay, her interests and travels are many and varied, some would even say strange. A graduate of Colby College in Maine, Proulx has lived in Vermont and is now in Wyoming, places that fostered her interest in gardening, fly fishing, and making cider (all of which she has written about), and led to her astute observations about people and landscapes. You can read about her keen sense of character and landscapes in her novels: Postcards *(1993), which won the PEN/Faulkner Award;* The Shipping News *(1994), which won both a Pulitzer Prize* and *National Book Award;* Accordion Crimes *(1996); and* That Old Ace in the Hole: A Novel *(2002). Proulx's short stories frequently appear in magazines such as the* New Yorker, *the* Atlantic Monthly, Harper's, *and* GQ, *some of which are reprinted in her books* Heart Songs and Other Stories *(1994) and the recent* Close Range *(1999). The essay that follows is part of a series—Writers on Writing—published by the* New York Times *where it appeared on May 10, 1999.*

What to Look For   Proulx's essay is as far removed from the lock-step, how-to essay as a chocolate mousse is from a Tootsie Roll, yet she is writing about a process—how she finds her sources of inspiration for her writing. As you read her essay, try to identify both the sources for her ideas and how she uses those sources and you will reveal the process that is embedded in the essay.

1   The Irish singer Christy Moore clips out "Don't Forget Your Shovel," a song I like not only for its tripping rhythm and sly social commentary but for its advice to the diggers of the world, a group to which I belong.

2   A whole set of metaphoric shovels is part of my tool collection, and for me the research that underlies the writing is the best part of the scribbling game. Years ago, alder scratched, tired, hungry, and on a late return from a fishing trip, I was driving through Maine when a hubbub on the sidewalk caught my eye: milling customers at a yard sale. I stop for yard sales.

3   Pay dirt. I found the wonderful second edition unabridged *Webster's New International Dictionary* with its rich definitions and hundreds of fine small illustrations. On a collapsing card table nearby sat *Harper's Dictionary of Classical Literature and Antiquities, The Oxford Companion to English Literature* and other weighty reference works, discards from a local library and the best catch of the trip.

4   I am an inveterate buyer of useful books on all possible subjects. Collectors pass up ex-libris books, but I need reading copies. And because I often fold down page corners and scribble in margins, it is best to keep me away from first editions.

5   On the jumbly shelves in my house I can find directions for replacing a broken pipe stem, a history of corncribs, a booklet of Spam recipes, a 1925 copy of *Animal Heroes of the Great War*

(mostly dogs but some camels); dictionaries of slang, dialect and regional English; a pile of Little Blue Books (none are blue) from the 1920's featuring titles like *How to Be a Gate-Crasher* and *Character Reading From the Face*. One of these, *Curiosities of Language,* treats us to the tortured orthography our grandparents thought hilarious:

> There was a young man, a Colonel,
> Who walked in the breezes volonel;
> He strolled in the aisles,
> Of the wooded maisles,
> And, returning, read in his jolonel.

6   This digging involves more than books. I need to know which mushrooms smell like maraschino cherries and which like dead rats, to note that a magpie in flight briefly resembles a wooden spoon, to recognize vertically trapped suppressed lee-wave clouds; so much of this research is concerned with four-dimensional observation and notation. These jottings go into cheap paper-covered notebooks that I keep in a desultory fashion, more often onto the backs of envelopes and the margins of newspapers, from there onto the floor of the truck or onto the stair landing atop a stack of faxes and bills.

7   The need to know has taken me from coal mines to fire towers, to hillsides studded with agate, to a beached whale skeleton, to the sunny side of an iceberg, to museums of canoes and of windmills, to death masks with eyelashes stuck in the plaster, to shipyards and log yards, old military forts, wildfires and graffiti'd rocks, to rough water and rusty shipwrecks, to petroglyphs and prospectors' diggings, to collapsed cotton gins, down into the caldera of an extinct volcano and, once or thrice in the middle distance, in view of a snouty twister.

8   I listen attentively in bars and cafes, while standing in line at the checkout counter, noting particular pronunciations and the rhythms of regional speech, vivid turns of speech and the duller talk of everyday life. In Melbourne I paid money into the hand of a sidewalk poetry reciter to hear "The Spell of the Yukon," in London listened to a cabby's story of his psychopath brother in Paris, on a trans-Pacific flight heard from a New Zealand engineer the peculiarities of building a pipeline across New Guinea.

9   The grand digging grounds are still the secondhand bookshops. Every trip ends with boxes of books shipped back, dusty old manuals

on the hide business or directions for the dances of Texas with footprints and dotted lines reeling across the pages. But bookstores are changing. Recently I rattled the latch of a favorite in Denver before I saw the sign announcing that it was forever closed, but the inventory could be "accessed" on the Internet. Another dealer, a specialist in local histories, operated from his living room for years and put out an interesting catalogue from time to time. Both the catalogue and a visit to his bookshelves are things of the past, rendered obsolete by chilly cyber-lists.

10 I rarely use the Internet for research, as I find the process cumbersome and detestable. The information gained is often untrustworthy and couched in execrable prose. It is unpleasant to sit in front of a twitching screen suffering assault by virus, power outage, sluggish searches, system crashes, the lack of direct human discourse, all in an atmosphere of scam and hustle.

11 Nor do I do much library research these days, though once I haunted the stacks. Libraries have changed. They are no longer quiet but rather noisy places where people gather to exchange murder mysteries. In bad weather homeless folk exuding pungent odors doze at the reading tables. One stands in line to use computers, not a few down for the count, most with smeared and filthy screens, running on creaky software.

12 I mourn the loss of the old card catalogues, not because I'm a Luddite, but because the oaken trays of yesteryear offered the researcher an element of random utility and felicitous surprise through encounters with adjacent cards: information by chance that is different in kind from the computer's ramified but rigid order.

13 This country swims in fascinating pamphlets. In a New Mexico greasy spoon I pick up a flyer that takes St. Paul sharply to task on the subjects of hair style, clothing and women. ("Shorts, miniskirts, halters, bikinis, etc., are all O.K. You don't have to listen to Paul. . . . God wants women to look nice and be in style with the times. As far as men, Jesus had long hair. Paul must have been a religious fanatic.") A hundred miles later I read a narrow sheet with advice on how to behave in the presence of a mountain lion. ("Do not make direct eye contact. . . . Try to appear as big as possible.")

14 Food and regional dishes are important research subjects. Some you can order in restaurants, but others exist only in out-of-print cookbooks and must be prepared at home, like a duck roasted inside a watermelon, a dish called Angel in a Cradle, or another

called the Atlanta Special, which sounds like a train, although the
ingredient list begins, "1 beaver (8 to 10 pounds.)"

15   I like to drive the West, making a slow drift over caliche and
gravel roads, volume cranked up and listening to music (this, too,
is research), usually regional subtexts of alternative genres. But two
that I never tire of hearing are Glenn Ohrlin singing "Barnacle Bill,
the Sailor," in his two-tone voice, and the good ol' boy Texas
country-and-western yodeler Don Walser with the Kronos String
Quartet, sliding a heartaching "Rose Marie" straight at me.

16   The truck wanders around intersecting roads as tangled as fishing line. At times topographic maps, compass bearings or keeping
the sun at my shoulder are better direction guides than signs, usually nonexistent or bullet-blasted into unreadability. The rules of
road drift are simple: Always take a branching side route, stop often, get out and listen, walk around, see what you see. And what
you see are signs, not direction signs but the others, the personal
messages. We live in a world of signs.

17   I am amazed when people mourn the loss of the Burma Shave
jingles. Better stuff is all around us, in public restrooms, in phone
booths, on rocks, stapled to telephone poles, stuck on lawns. I remember a large billboard that stood for many years on a back-
country road in Colorado. The community used it as a kind of enormous greeting card, welcoming home a son on leave from the
Navy, congratulating a child on her fifth birthday, inviting neighbors to a party.

18   The signs of urban panhandlers seem to indicate that many of
them took creative-writing courses. These messages are always
printed in neat capital letters: "WILL KILL FOR FOOD," "BIG DUMB
UGLY BUM NEEDS YOUR HELP," "MY MOTHER LOVED ME BUT
NOW SHE'S GONE."

19   The digging is never done because the shovel scrapes at life itself. It is not possible to get it all, or even very much of it, but I
gather what I can of the rough, tumbling crowd, the lone walkers
and the voluble talkers, the high lonesome signers, the messages
people write and leave for me to read.

Organization and Ideas

1. Paragraphs 1–3 introduce the essay and its central metaphor. What
does it lead you to expect from what follows?

2. What do you learn about Proulx's taste in books in paragraphs 3–5? About how she uses them?

3. When Proulx says that her "digging involves more than books" (paragraph 6), what is she referring to, what does she do? What is it that she does in paragraphs 7 and 8?

4. Paragraphs 9–12 describe changes, lost sources of information. What are they? What has been lost? What other sources does she mention in paragraphs 13–18?

5. Given your answers to the previous questions, make a list of the sources Proulx uses combined with the actions she takes to gather them. What general statement can you make about them? To what extent is that statement an adequate thesis for the essay?

Technique and Style

1. Proulx introduces the metaphor of digging in paragraph 1, then mentions it several times later in the essay (paragraphs 2, 3, 6, 9, and 19). In what ways is the metaphor appropriate for the process she describes? What does it add to the essay?

2. What is gained or lost by including the limerick in paragraph 5? What does it illustrate about Proulx's cast of mind?

3. Chose one of the paragraphs that brims with examples. What do they contribute to Proulx's point in the paragraph? To her thesis?

4. Reread the essay, noting the times Proulx mentions something relating to books or to writing. What reasons can you find for the frequency of the references?

5. Explain what line, if any, Proulx draws between research and inspiration. What evidence can you find for your opinion?

6. The last paragraph concludes the essay by summarizing without repeating. Reread the second sentence. What paragraph or paragraphs does "rough, tumbling crowd" refer to? "The lone walkers"? "The voluble talkers"? "The high lonesome singers"? "The messages people write and leave for me to read"?

Suggestions for Writing

Journal

1. In paragraph 10, Proulx has some harsh comments for the Internet. Use your journal to test out her assertions against your own experience.

2. Proulx coins the expression "road drift" for pleasurable and informative wandering around on side roads (paragraph 16). Recreate a time when you "followed the rules of road drift."

Essay

1. What are your sources of inspiration for your writing or for some aspect of your life? Jot them down along with the actions you take to obtain them, and you'll have the skeleton of an essay that you can model along the lines of Proulx's. If you prefer, you might choose to write about how you write, thinking of the central term as broadly as possible and not just from the point at which you start to produce words on paper or the screen. If that idea doesn't appeal, think about the last time you had to do research and retrace the process you went through.

2. *Multitasking* is the current buzzword for doing several things at the same time, and though it's not a word that Proulx would use, it does describe how she fuels her imagination. On a less grand scale, think of those times when you are doing several things simultaneously, choose one example, and write an essay in which you explain how you go about it.

ADDITIONAL WRITING ASSIGNMENTS

Using Process

1. Explain a familiar chore so that you make it less boring: washing the car, mowing the lawn, painting a room, cleaning out a closet, preparing for an exam, vacuuming.
2. Give a positive spin to a negative action: how to procrastinate, tell a white lie, stay awake in class, hide dislike.
3. Explain how to survive a difficult or unpleasant job: filing, reviving a computer crash, recycling, changing diapers, weeding.
4. Argue for the best way to party, study, enjoy a sport, find a parking space.

Evaluating the Essays

1. The essays by Will Cuppy and Dave Barry employ narration and description to set a humorous tone. Which does the better job? Back up your opinion with quotations from both essays.
2. Annie Proulx addresses a general audience on how she finds her sources of inspiration, while Naomi Wolf advises women on how to stand up for themselves. Yet both essays share a serious tone. What differences can you spot in the kind of seriousness the writers employ? Of the two, who is the more likeable? Believable? Answer those questions by analyzing the writers' tone.
3. To be effective, the steps or stages in an essay organized by process need to be subtle. Reread the essays by Laura Carlson and Dave Barry, paying particular attention to how they mark the various stages in their processes. Which does the better job and why? Quote from both essays to support your point.
4. Review the concept of *persona* (pp. 80, 81, 279–81) to have a clear understanding of how it operates and then think about how it functions in the five selections in this chapter. Of those five, which writer uses it most effectively? Write an essay in which you analyze how that writer uses persona. Use examples from several of them to bolster your argument.

On Using
Cause and
Effect

8

Process analysis focuses on *how;* causal analysis emphasizes *why.* Though writers examine both **cause and effect,** most will stress one or the other. Causal analysis looks below the surface of the steps in a process and examines why they occur; it analyzes their causes and effects, why *X* happens and what results from *X.* As a way of thinking, causal analysis is a natural one.

Let's say you've followed the directions that came with your new stereo system and have finally reached the moment of truth when it's ready. You load your favorite tape, push the switch marked "power"; it clicks, nothing happens. The receiver is on, as are the CD player and tape deck, but no sound comes out of the speakers. Probably you first check for the most immediate possible cause of the problem—the hookups. Are all the jacks plugged into the correct sources? Are they secure? Are the speaker wires attached correctly? If everything checks out, you start to search for less immediate causes, only to discover that the wrong switch was depressed on the receiver so that it's tuned to a nonexistent turntable. You push "Tape," and music fills the room. The problem is solved.

Essays that analyze cause and effect usually focus on one or the other. If you are writing about your hobby, which, let's say, happens to be tropical fish, you could emphasize the causes. You might have wanted a pet but were allergic to fur; you might have been fascinated with the aquarium in your doctor's office, and your aunt gave you two goldfish and a bowl. These reasons are causes that you would then have to sort out in terms of their importance. But if you wished to focus on effect, you might be writing on how your interest in tropical fish led to your majoring in marine biology.

You can see how causal analysis can be confusing in that a cause leads to an effect, which can then become another cause. This kind of causal chain undergirds Benjamin Franklin's point that "a little neglect may breed great mischief ... for want of a nail the shoe was lost; for want of a shoe the horse was lost; and for want of a horse the rider was lost." You can avoid the traps set by causal analysis if you apply some of the skills you use in division and classification and in process analysis:

1. Divide your subject into two categories—causes and effects.
2. Think about the steps or stages that are involved and identify them as possible causes or effects.
3. List an example or two for each possible cause or effect.
4. Sort out each list by dividing the items into primary or secondary causes and effects, that is, those that are relatively important and those that are relatively unimportant.

When you reach this final point, you may discover that an item you have listed is only related to your subject by time, in which case you should cross it out.

If you were writing a paper on cheating in college, for instance, your notes might resemble these:

	Possibilities	**Examples**	**Importance**
Causes	Academic pressure	Student who needs an A	Primary
	Peer pressure	Everybody does it	Primary
	System	Teachers tolerate it	Secondary
		No real penalty	
	Moral climate	Cheating on income taxes	Secondary
		False insurance claims	
		Infidelity	
		Breakup of family unit	
Effects	Academic	Grades meaningless	Primary
	Peers	Degree meaningless	Primary
	System	Erodes system	Secondary
	Moral climate	Weakens moral climate	Secondary

The train of thought behind these notes chugs along nicely. Looking at them, you can see how thinking about the moral climate might lead to speculation about the cheating that goes undetected on tax and insurance forms, and for that matter, the cheating that occurs in a different context, that of marriage. The idea of infidelity then sets off a causal chain: infidelity causes divorce, which causes the breakup of families. Pause there. If recent statistics show that a majority of students have cheated, and if recent statistics also reveal a large number of single-parent households, is it safe to conclude that one caused the other? No. The relationship is one of time, not cause. Mistaking a **temporal relationship** for a causal one is a **logical fallacy** technically called **post hoc reasoning.**

It is also easy to mistake a **primary cause** or effect for a **secondary** one. If the notes above are for an essay that uses a narrative framework, and if the essay begins by relating an example of a student who was worried about having high enough grades to get into law school, the principle behind how the items are listed according to importance makes sense. To bring up his average, the student cheats on a math exam, justifying the action by thinking, "Everybody does it." The essay might then go on to speculate about the less apparent reasons behind the action—the system and the moral climate. For the student who cheated, the grade and peer pressure are the more immediate or primary causes; the system and climate are the more remote or secondary causes.

Audience and Purpose

What you know or can fairly safely assume about the intended audience determines both what to say and how to say it. If you went straight from high school into a full-time job, for example, and wanted to write an essay about deciding five years later to enroll in college, you know your reader is familiar with both high school and college but knows nothing about you—your job and what led to your decision. The reality of your work—perhaps you found it wasn't sufficiently demanding and that your lack of a higher education stood in the way of promotion—and your expectations of what college will do to enrich your life are the reasons, the causes, behind your change in direction.

Perhaps your subject is less personal but still one that your reader knows something about, say the high school dropout rate. Like your reader, you know that it's high in your city because you remember a story in the local newspaper pointing that out. What you didn't know your reader probably doesn't know either: How high is high? Why do students drop out? What happens to them after that? You'll have to do some research to find out some answers (the news story is a good place to start), but you'll find plenty to say. And as you amass information on your topic, you'll start to sense a purpose. Perhaps you simply want to inform your reader about the magnitude of the problem, or perhaps you will want to argue that more needs to be done about it.

An awareness of the reader and that person's possible preconceptions can also guide your approach to the topic. If, for example, your topic is the single-parent family, and you want to dispel some ideas about it that you think are misconceptions, you might safely assume that your audience regards single-parent families as at best incomplete and at worst irresponsible. It's obvious that you won't win your argument by suggesting that anyone with such ideas is a fool and possibly a bigot as well; it's also obvious that making your point while not offending some readers requires a subtle approach. One way to avoid offense is to put yourself in the shoes of the reader who has the negative associations. Then just as you learned more about the topic and became enlightened, so, with any luck, may your reader.

Valid Causal Relationships

As noted earlier, it is easy to mistake a temporal relationship for a causal relationship and to assign significance to something relatively unimportant. That's another way of saying that evidence and logical reasoning are essential to cause-and-effect essays. If, for instance, you find yourself drawn to one example, you need to think about how to avoid resting your entire argument on that one example.

Writing about collegiate sports, for instance, you might have been struck by the story of a high school basketball star who wanted to play proball but wasn't good enough to go straight to the pros; yet he couldn't meet the admission requirements for an NCAA Division I basketball school. After playing at several junior colleges, he finally transferred to an NCAA I institution. There, he was tutored and received a lot of individual attention, so he was able to maintain his academic eligibility. Then one year short of graduation, all that support vanished because he had used up his time limit and was no longer eligible to play. The effect—no degree, little education, and few chances for review by pro scouts—was devastating. You want to write about it. You want to argue that college sports take advantage of high school athletes, but you have only one example. What to do?

You can use your one example as a narrative framework, one that is sure to interest your reader. But to make that example more than an attention-getting device that enlists the reader's emotions, you have a number of alternatives. If your research shows that a fair number of athletes have a similar story, then you have multiple examples to support your point. If only a few share the experience, you'll need to modify your thesis to argue that even a few is too many. And if you can't find any other examples, then you have to narrow your argument to fit what you have, arguing that this particular individual was victimized. While you can ask how many more like him there may be, you cannot state that they exist.

Organization and Ideas

Although a cause can lead to an effect that then becomes a cause leading to another effect and so on, most essays are organized around either one or the other: why high school students drop out, why a person returns to college, what happens if a college takes advantage of a basketball player, what effect does being a working mother in a one-parent household have on the children. That's not to say that if your essay focuses on cause, you have to avoid effect and vice versa. Whichever one you don't emphasize can make a good conclusion. Your introduction, however, is a good place for your thesis; the reader can then follow the logical relationships between ideas as you develop your main point.

Useful Terms

Cause and effect An examination of a topic to discover, explain, or argue why a particular action, event, situation, or condition occurred.

Logical fallacy An error in reasoning. Assigning a causal relationship to a temporal one and reaching a general conclusion based on one example are both logical fallacies.

Post hoc reasoning A logical fallacy in which a temporal relationship is mistaken for a causal one. The fact that one event preceded another only establishes a temporal not a causal relationship.

Primary cause The most important cause or causes.

Secondary cause The less important cause or causes.

Temporal relationship Two or more events related by time rather than anything else.

POINTERS FOR USING CAUSE AND EFFECT

Exploring the Topic

1. **Have you stated the topic as a question that asks why *X* happened?** What are the possible causes? The probable causes? Rank the causes in order of priority.
2. **Have you stated the topic as a question that asks what results from *X*?** What are the possible effects? The probable effects? Rank the effects in order of priority.
3. **Is a temporal relationship involved?** Review your lists of causes and effects, and rule out any that have only a temporal relationship to your subject.
4. **Which do you want to emphasize, cause or effect?** Check to make sure your focus is clear.
5. **What is your point?** Are you trying to show that something is so or to explore your topic? Are you making an argument?
6. **What evidence can you use to support your point?** Do you need to cite authorities or quote statistics? If you depend on personal experience, are you sure your experience is valid, that is, representative of general experience?
7. **What does your reader think?** Does your audience have any preconceived ideas about your topic that you need to account for? What are they? How can you deal with them?
8. **Do you need to define any terms?** What words are crucial to your point? Are any of them abstract and, therefore, need to be defined? Have you used any technical terms that need definition?
9. **What role do you want to play in the essay?** Are you an observer or a participant? Do you intend to inform, persuade, or entertain? What point of view best serves your purpose?

Drafting the Paper

1. **Know your reader.** Figure out what attitudes your reader may have about your topic. If the causal relationship you are discussing is unusual, you might want to shape your initial attitude

so that it is as skeptical as your reader's. On the other hand, you may want to start with a short narrative that immediately puts the reader on your side. How much does your reader know about your topic? If you are the expert, make sure you explain everything that needs to be explained without being condescending.

2. **Know your purpose.** Adjust your tone and persona to suit your purpose. If you are writing a persuasive paper, make sure your persona is credible and that you focus your ideas to change the mind of a reader or, short of that, so your ideas make the reader rethink the position. If you are writing an informative paper, choose a persona and tone that will interest the reader. Tone and persona are even more crucial to essays written to entertain, in which the tone can range from ironic to lighthearted.

3. **Emphasize a cause or effect.** Essays that focus on cause will probably cover a variety of reasons that explain the result. Though there may be only one effect or result, you may want to predict other possible effects in your conclusion. For instance, an essay that explores the causes of violence may examine a number of reasons or causes for it but may then conclude by speculating on the possible effects of a rising crime rate. On the other hand, essays that focus on effect will more than likely cover a number of possible effects that are produced by a single cause, though again you may want to speculate on other causes. If you are writing about the effects of smoking, at some point in the essay you may want to include other harmful substances in the air such as dust, hydrocarbons, and carbon monoxide.

4. **Check for validity.** Don't hesitate to include quotations, allusions, statistics, and studies. Choose your examples carefully to buttress the relationship you are trying to establish, and be sure you don't mistake a temporal relationship for a causal one.

5. **Make a point.** The cause-and-effect relationship you examine should support an assertion: video games not only entertain, they also stimulate the mind and improve coordination; video games are not only habit-forming, they are also addictive.

6. **Proofread.** Check to make sure you are using *affect* and *effect* correctly. While a handbook will provide a longer explanation, the short one is to think of *affect* as a verb and *effect* as a noun. That's not always true, but it is most of the time.

Tiffany Stephenson—An Apology

Bjorn Skogquist

Bjorn Skogquist came to Concordia College in Moorhead, Minnesota, with a firm interest in drama (having been in productions at Anoka High School that were recognized for excellence by the Kennedy Center for the Performing Arts) but a distinct aversion to writing. His freshman year, however, when his instructor, James Postema, encouraged him to "include anything I wanted, anything that I felt to be important," Skogquist "began to find it rather easy, and in a way, almost entertaining." He comments, "About halfway through, after I had written about various mishaps and comical incidents in my life, I decided to write about the things that a person would rather forget." The result is the essay that follows, although the name of the subject has been changed to Tiffany Stephenson. Skogquist relates "one of those things that I would rather forget, but instead of forgetting it, I apologized. It was something that I began and couldn't put down until I had finished."

What to Look For   If you find yourself thinking about an incident that occurred to you and mulling over its effect, you may well be on the way to an essay that takes a personal narrative and reexamines it through the lens of cause and effect. That is what Bjorn Skogquist does with what happened to him in the fourth grade. As you read the essay, look for the ways he handles different time periods—what had been happening before he entered his new school, his first day there, the incident that occurred, and the present.

1   When I was in the fourth grade, I moved from a small Lutheran school of 100 to a larger publicly funded elementary school. Lincoln Elementary. Wow. Lincoln was a big school, full of a thousand different attitudes about everything from eating lunch to how to treat a new kid. It was a tough time for me, my first year, and more than anything, I wanted to belong.

2   Many things were difficult; the move my family had just made,
trying to make new friends, settling into a new home, accepting a
new stepfather. I remember crying a lot. I remember my parents
fighting. They were having a difficult time with their marriage, and
whether it was my stepfather's drinking, or my mother's stubborn-
ness, it took an emotional toll on both me and my siblings. Despite
all this, the thing that I remember most about the fourth grade is
Tiffany Stephenson.

3   The first day of fourth grade at Lincoln Elementary School was
an emptiness, and it felt enormous. I wasn't the only one who felt
this way, but I was too absorbed in my own problems to notice
anyone else's. I was upset that my father, my blood father, was in
the hospital for abusing alcohol. Among other things, he was a
schizophrenic. I was too young to understand these diseases, but I
understood all too well that my daddy was very sick, and that I
couldn't see him any more.

4   My first day at Lincoln was a very real moment in my life. The
weather was both cloudy and intolerably sunny at the same time.
Maybe it wasn't that the sun was so bright, maybe it was just that our
eyes were still adjusted to morning shadows. It was one of those sequences that somehow stand out in my memory as unforgettable. I remember feeling gray inside. I think that all of us felt a little gray, and I
would guess that most of us remember that first day as you might remember your grandmother's funeral, whether you liked it or not.

5   I walked in and sat near the back of the class, along with a few others. If you were different or weird or new, from another planet, you sat
in the back because those were the only desks left. I sat at the far left
of the room, in the back near the windows. For a while I just stared
out into the playground, waiting for recess to come. Our teacher, Mrs.
Bebow, came into the room and started talking to us. I don't remember exactly what she said that day, because I wasn't listening. I was
numb to the world, concentrating solely on that playground. She
seemed distant, far away, and I think that my whole day might have
stayed numb if it weren't for a boy named Aaron Anderson.

6   Aaron, who sat to my right, leaned over and whispered, "My
name's Aaron. And that's Tiffany Stephenson. Stay away from her.
She's fat and ugly and she stinks." At that, a few others laughed, and
I felt the numbness leaving me. Mrs. Bebow remarked that if we had
something so terribly amusing to say, everyone had a right to know

just what it was. Of course, we all quieted down. Then I asked
which one was Tiffany, and Aaron pointed. There she was, coloring
contentedly, sitting alone in the corner, in the very back, just like
me. She was not fat or ugly, and as far as I knew, she didn't stink either. I even remember thinking that she was cute, but I quickly dismissed the thought because I already had a new friendship, even
though it was in the common disgust of Tiffany Stephenson.

7   While all this was happening, our teacher Mrs. Bebow managed
to take roll, after which she proceeded to lecture the boys on good
behavior and then the girls on being young ladies. Every time she
turned her back, airplanes and garbage flew across the room at
Tiffany, along with a giggle. I don't think Tiffany Stephenson
thought too much of us, that day or ever.

8   A few days later, one of the girls passed Tiffany a note. It ended
up making her cry, and it got the girl a half an hour of detention. I
was too busy trying to fit in to notice though, or didn't notice, or
was afraid to notice, or simply didn't care.

9   That fall, both the boys and girls would go up to Tiffany on the
playground and taunt her. They made absurd accusations, accusations about eating boogers at lunch, or about neglecting to wear
underwear that day. Interestingly, this was the only activity that we
participated in where a teacher didn't command, "OK, boys and
girls need to partner up!" What we did to Tiffany Stephenson was
mean, but in using her we all became common allies. I wonder if
the teachers knew what we were up to when we made our next
move, or if they thought that we were actually getting along. I think
they knew at first, but we got craftier as time passed. And Tiffany
had quit telling the teacher what happened. She knew that when
we were ratted on, her taunts got worse. And they did get worse.
We were mean, but we kept on because there was no one to stand
out and say, "Enough."

10   When I think about that year, and about Tiffany, I remember that
she was almost always alone. Toward the second half of the year, a
retarded girl named Sharon Olsen befriended her. Sharon and
Tiffany were a lot alike. They spent most of their time together coloring and drawing pictures, and those pictures always found their
way to the prize board at the end of the week. The teacher knew
that they needed a little encouragement, but mostly that "encouragement" ended up making us hate them more. We picked on
Sharon a lot too, but not as much as we targeted Tiffany.

11   Through the long winter, our taunts became hateful jeers, and our threats of pushing and shoving became real acts. We carried our threats out against Tiffany, but with no real reason to hate her. A couple of times when we walked down to lunch, we even pushed her around the corner to an area under the stairs. We knew that if no other classes followed us, we could get away with our plan, which was to tease her until tears flowed. We always asked her if she was scared. She never gave us the right answer. In a quiet voice she would reply, "No. Now leave me alone." Sometimes we left her alone, and sometimes we just laughed. Tiffany must have felt so very scared and alone, but she had more than us, she had courage. We didn't care. The more we could scare her, the better, the closer, the stronger knit we somehow felt.

12   One afternoon, heading for lunch, a few of us stayed behind and blocked the doorway. Tiffany was there, alone again, and cornered by three boys. Looking back, I realized why we began pushing her around. We felt unbelievably close, so close to each other through our hatred. It was a feeling that I have experienced only a few times since. And not only was the experience ours to cherish, it was a delight for Mrs. Bebow's entire fourth grade class. We were a purpose that afternoon, and we knew it. Looking back to that moment, I feel more remorse for my coldness than I have felt for any other passing wrong. But then, there, I felt alive, unafraid, and strangely whole.

13   That afternoon changed me forever.

14   By the time we sent Tiffany Stephenson to the green linoleum, she was no longer a person. Her full name, given to her at birth as a loving gesture, was now a fat, smelly, ugly title. There, on the green linoleum of Mrs. Bebow's fourth grade classroom, amidst the decorations and smell of crayfish aquariums, Tiffany Stephenson received many kicks, punches and unkind words. We didn't kick or punch her very hard, and the things we said weren't especially foul, but they were inhuman. This event was the culmination of the inhumane hate and vengeance that had been growing inside of us all year long. And yet, if any one of us stopped for a second to look, to really take a good look at who it was lying there on the ground, curled up in a ball crying, we would have realized that she was one of us.

15   At the beginning of the year, all of us had felt like we were in the back of the room. We were all unknowns. But somehow during

that year we had put ourselves above her by force, and I admit that for a long time I couldn't see my wrong. But I had wronged. I had caused someone pain for my own personal ambitions. I was now popular, and it was at Tiffany Stephenson's expense. I was a coward, stepping on her courage for one moment in the warm sunlight, above my own pale clouds.

16   Only recently do I realize my error. I wish I could have been the one to say, on that first fall afternoon, "Tiffany's not ugly, fat or stinky. She's just like you and me, and we're all here together." Really, I wish anyone would have said it. I know now that people need each other, and I wish I could tell the fourth grade that we could all be friends, that we could help each other with our problems. I wish that I could go back. But all I can do is apologize. So Tiffany, for all my shortcomings, and for sacrificing you for the sake of belonging, please forgive me.

Organization and Ideas

1. What paragraph or paragraphs introduce the narrative?
2. Trace the causal relationships in paragraphs 1–5 and 6–14. What does the author feel and why?
3. Paragraphs 15 and 16 sum up the incident that occurred "that afternoon." What did the author realize then? Now?
4. Consider all the cause-and-effect relationships in the narrative and state the thesis of the essay.
5. What is the emotional effect of the essay? How does Skogquist achieve it?

Technique and Style

1. Tiffany Stephenson's name first appears in paragraph 2 but not again until paragraph 6. Explain what is gained by the delay.
2. How does the author try to connect his experience with that of the reader? Why might he have chosen to do that?
3. In paragraph 15 Skogquist says "I was a coward, stepping on her courage for one moment in the warm sunlight, above my own pale clouds." What does he mean by "the warm sunlight, above my own pale clouds"?
4. Paragraph 13 consists of one sentence. Explain its function and effect.
5. Skogquist gives his audience a lot of information about his family. Explain why he may have chosen to do that and what it contributes to the essay.

Suggestions for Writing

Journal

1. Do you identify with the author or with Tiffany Stephenson?
2. If you were Tiffany Stephenson, would you forgive Skogquist? Why or why not?

Essay

1. Write your own personal narrative about an experience in which you explore the effect it had on you. Like Skogquist, you will probably want to have a dual perspective: the effects then and now. For a subject, consider your first
   day at a new school
   attempt at a sport
   acquaintance with death
   friendship
   visit to the dentist or doctor or hospital
2. Place yourself in Tiffany Stephenson's position and write the essay from her point of view, looking back on the fourth grade from a time much later.

When Music Heals Body and Soul

Oliver Sacks

For Oliver Sacks, medicine is a family tradition. Born in England to parents who were both physicians, he is one of three sons who became doctors. Armed with a medical degree from Oxford University, Sacks moved to the United States for his internship and residency and is now Clinical Professor of Neurology at the Albert Einstein College of Medicine in New York. Sacks is probably best known for his book Awakenings *(1974), an account of his work with "frozen" patients that was made into a film in 1990, starring Robin Williams and Robert De Niro. His other medical works include* The Man Who Mistook His Wife for a Hat *(1985),* An Anthropologist on Mars *(1995), and* Island of the Colorblind *(1998). Sacks' autobiographical books are* A Leg to Stand On *(1989), where he recounts the accident he refers to in his essay below, and* Uncle Tungsten: Memories of a Chemical Boyhood *(2001). Though Sacks calls himself a "lonely person, not at ease socially," it's obvious that he cares deeply about people in general and the link between "body and soul" in particular. The essay reprinted here was published in* Parade Magazine, *on March 31, 2002.*

What to Look For   It's often difficult for someone in a highly technical field to write in a way that is understood by ordinary readers. That's the problem Sacks faces when he describes a number of medical cases and neurological symptoms. As you read his essay, check to see if his prose is clear and comprehensible.

1   All of us have all sorts of personal experiences with music. We find ourselves calmed by it, excited by it, comforted by it, mystified by it and often haunted by it. It can lift us out of depression or move us to tears. I am no different. I need music to start the day and as company when I drive. I need it, propulsively, when I go for swims and runs, I need it, finally, to still my thoughts when I retire, to usher me into the world of dreams.

2   But it was only when I became a patient myself that I experienced a *physical* need for music. A bad fall while climbing a mountain in Norway had left me incapacitated by damage to the nerves and muscles of one leg. After surgery to repair the torn tendons in my leg, I settled down to await some return of function in the torn nerves.

3   With the leg effectively paralyzed, I lost all sense of its existence—indeed, I seemed to lose the very *idea* of moving it. The leg stayed nonfunctional for the longest 15 days of my life. These days were made longer and grimmer because there was no music in the hospital. Radio reception was bad. Finally, a friend brought me a tape recorder along with a tape of one of my favorite pieces: the Mendelssohn *Violin Concerto.*

4   Playing this over and over gave me great pleasure and a general sense of being alive and well. But the nerves in my damaged leg were still healing. Two weeks later, I began to get small twitches in the previously flaccid muscle and larger sudden, involuntary movements.

5   Strangely, however, I had no impulse to walk. I could barely remember how one would go about walking—until, unexpectedly, a

day or two later, the *Violin Concerto* played itself in my mind. It seemed, suddenly, to lend me its own energy, and I recovered the lost rhythm of walking—like remembering a once-familiar but long-forgotten time. Only then did walking regain its natural, unconscious, kinetic melody and grace.

6   Music can have the same effect on the neurologically impaired. It may have a power beyond anything else to restore them to themselves—at least in the precious few minutes that it lasts.

7   For reasons we do not yet understand, musical abilities often are among the last to be lost, even in cases of widespread brain damage. Thus, someone who is disabled by a stroke or by Alzheimer's or another form of dementia may still be able to respond to music in ways that can seem almost miraculous.

8   After a stroke, patients may suffer from *aphasia*, the inability to use or comprehend words. But the ability to sing words is rarely affected, even if an aphasic cannot speak them. Some patients can even be "reminded" in this way of words and grammatical constructions they have "forgotten." This, in turn, may help them start to regain old neural pathways for accessing language or to build new pathways in their place. Music becomes a crucial first step in a sequence followed by spontaneous improvement and speech therapy.

9   Some of my patients with strokes or Alzheimer's are unable to carry out a complex chain of actions: to dress, for example. Here, music can work as a mnemonic—a series of promptings in the form of verse or song, as in the childhood rhyme "One, two, buckle my shoe."

10   My patient Dr. P. had lost the ability to recognize or identify even common objects, though he could see perfectly well. He was unable to recognize a glove or a flower when I handed it to him, and he once mistook his own wife for a hat. This condition was almost totally disabling—but he discovered that he could perform the needs and tasks of the day if they were organized in song. And so he had songs for dressing, songs for eating, songs for bathing, songs for everything.

11   As a result of a brain tumor, my patient Greg has not been able to retain any new memories since the 1970s. But if we talk about or play his favorite Grateful Dead songs, his amnesia is bypassed. He becomes vividly animated and can reminisce about their early concerts.

12   I first saw the immense therapeutic powers of music 30 years ago, in the postencephalitic patients I later wrote about in

Awakenings. These 80 individuals all were victims of *encephalitis lethargica,* the viral sleeping sickness that swept the globe just after World War I. When I came to Beth Abraham Hospital in the Bronx in 1966, most of them had been "frozen," absolutely motionless, for decades.

13   Their voices, if they could speak, lacked tone and force; they were almost spectral. Yet these patients were able to *sing* loudly and clearly, with a normal range of expressiveness and tone. Among those who could walk and talk—though only in a jerky, broken way—music gave their movement or speech the steadiness and control it usually lacked.

14   We could observe this effect on the patients' electroencephalograms. If we found music that worked, their EEGs—often exceedingly slow, reflecting their frozen states—would become faster and more regular. We noted this when patients listened to music or sang it or played it—even when they imagined it.

15   Take Rosalie B., a patient who had a severe form of parkinsonism. She tended to remain transfixed for hours a day, completely motionless, stuck, usually with one finger on her spectacles. But she knew all of Chopin's works by heart, and we had only to say "Opus 49" to see her whole body, posture and expression change. Her parkinsonism would vanish as soon as she even imagined Chopin's *Fantaisie in F minor.* Her EEG would become normal at the same instant the Chopin played itself in her mind.

16   Clearly, human brains are able to tenaciously hold and replay musical stimuli. This is why tunes may repeat themselves endlessly, sometimes maddeningly, in the mind. Musical hallucinations are far more common than visual hallucinations. There even seems to be a sort of normal "reminiscence" or "recycling" of early musical memories, especially in the aging brain.

17   To help, however, the music must be the right kind for each patient—music that has meaning and evokes feeling for that individual. Music therapists who work with a geriatric population often find that only old popular songs can bring such patients to life. While singing them, these patients are able to find a brief but intense sense of community and connectedness with their past lives—and perhaps a deep emotional catharsis.

18   This almost universal responsiveness to music is an essential part of our neural nature. Though analogies often are made to birdsong or animal cries, music in its full sense—including complexities of rhythm and harmony, of pace, timbre and tonality no less than of

melody—seems to be confined to our own species, like language. Why this should be so is still a mystery. Our research is only now beginning to unlock those secrets.

Organization and Ideas

1. What kind of music do you enjoy? How does it affect you?
2. To what extent are your responses similar to those Sacks describes in paragraph 1?
3. Trace the pattern of general and particular through the essay. How would you describe it?
4. How does music affect Sacks' recovery? Those who are neurologically damaged?
5. Consider all the effects Sacks shows that music can have on people and in one sentence state what you find to be his thesis.

Technique and Style

1. Paragraphs 10–15 set out a number of examples. What do they add to the essay?
2. You may be familiar with *Parade Magazine,* for it accompanies many a Sunday newspaper. Its readership is about as general as one can be, yet Sacks is very much of a specialist. How well does he tailor his knowledge to his audience?
3. Sacks blends personal narrative with examples from his medical practice. How effective is his use of the subjective and the objective?
4. Sacks focuses on the effects of music. To what extent does he bring in causal analysis?
5. Paragraphs 16–18 provide the essay's conclusion. How satisfactory is it? Explain.

Suggestions for Writing

Journal

1. In what ways is the title of the essay appropriate? What others can you think of?
2. What surprises you most in Sacks' essay? Explain why.

Essay

1. Almost everyone uses leisure time to relax by pursuing some form of pleasure. Think about what you do for day-to-day fun and make a list of what you come up with. Choose one subject and consider why you do it as well as its effects on you. Then draft an essay in which you

explain what you do and why. You may want to emphasize cause rather than effect or vice versa. Suggestions:

    talking to friends
    playing a sport
    watching television
    pursuing a hobby
    exercising

2. Think about the ways in which music affects you and explore that subject in an essay. You might begin by defining the kind of music you like and then go on to analyze its effect.

Wrestling with Myself

George Felton

When not teaching writing and copywriting at the Columbus College of Art and Design, George Felton is a freelance writer whose topics cover the hot spots of popular culture—Richard Simmons, the "Healthism" craze, not understanding how things work, and the like. Here, he investigates his (and our) fascination with pro wrestling. The essay was originally published in Sun Magazine, *the supplement to the* Baltimore Sun, *on November 11, 1990. Felton has also published his work in the* New York Times, Newsweek, *and* Advertising Age *and has been a contributor to the Bread Loaf Writers' Conference.*

What to Look For   Felton's audience is composed of readers who share his enthusiasm for pro wrestling, those who regard it as silly or worse, and those who know little if anything about it. At times, you may find yourself faced with a similar variety of readers, which is when you can employ some of the techniques Felton uses. As you read his essay, look for the ways he addresses the attitudes of these various readers.

1   It's Saturday morning, 11 a.m., right after the cartoons: time for "The NWA Main Event." As I watch the ringside announcer set up today's card, a huge wrestler—topless and sweating, wearing leather chaps and a cowboy hat, carrying a lariat with a cowbell on

it—bursts into the frame, grabs the announcer by his lapels, and, chunks of tobacco spraying out of his mouth, begins to emote: "Well lookee here, this is just what eats in my craw. . . . I don't care if you're the president or the chief of police, it don't matter, I'm gonna do what I wanna do," and what he mostly wants to do is wrassle somebody good for once—enough nobodies in the ring, enough wimps running the schedule. As quickly as he spills into camera, he veers out, having delivered exactly the 20-second sound bite required. Our announcer blithely sends us to a commercial, and another Saturday's wrestling hour has begun. I feel better already.

2   I soon find out this cowboy's name is Stan Hanson, he's from Border, Texas, and lately he's been getting disqualified in all his matches for trying to kill his opponents and then "hogtying" them with his lariat. We get to watch a recent match in which he kicks some poor guy's stomach furiously with his pointed-toe cowboy boots and drop-slams his elbow into his neck and, after getting him down, hits him over the head with the cowbell, and first whips, then strangles him with his lariat. It's great stuff, with the bell ringing madly and the referee waving his arms, but Stan's already yanked the guy outside the ring onto the apron and he's still on top, trying to kill him.

3   Why do I love this? Why am I crazy about Stan Hanson, who's old and fat and a man the announcer warns us "ought to be in a straitjacket and chains"? Because he personifies the great redemption of pro wrestling, the way it delivers me from civilization and its discontents. Not only is Stan Hanson mad as hell and not taking it anymore, but he's doing it all for me—getting himself disqualified so that I won't run the risk myself, but inviting me to grab one end of the rope and pull. He is my own id—the hairy beast itself—given a Texas identity and a push from behind, propelled out there into the "squared circle" where I can get a good look at it: sweat-soaked, mean, kicking at the slats, looking for an exposed neck. My heart leaps up, my cup runneth over.

4   Obviously I can't tell my friends about too much of this. If I even mention pro wrestling, they just stare at me and change the subject. They think I'm kidding. I am not supposed to like pro wrestling—its demographics are too downscale, its Dumb Show too transparent. They complain that it's fake and silly, which to me are two of its great charms. If it were real, like boxing, it'd be too painful to watch, too sad. I like knowing it's choreographed: the staged mayhem

lets me know someone has studied me and will toss out just the meat the dark, reptilian centers of my brain require to stay fed and stay put. Sadomasochism? Homoeroticism? I am treated to the spectacle of Ric "The Nature Boy" Flair, astride the corner ropes and his opponent. His fist may be in the air, triumphant, but his groin is in the other guy's face, and he keeps it there. For once the ringside announcers are speechless as we all stare, transfixed, at this clearest of symbolic postures. Consciously I am squirming, but my reptilian center feels the sun on its back.

5   Racism? Ethnocentrism? Am I unsettled about Japanese hegemony? No problem. There is, in the World Wrestling Federation, a tag team of scowling, unnervingly business-oriented Japanese toughs—the Orient Express, managed by Mr. Fuji—who invite me to hate them, and of course I do. Their failure is my success, and I don't even have to leave the living room. Two oversized, red-trunked Boris types used to parade around the ring under a red flag and insist, to our booing, on singing the Russian national anthem before wrestling. Since the Cold War has become passé, however, I've noticed matches pitting Russians *against each other,* and that, as my newspaper tells me, is not passé. I hear groans of delight from below, as this reprise of Cain and Abel croons its libidinal tune.

6   I mean where else can I take my id out for a walk, how else to let it smell the sweaty air, root its nose through the wet leaves? Cartoons? No amount of Wile E. Coyote spring-loaded bounces, no pancakings of Roger Rabbit, none of the whimsical annihilations of Cartoonville can approximate the satisfactions of a real boot in a real belly, a man's head twisted up in the ropes, the merry surfeit of flying drop kicks, suplexes, sleeper holds, and heart punches, all landed somewhere near real bodies. Pro sports? I get more, not less, neurotic rooting for my teams—my neck muscles ache, my stomach burns with coffee, after enduring another four-hour Cleveland Browns loss on TV. The Indians? Don't even get me started. The violence of movies like *The Last Action Hero* and *Cliffhanger?* Needlessly complicated by storyline.

7   No, give it to me straight. Wrestling may be a hybrid genre—the epic poem meets Marvel Comics via the soap opera—but its themes, with their medieval tone, could hardly be simpler: warrior kings doing battle after battle to see who is worthy, women pushed almost to the very edges of the landscape, *Beowulf's* heroic ideal

expressed in the language of an after-school brawl: "I wanna do what I wanna do. You gonna try to stop me?"

8   I also appreciate the pop-culture novelty of pro wrestling, its endearing way of creating, a little smudged and thick-fingered, but with a great earnest smile ("Here, look at this!") new *bêtes noires* for our consumption. One of the newest is something called Big Van Vader, a guy in a total upper torso headgear that looks like Star Wars Meets a Mayan Temple. He carries a stake topped with a skull and can shoot steam out of ventricles on his shoulders, but it looks like all he can do to keep from toppling over. He's horrifying and silly all at once, an atavistic nightdream wearing a "Kick Me" sign.

9   Such low rent Show Biz, this admixture of the asylum and the circus, is central to wrestling's double-tracked pleasure. Its emotional *reductio ad absurdum* taps my anger like a release valve, but its silliness allows me to feel superior to it as I watch. I can be dumb and intelligent, angry and amused, on all fours yet ironically detached, all at the same moment.

10   It's a very satsifying mix, especially since my life between Saturdays is such an exercise in self-control, modesty, and late twentieth-century angst. To my students I am the helpful Mr. Felton. To my chairman I am the responsible Mr. Felton. To virtually everybody and everything else I'm the confused and conflicted Mr. F. My violence amounts to giving people the finger, usually in traffic. When I swear I mutter. To insults I quickly add the disclaimer, "just kidding," a move I learned from watching David Letterman temper his nastiness. I never yell at people, threaten them, twist my heel into their ears, batter their heads into ring posts, or catch them flush with folding chairs. I don't wear robes and crowns and have bosomy women carry them around for me, either. In short, I never reduce my life to the satisfying oversimplification I think it deserves.

11   I'm a wimp. Just the sort of guy Cactus Jack or old Stan himself would love to sink his elbows into, a sentiment with which I couldn't agree more. And that brings us to the deepest appeal of pro wrestling: It invites me to imagine the annihilation of my own civilized self. When Ric Flair jabs his finger into the camera and menaces his next opponent with, "I guarantee you one thing— Junkyard Dog or no Junkyard Dog, you're going to the hospital," when another of the Four Horsemen growls, "I'm gonna take you apart on national television," the real thrill is that they're coming for

me. And when Stan offers me one end of the rope, we both know just whose neck we're pulling on. Ah, redemption.

Organization and Ideas

1. What paragraph or paragraphs make up Felton's introduction? What are the reasons for your choice?
2. Paragraphs 4 and 5 rely heavily on examples. What ideas do Felton's examples illustrate?
3. Comparisons take up much of paragraphs 6 and 10. What are the comparisons? What are Felton's points in using them?
4. Where in the essay does Felton discuss the effect pro wrestling has on him? Felton saves his most important reason till his last paragraph. Putting that reason together with the others in the essay, state Felton's thesis in your own words.
5. If you watch professional wrestling, how accurate do you find Felton's view? If you do not watch it, to what extent does Felton persuade you to give it a try?

Technique and Style

1. Felton uses dashes in paragraphs 1, 3, and 7. After examining those examples, what conclusions can you draw about the proper function of dashes?
2. What impression do you have of Felton's persona? Explain whether it fits his self-description in paragraphs 10 and 11.
3. Both the first and last paragraphs use dialogue. What does it add?
4. Paragraph 3 is riddled with allusions: to Freud's *Civilization and Its Discontents*, to the film *Network*, to a poem by Wordsworth, to the *Bible*. What do these allusions contribute to Felton's persona? To the essay as a whole?
5. Although the essay is written in first person, Felton uses *we* in paragraphs 2 and 11. Who does *we* refer to? What is gained or lost by switching pronouns?

Suggestions for Writing

Journal

1. Which category of readers do you belong to—wrestling fan, wrestling debunker, wrestling innocent, or some other? Evaluate the effectiveness of the essay from your perspective.

2. Felton maintains that pro wrestling appeals to the id, to "the hairy beast itself." What other sports can you think of that appeal to the id? Select one and detail its appeal.

Essay

1. Whether or not you are a fan, there's no arguing with the popularity of watching sports events. Select a sport that you enjoy or one of which you cannot understand the appeal, and use it as the subject for an essay in which you explain or speculate on its popularity. Suggestions:
   football or baseball
   tennis or golf
   racing (cars, horses, dogs)
   roller derby, amazon contests, demolition derby
   motocross
2. Assuming you actively participate in a sport, think about why you do it and how it affects you. Write an essay in which you explain what you discover.

Black Men and Public Space

Brent Staples

Any woman who walks along city streets at night knows the fear Brent Staples speaks of, but in this essay we learn how that fear can also affect the innocent. We see and feel what it is like to be a tall, strong, young black man who enjoys walking at night but innocently terrifies any lone woman. His solution to his night walking problems gives a nice twist to nonviolent resistance.

Brent Staples holds an MA and PhD in psychology from the University of Chicago. A former reporter for the Chicago Sun-Times, *Staples became the assistant metropolitan editor of the* New York Times, *then editor of the* New York Times Book Review, *and now writes on politics and culture for the* New York Times *editorial board. His memoir,* Parallel Time: Growing Up in Black and White, *was published by Pantheon Books in 1994 and has been hailed as one of the best coming-of-age books in recent years. The essay reprinted here was first published in* Harper's Magazine *in 1986. He's still whistling.*

> **What to Look For**   Before you read the essay, look up the dash
> in a handbook of usage so you'll be on the lookout for Staples' use
> of it. He uses it in two different ways, but always appropriately.

1     $\mathbf{M}$y first victim was a woman—white, well-dressed, probably in
her early twenties. I came upon her late one evening on a deserted
street in Hyde Park, a relatively affluent neighborhood in an otherwise mean, impoverished section of Chicago. As I swung onto the
avenue behind her, there seemed to be a discreet, uninflammatory
distance between us. Not so. She cast back a worried glance. To
her, the youngish black man—a broad 6 feet 2 inches with a beard
and billowing hair, both hands shoved into the pockets of a bulky
military jacket—seemed menacingly close. After a few more quick
glimpses, she picked up her pace and was soon running in earnest.
Within seconds she disappeared into a cross street.

2   That was more than a decade ago. I was 22 years old, a graduate
student newly arrived at the University of Chicago. It was in the
echo of that terrified woman's footfalls that I first began to know
the unwieldy inheritance I'd come into—the ability to alter public
space in ugly ways. It was clear that she thought herself the quarry
of a mugger, a rapist, or worse. Suffering a bout of insomnia, however, I was stalking sleep, not defenseless wayfarers. As a softy who
is scarcely able to take a knife to a raw chicken—let alone hold one
to a person's throat—I was surprised, embarrassed, and dismayed
all at once. Her flight made me feel like an accomplice in tyranny. It
also made it clear that I was indistinguishable from the muggers
who occasionally seeped into the area from the surrounding ghetto.
That first encounter, and those that followed, signified that a vast,
unnerving gulf lay between nighttime pedestrians—particularly
women—and me. And I soon gathered that being perceived as dangerous is a hazard in itself. I only needed to turn a corner into a
dicey situation, or crowd some frightened, armed person in a foyer
somewhere, or make an errant move after being pulled over by a
policeman. Where fear and weapons meet—and they often do in
urban America—there is always the possibility of death.

3   In that first year, my first away from my hometown, I was to become thoroughly familiar with the language of fear. At dark, shadowy intersections, I could cross in front of a car stopped at a traffic

light and elicit the *thunk, thunk, thunk, thunk* of the driver—black, white, male, or female—hammering down the door locks. On less traveled streets after dark, I grew accustomed to but never comfortable with people crossing to the other side of the street rather than pass me. Then there were the standard unpleasantries with policemen, doormen, bouncers, cabdrivers, and others whose business it is to screen out troublesome individuals *before* there is any nastiness.

4   I moved to New York nearly two years ago and I have remained an avid night walker. In central Manhattan, the near-constant crowd cover minimizes tense one-on-one street encounters. Elsewhere—in SoHo, for example, where sidewalks are narrow and tightly spaced buildings shut out the sky—things can get very taut indeed.

5   After dark, on the warrenlike streets of Brooklyn where I live, I often see women who fear the worst from me. They seem to have set their faces on neutral, and with their purse straps strung across their chests bandolier-style, they forge ahead as though bracing themselves against being tackled. I understand, of course, that the danger they perceive is not a hallucination. Women are particularly vulnerable to street violence, and young black males are drastically overrepresented among the perpetrators of that violence. Yet these truths are no solace against the kind of alienation that comes of being ever the suspect, a fearsome entity with whom pedestrians avoid making eye contact.

6   It is not altogether clear to me how I reached the ripe old age of 22 without being conscious of the lethality nighttime pedestrians attributed to me. Perhaps it was because in Chester, Pennsylvania, the small, angry industrial town where I came of age in the 1960s, I was scarcely noticeable against a backdrop of gang warfare, street knifings, and murders. I grew up one of the good boys, had perhaps a half-dozen fistfights. In retrospect, my shyness of combat has clear sources.

7   As a boy, I saw countless tough guys locked away; I have since buried several, too. They were babies, really—a teenage cousin, a brother of 22, a childhood friend in his mid-twenties—all gone down in episodes of bravado played out in the streets. I came to doubt the virtues of intimidation early on. I chose, perhaps unconsciously, to remain a shadow—timid, but a survivor.

8   The fearsomeness mistakenly attributed to me in public places often has a perilous flavor. The most frightening of these confusions occurred in the late 1970s and early 1980s, when I worked as

a journalist in Chicago. One day, rushing into the office of a magazine I was writing for with a deadline story in hand, I was mistaken
for a burglar. The office manager called security and, with an ad
hoc posse, pursued me through the labyrinthine halls, nearly to my
editor's door. I had no way of proving who I was. I could only
move briskly toward the company of someone who knew me.

9   Another time I was on assignment for a local paper and killing
time before an interview. I entered a jewelry store on the city's affluent Near North Side. The proprietor excused herself and returned
with an enormous red Doberman pinscher straining at the end of a
leash. She stood, the dog extended toward me, silent to my questions, her eyes bulging nearly out of her head. I took a cursory look
around, nodded, and bade her good night.

10   Relatively speaking, however, I never fared as badly as another
black male journalist. He went to nearby Waukegan, Illinois, a couple of summers ago to work on a story about a murderer who was
born there. Mistaking the reporter for the killer, police officers
hauled him from his car at gunpoint and but for his press credentials would probably have tried to book him. Such episodes are not
uncommon. Black men trade tales like this all the time.

11   Over the years, I learned to smother the rage I felt at so often being taken for a criminal. Not to do so would surely have led to
madness. I now take precautions to make myself less threatening. I
move about with care, particularly late in the evening. I give a wide
berth to nervous people on subway platforms during the wee
hours, particularly when I have exchanged business clothes for
jeans. If I happen to be entering a building behind some people
who appear skittish, I may walk by, letting them clear the lobby before I return, so as not to seem to be following them. I have been
calm and extremely congenial on those rare occasions when I've
been pulled over by the police.

12   And on late-evening constitutionals I employ what has proved to
be an excellent tension-reducing measure: I whistle melodies from
Beethoven and Vivaldi and the more popular classical composers.
Even steely New Yorkers hunching toward nighttime destinations
seem to relax, and occasionally they even join in the tune. Virtually
everybody seems to sense that a mugger wouldn't be warbling
bright, sunny selections from Vivaldi's *Four Seasons*. It is my equivalent of the cowbell that hikers wear when they know they are in
bear country.

Organization and Ideas

1. Reread paragraph 1. What expectations does it evoke in the reader? For paragraph 2, state in your own words what Staples means by "unwieldy inheritance." What effects does that inheritance have?
2. The body of the essay breaks into three paragraph blocks. In paragraphs 3–5, what effects does the author's walking at night have on others? On himself?
3. In paragraphs 6 and 7, Staples refers to his childhood. Why had he been unaware of his effect on others? What effect did the streets he grew up on have on him?
4. Summarize the causes and effects Staples brings out in paragraphs 11 and 12, and in one sentence, make a general statement about them. What does that statement imply about being a black male? About urban life? About American culture? Consider your answers to those questions, and in one sentence state the thesis of the essay.
5. Who are the "victims" in Staples' essay? What are they victims of?

Technique and Style

1. A large part of the essay's impact lies in the ironic contrast between appearance and reality. What details does Staples bring out about himself that contrast with the stereotype of the mugger?
2. In paragraph 1, Staples illustrates the two uses of the dash. What function do they perform? Rewrite either of the two sentences so that you avoid the dash. Which sentence is better and why?
3. Trace Staples' use of time. Why does he start where he does? Try placing the time period mentioned in paragraphs 6 and 7 elsewhere in the essay. What advantages does their present placement have? What is the effect of ending the essay in the present?
4. Examine Staples' choice of verbs in the second sentence of paragraph 5. Rewrite the sentence using as many forms of the verb *to be* as possible. What differences do you note?
5. Staples concludes the essay with an analogy. In what ways is it ironic? How does the irony tie into the essay's thesis?

Suggestions for Writing

Journal

1. To what extent do you identify with the women in the essay? With Staples? With both? Explain.
2. Think about a time when, intentionally or unintentionally, you threatened or intimidated someone. Describe either the causes or effects.

Essay

1. You can develop either of the journal ideas above into a full-fledged essay. Or, if you prefer, think about a situation in which you have been stereotyped and that stereotype determined your effect on others. Among the physical characteristics that can spawn a stereotype are

   age
   race
   gender
   physique
   clothing

2. All of us have been in a situation in which we felt threatened. Select an incident that occurred to you and describe its effect on you.

When Here Sees There

George Packer

George Packer grew up in California, graduated from Yale, served with the Peace Corps in Togo, West Africa, returned to the United States, and between work on construction jobs and in shelters for the homeless, began his career as a writer. His first book, The Village of Waiting *(1988), focuses on his time in Africa and was followed by two novels:* The Half Man *(1991), set in Asia, and* Central Square *(1998), set in Cambridge, Massachusetts. Preferring to write nonfiction, he has been published by* Harper's, Double Take, Dissent, Salon, *and the* New York Times, *and his essays are included in the* 1997 *Pushcart Prize collection as well as the* Art of the Essay. *His* Blood of the Liberals *(2000) focuses on the "power of bloodlines and the lifeblood of politics" (Publisher's Weekly) as reflected in his family's history. Packer has taught at Harvard, Bennington, and Sarah Lawrence. His essay on the effects of the global media appeared in the* New York Times Magazine *on April 21, 2002.*

> **What to Look For**   Causes and effects can easily be abstract and soulless unless examples bring them to life. As you read Packer's essay, be on the lookout for how he uses examples and what they contribute.

1   An Arab intellectual named Abdel Monem Said recently surveyed the massive anti-Israel and anti-American protests by Egyptian students and said: "They are galvanized by the images that they see on television. They want to be like the rock-throwers." By now everyone knows that satellite TV has helped deepen divisions in the Middle East. But it's worth remembering that it wasn't supposed to be this way.

2   The globalization of the media was supposed to knit the world together. The more information we receive about one another, the thinking went, the more international understanding will prevail. An injustice in Thailand will be instantly known and ultimately remedied by people in London or San Francisco. The father of worldwide television, Ted Turner, once said, "My main concern is to be a benefit to the world, to build up a global communications system that helps humanity come together." These days we are living with the results—a young man in Somalia watches the attack on the south tower live, while Americans can hear more, and sooner, about Kandahar or Ramallah than the county next to theirs.

3   But this technological togetherness has not created the human bonds that were promised. In some ways, global satellite TV and Internet access have actually made the world a less understanding, less tolerant place. What the media provide is superficial familiarity—images without context, indignation without remedy. The problem isn't just the content of the media, but the fact that while images become international, people's lives remain parochial—in the Arab world and everywhere else, including here.

4   "I think what's best about my country is not exportable," says Frank Holliwell, the American anthropologist in *A Flag for Sunrise*, Robert Stone's 1981 novel about Central America. The line kept playing in my mind recently as I traveled through Africa and watched, on television screens from Butare, Rwanda, to Burao, Somalia, CNN's coverage of the war on terrorism, which was shown like a mini-series, complete with the ominous score. Three months after the World Trade Center attacks, I found myself sitting in a hotel lobby by Lake Victoria watching Larry King preside over a special commemoration with a montage of grief-stricken American faces and flags while Melissa Etheridge sang "Heal Me." Back home, I would have had the requisite tears in my eyes. But I was in Africa, and I wanted us to stop talking about ourselves in front of strangers.

Worse, the Ugandans watching with me seemed to expect to hear nothing else. Like a dinner guest who realizes he has been the subject of all the talk, I wanted to turn to one of them: "But enough about me—anything momentous happening to you?" In CNN's global village, everyone has to overhear one family's conversation.

5   What America exports to poor countries through the ubiquitous media—pictures of glittering abundance and national self-absorption—enrages those whom it doesn't depress. In Sierra Leone, a teenage rebel in a disarmament camp tried to explain to me why he had joined one of the modern world's most brutal insurgencies: "I see on television you have motorbikes, cars. I see some of your children on TV this high"—he held his hand up to his waist—"they have bikes for themselves, but we in Sierra Leone have nothing." Unable to possess what he saw in images beamed from halfway around the world, the teenager picked up an automatic rifle and turned his anger on his countrymen. On generator-powered VCR's in rebel jungle camps, the fantasies of such boy fighters were stoked with Rambo movies. To most of the world, America looks like a cross between a heavily armed action hero and a Lexus ad.

6   Meanwhile, in this country the aperture for news from elsewhere has widened considerably since Sept. 11. And how does the world look to Americans? Like a nonstop series of human outrages: Just as what's best about America can't be exported, our imports in the global-image trade hardly represent the best from other countries either. Of course, the world *is* a nonstop series of human outrages, and you can argue that it's a good thing for Americans, with all our power, to know. But what interests me is the psychological effect of knowing. One day, you read that 600 Nigerians have been killed in a munitions explosion at an army barracks. The next day, you read that the number has risen to a thousand. The next day, you read nothing. The story has disappeared—except something remains, a thousand dead Nigerians are lodged in some dim region of the mind, where they exact a toll. You've been exposed to one corner of human misery, but you've done nothing about it. Nor will you. You feel—perhaps without being conscious of it—an impotent guilt, and your helplessness makes you irritated and resentful, almost as if it's the fault of those thousand Nigerians for becoming your burden. We carry around the mental residue of millions of suffering human beings for whom we've done nothing.

7   It is possible, of course, for media attention to galvanize action. Because of a newspaper photo, ordinary citizens send checks or pick up rocks. On the whole, knowing is better than not knowing; in any case, there's no going back. But at this halfway point between mutual ignorance and true understanding, the "global village" actually resembles a real one—in my experience, not the utopian community promised by the boosters of globalization but a parochial place of manifold suspicions, rumors, resentments and half-truths. If the world seems to be growing more, rather than less, nasty these days, it might have something to do with the images all of us now carry around in our heads.

Organization and Ideas

1. The introduction, paragraphs 1 and 2, sets out the present effect of global television coverage versus the expected effect. What are those effects?

2. Sum up the unintended effects of satellite television. How accurate is Packer's explanation of "superficial familiarity" (paragraph 3)?

3. What support does Packer provide for his assertion that "To most of the world, America looks like a cross between a heavily armed action hero and a Lexus ad" (paragraph 5). Is his assertion valid?

4. In paragraph 6, Packer reverses the perspective, with America viewing the news of the world. What is the effect of that news?

5. To what extent is Packer's essay optimistic, pessimistic, or some combination of the two?

Technique and Style

1. What do you learn about Packer's travels? What does that add to his persona?

2. Take another look at the title. How effective is it?

3. Reread the essay noting Packer's use of "global village." What are the term's positive associations? Negative ones?

4. Packer switches from an objective point of view to first person, back to objective, and then to "you" in paragraph 6. What reasons can you think of for those changes?

5. The concluding paragraph begins with the positive effects of the global media and then ends with the negative. How successful is the last paragraph?

Suggestions for Writing

Journal

1. To what extent are you affected by world events? How do they affect you?
2. How do you learn about what is going on in the world? To what extent do you trust your sources and why?

Essay

1. Most of us would agree that the media emphasizes violence, but how that affects us is open to debate. Some of that violence is intended, such as what is involved in crimes and depicted in books, films, and other examples from the popular culture. Some, however, is accidental, as in automobile accidents. Think about violence and the role it plays in our society. Perhaps you wish to speculate on what causes it or on its effects. If you have witnessed it in person, you could write about its effect on you, though you may find that topic too personal; in which case, you can always turn to the media and the electronic world around you to find a topic. Suggestions:
   film
   books
   television
   video games
   the Internet
2. An unintended effect of the "globalization of the media" and the spread of the World Wide Web is the rise of conspiracy theories. Think of several significant events—such as a terrorist attack or an assassination—and then choose one so that you can research the known facts and use the Web to explore the various theories attached to it. The result will be an essay in which you speculate about the causes of the theories.

ADDITIONAL WRITING ASSIGNMENTS

Using Cause and Effect

1. Consider the causes of a problem that can arise in a familiar setting and its solution, a problem that might occur at work, school, home, a sports event, between friends, within a marriage.
2. Analyze why you like what you like, your taste in hangouts, classes, teams, celebrities, food, films.
3. Predict the future by analyzing why *x* is going to win a political race, crucial game, championship, stardom, prize, contest.
4. Use your library or the Internet to research the causes of a particular disease, accident, chemical reaction, environmental problem, safety measure.

Evaluating the Essays

1. Both Bjorn Skogquist and Brent Staples deal with how each affects others, depending upon narration and example to support their theses. Of the two, which do you more closely identify with and why? The answer will be your thesis for an essay built around effect.
2. Oliver Sacks explains the healing power of music, while George Packer examines the destructive power of global media coverage. Compare the two essays to determine which does a better job of explaining effects. Use evidence from both essays to make your point.
3. The idea of identification runs through the essays by George Felton and George Packer, though both writers treat it differently. Felton's interest is personal; pro wrestling provides a way for him "to take my id out for a walk" (p. 256). Packer's interest is general; he observes how people identify with "Rambos" and envy the products of a consumer culture. Felton's identification is harmless; the one Packer examines can be lethal. Which do you find the more interesting and why?
4. The essays in this chapter take up widely differing topics—the effects of music, teasing, the media, pro wrestling, of being young, black and strong—yet all depend upon example, narration, and description to investigate and explain their subjects. Of the five, who faces the most difficult topic? How well does the writer deal with it? Use examples from the other essays for comparison.

On Using Argument

Up to this point, this book has focused on patterns of organization that can be used singly and in combination for various aims—to express how you feel, to explain, and, to a lesser extent, to argue. Those modes or patterns are the means to an end, ways to achieve your goal of self-expression, exposition, or argument. This chapter directly addresses the goal of argument, but because book after book has been written on the art of argument, think of what you have here as a basic introduction. In this chapter you will discover how to construct a short argumentative essay and how the various modes are used to support that aim. It's only appropriate, therefore, that the discussion start with a definition.

In everyday speech, **argument** is so closely associated with *quarrel* or *fight* that it has a negative connotation, but that connotation does not apply to essays. If you were to analyze an essay by examining its argument, you would be looking at the writer's major assertion and the weight of the evidence on which it rests. That evidence should be compelling, because the ideal is for the reader to adopt the writer's view. In writing argumentative papers, you might want to go further than that and call for a particular action, but most of the time you'll probably work at convincing your reader at least to keep reading and at best share your position. Many of the subjects of argumentative essays are ones your readers already have an opinion about, so if all you accomplish is having someone who disagrees with you keep on reading, you have constructed a successful argument.

Because an argumentative essay bases its thesis primarily on reason, the word *logic* may pop into your mind and raise images of mathematical models and seemingly tricky statements stringing together sentences beginning with *if*s and leading to one starting with *therefore*. Don't worry. The kind of argumentative essays you will be asked to write extends the kinds of essays you've written all along: your thesis is the heart of your argument, and examples, definitions, descriptions and the like provide supporting evidence.

It's useful to distinguish between self-expression and argument. Open your local newspaper to the editorial pages, and you'll probably find examples of both. If you found a letter to the editor that rants about the financial "sins" of the Democratic party and describes the "sinners" as "dishonest, lying, cheats," it's unlikely a Democrat will finish it. The writer was letting off steam rather than trying to argue a point, steam based on emotion, not reason. But an editorial on the same page on the same general subject will use reason. Such an editorial may well state that although the media's focus highlights abuses within the Democratic party, the Republicans are not altogether innocent. Both Democrats and Republicans are apt to read the editorial all the way through, and many from both parties may come to agree with the editor's thesis.

If you brainstorm the subject as a whole, not just your position on it, you can avoid relying on emotion instead of reason. Phrase the subject as a question, and then list the pros and cons.

If you are writing on gambling, for instance, you would ask, "Should gambling be legalized?" Then you would define your terms: Who would be legalizing it—the federal government, the state, the county, the city? What kind of gambling is involved—betting on horse races, on sports? Playing games such as bingo, video poker, slot machines, roulette? Buying tickets for a lottery? Answering those kinds of questions will help you to draw up your pros and cons more easily because your focus will be more specific. Once you've listed the arguments that can be used, you can then sort through them, noting evidence you can cite and where to find it. Having done all that, you then are in a position to choose which side you wish to take, and you know the arguments that can be used against you.

Reason is the backbone of argumentative writing, and to use it successfully, you will probably need to research your subject. Once your argument begins to take shape, however, you will find that dealing with one or two of the opposing views will not only strengthen your own case but will also earn you some points for fairness.

Argumentative writing ranges from the personal to the abstract and draws on the various patterns that can be used to structure an essay. For instance, waiting tables in a restaurant may have convinced you that tips should be automatically included in the bill. To make the case that the present system is unfair to those in a service trade, you might draw primarily on your own experience and that of others, though you need to make sure that your experience is representative. If you don't, your reader may discount your argument, thinking that one example isn't sufficient evidence. A quick check among others who are similarly employed or a look at government reports on employment statistics should show that your example is typical and, therefore, to be trusted.

The technical term for an entire argument based on only one example is **hasty generalization,** one of many logical fallacies that can occur in argumentative writing. **Logical fallacies** are holes or lapses in reasoning and, therefore, to be avoided. If you were to argue that the reader should consider only the present system of tipping or the one you propose, you will be guilty of **either-or reasoning,** which is false because it permits no middle ground such as requiring a minimum tip of 10 percent. Quote Michael Jordan on the subject and you will be citing **false authority;** he knows basketball but not the restaurant industry. And obviously, if you call a 10-percent tipper a cheap idiot, you will be accused quite rightly of name-calling, the **ad hominem** (to the person) fallacy.

Say you noticed one evening that as closing time loomed, your tips got smaller. Is that because people who dine late tip minimally or because your customers felt rushed or because someone miscalculated the tip or some unknown reason? If you conclude that people who dine late are poor tippers, you may well be mistaking a temporal relationship for a causal one. Two events may occur at times close to each other (small tip, late hour) without implying a valid cause-and-effect relationship. To confuse the two is called **post hoc reasoning.**

Often the best topic for an argumentative essay is the one you come up with on your own, but at times you may be assigned a topic. If so, your chances for success increase if you shape the topic so that you can connect to it. Because you already know something about the subject, you have done some thinking about it instead of starting from scratch or using secondhand opinions. Even abstract topics such as euthanasia can be made concrete and will probably be the better for it.

You may know little about mercy killing, but you probably have had a member of your family who was terminally ill. Would euthanasia have been an appropriate alternative? Should it have been? In addition to using your own experience, consider using your local newspaper as a resource. Newspaper accounts and editorials can also help give form and focus to an abstract issue, as can book and periodical sources, and of course there's the Internet. The Web provides instant access to a huge and unfiltered amount of information, but always check out who or what is behind the information. Anyone can put anything on the Web. And does.

Audience and Purpose

Audience plays a greater role in argument than in any other type of writing, and therein lies a problem: you must adapt both form and content to fit your audience, while at the same time maintaining your integrity. If you shape your argumentative position according to its probable acceptance by your readers rather than your own belief, the result is propaganda or sensationalism, not argument. Knowingly playing false with an audience by omitting evidence or shaping facts to fit an assertion or by resorting to logical fallacies are all dishonest tricks.

Imagine, for example, that you are on the staff of your campus newspaper and have been given the assignment of investigating the rumors that the Dean of the College of Business is going to resign. You know that the dean has been fighting with the president of your university, arguing that the College of Business is "grossly underfunded," a phrase you found in an earlier story on university finances. But you also read an interview with the dean and know that she has close ties to the local business community and may be offered a job heading a local company. Add to that your suspicion that not many colleges of business have deans who are women, a suspicion borne out by statistics you can quote, and you begin to scent a story. If you choose to write one that plays up the conflict with the president and implies sexism while ignoring the possibility of the dean's being hired away from the university, you are not being true to your evidence and are, therefore, misleading your readers.

Within honest bounds, however, you have much to draw on, and a sense of what your audience may or may not know and of what the audience believes about a topic can guide you. Even if your topic is familiar, what you have to say about it will be new information. Censorship is a tired subject, but if you were to write on the banning of a particular book from a particular public school library, you would probably give the topic a new twist or two. A concrete example, often in the form of a short introductory narrative, makes an abstract issue more accessible and is apt to keep your reader reading.

If your subject is one many readers know little about, then you can begin by explaining the issue and its context. If your classmates are your readers, for example, they will know little about your personal life. And if you have an aunt whose health insurance was cancelled after her cancer returned, the action may compel you to research an insurance company's right to drop those it insures. Put your indignation together with what you discovered through your research and what your classmates don't know, and you have all the makings of a successful argumentative paper protesting what you see as an injustice.

Whether you start with what your audience does or does not know or with a narrative that illustrates the general situation and makes it concrete, your aim is to try to convince your readers to adopt your convictions, perhaps even to act on them.

Appealing to Reason, Emotion, and Persona

The appeal of **reason,** what the ancient Greeks called *logos,* is crucial. To present a logical pattern of thought, you will probably find yourself drawing on one or more modes, particularly definition, comparison, and cause and effect. If, for instance, you have a part-time job at a fast-food franchise, you may have noticed that most of the other employees are also part-time. The situation may strike you as exploitive, and you want to write about it.

You might start sketching out a first draft with the example of your job, then define what part-time means, using cause and effect to argue that franchise companies that depend primarily on part-time labor exploit their workers to create greater profits for the company. As you work, you will find that you are laying out a line of reasoning, the assertions—probably the topic sentences for paragraphs or paragraph clusters—that support your thesis. You will also have to do some research so that you place your example in a larger context, showing that it is clearly typical. Then, armed with some facts and figures, you can test your thesis and supporting sentences:

1. Am I making an assertion? Test the sentence by checking to see if it states an opinion.

    If yes, go to question 2.

    If no, review pp. 3–4 and revise the sentence.

2. Is the assertion supported by evidence? List the evidence and sources.

    If yes, go to question 3.

    If no, research the topic to gather more evidence.

3. Is the evidence sufficient? Check it to make sure it's directly re-lated to the assertion.

> If yes, the assertion checks out.
>
> If no, gather more evidence.

If your thesis and supporting sentences check out, then you know your argument rests on reason.

Logical thinking must undergird all argumentative essays, even those that use an **emotional** appeal, or *pathos*, an appeal that often rests on example, description, and narration. In the example of the essay about health insurers, you would be using an emotional appeal if you began your essay with a brief narrative of your aunt's battle with cancer and the crisis caused by her loss of health insurance. And although the bulk of the essay would be taken up with the essay's appeal to reason, you might choose to close with an emotional appeal, perhaps reminding your readers of the number of people who cannot afford any kind of medical insurance and calling for a general reform of health care.

But the emotional appeal has its dangers, particularly when you are close to the subject. You would not want your description of your aunt's problems to slide into the melodramatic, nor would you want to create so powerful an impression that anything that comes after, which is the heart of your argument, is anticlimactic. Emotional appeals are often best left to snagging the reader's attention or calling for action—rela-tively small roles—than serving a primary function in the essay. Emotion will have an impact; reason will carry the argument.

The ethical appeal or *ethos;* rests on a credible **persona** and is more subtle than the others; the writer is not appealing directly to the reader's emotions or intellect but instead is using his or her persona to lend cre-dence to the essay's major assertion. The point gets tricky. A fair and honest writer is one who is fair and honest with the reader. Such a writer takes on a persona, not like donning a mask to hide behind but like selecting a picture to show those elements in the personality that represent the writer at his or her best.

To understand how persona functions, think of the last time you took an essay test. What you were writing was a mini-argument maintaining that your answer to the question is a correct one. Your persona, which you probably didn't even think about, was intended to create a sense of authority, the idea that you knew what you were writing about. You are so used to writing within an academic context, that the elements of your persona come naturally. The tone you use for essay tests is more formal than informal, which means that your choice of words, your diction, is more elevated than conversational. And if a technical vocabulary is appropriate—the vocabulary of physics, sociology, the arts, and the like—you use it. Successful essay answers also use evidence and are tightly organized so that the line of thought is clear and compelling, all of which comes under the appeal of reason, but don't underestimate the appeal of persona. If two test answers contain the exact same information, the one that is written in the more sophisticated style that implies a more thoughtful response is apt to receive the higher grade.

Logical Fallacies

Logical fallacies abuse the various appeals. The introduction to this chapter has already pointed out the more obvious ones—hasty generalization, false authority, name-calling, post hoc and either-or reasoning—but there are many others as well. Advertising and political campaigns are often crammed with them.

If you receive a flyer asking you to vote for a candidate for the school board because he is a Vietnam veteran who has a successful law practice, the logic doesn't follow, a literal translation of the Latin term **non sequitur:** the claim leaves you wondering what being a veteran and an attorney have to do with the duties of a member of the school board. And if the flyer goes on to maintain that because the candidate has three children he can understand the problems of students in the public schools when you know that his three children go to private schools, then you've spotted a **false analogy,** a double one—public and private schools are quite different, and three children from the family of a professional are not representative of the public school student population.

Such a flyer is also guilty of **begging the question,** another fallacy. The main question for a school board election is "Can this person make a positive contribution?" Being a Vietnam veteran and the father of three children doesn't answer that question. A **shift in definition** is another form of begging the question. If this hypothetical candidate also claims to be a "good citizen" and then goes on to define that term by example, citing service to his country and fatherhood as proof, then as a voter, you're left with a very narrow definition. Good citizenship involves much more.

Often when you read or hear about the holes in an argument, you may also hear the term **straw man.** With this technique (yet another form of begging the question), your attention is drawn away from the main point, and instead the argument focuses on a minor point with the hope that by demolishing it, the main one will also suffer. Imagine that there's a move to increase local taxes, and you want to argue against it in a letter to the local paper. As you consider the points you can make, you come up with a short list: that the taxes are already high, that existing funds are not being spent wisely, and that all that the taxes support—schools, roads, government and the like—while not outstanding are adequate. You start to gather information to use as evidence for each of these points (probably discovering several more) and run across a news story about a large amount of local taxpayers' money having been spent on rebuilding a bridge on a back road that averaged all of three cars a day. If you were to stop there and construct a thesis arguing taxes should not be raised because of waste in government, then making your case by basing it on the example of the building of the bridge, you would be constructing a straw man argument, one that avoids the major issues.

Organization and Ideas

The thesis of an argumentative essay should be readily identifiable: it is the conviction that you want an audience to adopt. Sometimes the thesis may be stated in the title, but more often you will state your position early on, then back it up with evidence in the body of your essay. If you organize your ideas by moving from the general (the thesis) to the particular (the evidence), you are using **deductive reasoning.** Most of the argumentative essays you run across will be using this kind of logical organization. As for the order in which you choose to present the evidence on which your thesis rests, you'll probably arrange it from the least important to the most important so that the essay has some dramatic tension. Putting the most important first doesn't leave you anywhere to go, rather like knowing from the start that the butler did it.

Although some times you may want to put your thesis as your first sentence, usually you will want to lead up to it, *introduce* it in the literal sense. Starting right off with the thesis will probably strike the reader as too abrupt, too sudden, a bit like being hit over the head. Often an argumentative essay will begin with a narrative or some explanation, ways of setting the scene so that when the thesis appears, it seems natural. As for the ending, you may want to return to the same narrative or information you started with or call for action or point out what may happen unless your view is adopted. Remember, by the time your reader finishes reading what you have to say, if all you have done is make the person reconsider ideas and rethink the argument, you will have succeeded. It's rare, though not impossible, for one essay to change a person's mind.

Now and then, you'll find yourself reading an argument that is organized by moving from the particular to the general, from evidence to thesis. What you have then is called **inductive reasoning,** and it's usually more difficult to write because it demands tight focus and control. Think of the essay's organization as a jigsaw puzzle. Your reader has to recognize each piece as a piece, and you have to build the evidence so that each piece falls into a predetermined place. The completed picture is the thesis.

If you want to construct an essay using inductive reasoning, you may find it easier to do if in your first draft you state your thesis at the beginning, baldly, just so you stay on track. Then, when you've shaped the rest of the paper, you simply move the thesis from the beginning to the last paragraph, perhaps even the last sentence.

You'll find that the essays in this section represent both kinds of organization, so you'll have a chance to see how others have developed their ideas to argue a particular point.

Useful Terms

Ad hominem argument Name-calling, smearing the person instead of attacking the argument. A type of logical fallacy. Smearing the group the person belongs to instead of attacking the argument is called an *ad populum* logical fallacy.

Appeal to emotion Playing or appealing to the reader's emotions.

Appeal to persona The appeal of the writer's moral character that creates the impression that the writer can be trusted and, therefore, believed.

Appeal to reason Presenting evidence that is logical, well thought out, so as to be believed.

Argument The writer's major assertion and the evidence on which it is based.

Begging the question Arguing off the point, changing direction. A type of logical fallacy.

Deductive reasoning Reasoning that moves from the general to the particular, from the thesis to the evidence.

Either-or reasoning Staking out two extremes as the only alternatives and, therefore, excluding anything in between. A type of logical fallacy.

False analogy An analogy that does not stand up to logic. A type of logical fallacy.

False authority Citing an expert on one subject as an expert on another. A type of logical fallacy.

Hasty generalization Reasoning based on insufficient evidence, usually too few examples. A type of logical fallacy.

Inductive reasoning Reasoning that moves from the particular to the general, from the evidence to the thesis.

Logical fallacy An error in reasoning, a logical flaw that invalidates the argument.

Non sequitur Literally, it does not follow. No apparent link between points. A type of logical fallacy.

Persona The character of the writer that comes through from the prose.

Post hoc reasoning Assuming a causal relationship where a temporal one exists. A type of logical fallacy.

Shifting definition Changing the definition of a key term, a form of begging the question. A type of logical fallacy.

Straw man Attacking and destroying an irrelevant point instead of the main subject.

POINTERS FOR USING ARGUMENT

Exploring the Topic

1. **What position do you want to take toward your subject?** Are you arguing to get your audience to adopt your thesis or to go further and take action? What is your thesis? What action is possible?

2. **How is your audience apt to respond to your assertion if you state it baldly?** How much background do you need to provide? Do you need to use definition? What arguments can the reader bring against your assertion?

(Continued)

3. **What examples can you think of to illustrate your topic?** Are all of them from your own experience? What other sources can you draw upon?
4. **How can you appeal to your readers' emotions?** How can you use example, description, and narration to carry your emotional appeal?
5. **How can you appeal to your readers' reason?** How can you use example, cause and effect, process, comparison and contrast, analogy, or division and classification to strengthen your logic?
6. **What tone is most appropriate to the kind of appeal you want to emphasize?** Does your persona fit that tone? How can you use persona to support your argument?

Drafting the Paper

1. **Know your reader.** Estimate how familiar your reader is with your topic and how, if at all, the reader may react to it emotionally. Keeping those ideas in mind, review how the various patterns of development may help you contend with your audience's knowledge and attitudes, and decide whether your primary appeal should be to emotion or reason.

   Description, narration, and example lend themselves particularly well to emotional appeal; process, cause and effect, comparison and contrast, analogy, example, and division and classification are useful for rational appeal. Use definition to set the boundaries of your argument and its terms as well as to clear up anything the reader may not know.

2. **Know your purpose.** Depending on the predominant appeal you find most appropriate, your essay will tend toward persuasion or argument; you are trying to get your reader not only to understand your major assertion but also to adopt it and perhaps even to act on it. Short of that, a successful writer of argument must settle for the reader's "Well, I hadn't thought of it that way" or "Maybe I should reconsider."

   The greatest danger in argumentative writing is to write to people like yourself, ones who already agree with you. You need not think of your audience as actively hostile, but to stay on the argumentative track, it helps to reread constantly as you write, playing the devil's advocate.

3. Acknowledge the opposition. Even though your reader may be the ideal—someone who holds no definite opposing view and indeed is favorably inclined toward yours but hasn't really thought the topic through—you should bring out one or two of the strongest arguments against your position and demolish them. If you don't, the reader may, and there goes your essay. The ideal reader is also the thinking reader who says, "Yes, but. . . . "

4. Avoid logical pitfalls. Logical fallacies can crop up in unexpected places; one useful way to test them is to check your patterns of development. If you have used examples, does your generalization or assertion follow? Sometimes the examples are too few to support the assertion, leading to a hasty generalization; sometimes the examples don't fit, leading to begging the question or arguing off the point or misusing authority; and sometimes the assertion is stated as an absolute, in which case the reader may think of an example that is the exception, destroying your point.

If you have used analogy, double-check to see that the analogy can stand up to scrutiny by examining the pertinent aspects of the things compared. If you have used cause and effect, you need to be particularly careful. Check to see that the events you claim to have a causal relationship do not have a temporal one instead; otherwise, you fall into the post hoc fallacy. Also examine causal relationships to make sure that you have not merely assumed the cause in your statement of effect. If you claim that "poor teaching is a major cause of the high dropout rate during the freshman year in college," you must prove that the teaching is poor; if you don't, you are arguing in a circle or begging the question.

Non sequiturs can also obscure cause-and-effect relationships when an element in the relationship is missing or nonexistent. Definition also sets some traps. Make sure your definition is not only fully stated but also commonly shared and consistent throughout.

5. Be aware of your persona. The ethical appeal, the rational appeal, and the emotional appeal are fundamental concepts of argument, and it is the persona, together with tone, that provides the ethical appeal. To put it simply, you need to be credible.

(Continued)

If you are writing on an issue you feel strongly about and, for example, are depending primarily on an appeal to reason, you don't want to let your dispassionate, logical persona slip and resort to name-calling (formally known as arguing ad hominem or ad populem). That's obvious.

Not so obvious, however, is some slip in diction or tone that reveals the hot head behind the cool pen. Your reader may feel manipulated or use the slip to discount your entire argument, all because you lost sight of the ethical appeal. Tone should vary, yes, but never to the point of discord.

6. **Place your point where it does the most good.** Put each of your paragraphs on a separate piece of paper so that you can rearrange their order as you would a hand of cards. Try out your major assertion in different slots. If you have it at the beginning, try it at the end and vice versa. Or extend the introduction so that the thesis comes closer to the middle of the paper. See which placement carries greater impact.

You may want to organize your material starting with examples that lead up to the position you wish to attack and to the conviction you are arguing for; in that case your thesis may occur somewhere in the middle third or at the end of the paper. On the other hand, you may want to use deduction—starting with the opposition, stating your position, and then spending 90 percent of the remaining essay supporting your case. Remember that you want to win your reader over, so put your thesis where it will do the greatest good.

Last Rites for Indian Dead

Suzan Shown Harjo

Suzan Shown Harjo is a columnist for Indian Country Today, *the foremost Native American newspaper, but, as her biography on the paper's Web site states, she is also "poet, writer, lecturer, curator and policy advocate." President and Executive Director of the Morning Star Institute, a national Indian organization dedicated to promoting their rights, cultures, traditions, and arts, Harjo was the first Native American to be honored by the Stanford University Haas Center for Public Policy. The essay that follows typifies her activism and her effectiveness. Writing as a Cheyenne, Suzan Shown Harjo points to a problem that affects Native Americans and, she argues, that raises an ethical issue for the rest of us. Her essay, which appeared on the editorial page of the* Los Angeles Times *in September of 1989, is a good example of deductive reasoning. And her argument was effective: Congress passed the Native American Graves Protection and Repatriation Act in 1990.*

What to Look For   Conclusions are often difficult to write, but one way of ending an argumentative essay is to call for a specified action. That is what Harjo does for her essay, and it's a technique you can adapt for your own arguments.

1   What if museums, universities, and government agencies could put your dead relatives on display or keep them in boxes to be cut up and otherwise studied? What if you believed that the spirits of the dead could not rest until their human remains were placed in a sacred area?

2   The ordinary American would say there ought to be a law—and there is, for ordinary Americans. The problem for American Indians is that there are too many laws of the kind that make us the archaeological property of the United States and too few of the kind that protect us from such insults.

3   Some of my own Cheyenne relatives' skulls are in the Smithsonian Institution today, along with those of at least 4500

other Indian people who were violated in the 1800s by the U.S. Army for an "Indian Cranial Study." It wasn't enough that these unarmed Cheyenne people were mowed down by the cavalry at the infamous Sand Creek massacre; many were decapitated and their heads shipped to Washington as freight. (The Army Medical Museum's collection is now in the Smithsonian.) Some had been exhumed only hours after being buried. Imagine their grieving families' reaction on finding their loved ones disinterred and headless.

4   Some targets of the Army's study were killed in noncombat situations and beheaded immediately. The officer's account of the decapitation of the Apache chief Mangas Coloradas in 1863 shows the pseudoscientific nature of the exercise. "I weighed the brain and measured the skull," the good doctor wrote, "and found that while the skull was smaller, the brain was larger than that of Daniel Webster."

5   These journal accounts exist in excruciating detail, yet missing are any records of overall comparisons, conclusions or final reports of the Army study. Since it is unlike the Army not to leave a paper trail, one must wonder about the motive for its collection.

6   The total Indian body count in the Smithsonian collection is more than 19,000, and it is not the largest in the country. It is not inconceivable that the 1.5 million of us living today are outnumbered by our dead stored in museums, educational institutions, federal agencies, state historical societies and private collections. The Indian people are further dehumanized by being exhibited alongside the mastodons and dinosaurs and other extinct creatures.

7   Where we have buried our dead in peace, more often than not the sites have been desecrated. For more than 200 years, relic hunting has been a popular pursuit. Lately, the market in Indian artifacts has brought this abhorrent activity to a fever pitch in some areas. And when scavengers come upon Indian burial sites, everything found becomes fair game, including sacred burial offerings, teeth and skeletal remains.

8   One unusually well-publicized example of Indian grave desecration occurred two years ago in a western Kentucky field known as Slack Farm, the site of an Indian village five centuries ago. Ten men—one with a business card stating "Have Shovel, Will Travel"—paid the landowner $10,000 to lease digging rights between planting seasons. They dug extensively on the 40-acre farm, rummaging

through an estimated 650 graves, collecting burial goods, tools and ceremonial items. Skeletons were strewn about like litter.

9   What motivates people to do something like this? Financial gain is the first answer. Indian relic-collecting has become a multi-million-dollar industry. The price tag on a bead necklace can easily top $1000; rare pieces fetch tens of thousands.

10   And it is not just collectors of the macabre who pay for skeletal remains. Scientists say that these deceased Indians are needed for research that someday could benefit the health and welfare of living Indians. But just how many dead Indians must they examine? Nineteen thousand?

11   There is doubt as to whether permanent curation of our dead really benefits Indians. Dr. Emery A. Johnson, former assistant surgeon general, recently observed, "I am not aware of any current medical diagnostic or treatment procedure that has been derived from research on such skeletal remains. Nor am I aware of any during the 34 years that I have been involved in American Indian . . . health care."

12   Indian remains are still being collected for racial biological studies. While the intentions may be honorable, the ethics of using human remains this way without the full consent of relatives must be questioned.

13   Some relief for Indian people has come on the state level. Almost half of the states, including California, have passed laws protecting Indian burial sites and restricting the sale of Indian bones, burial offerings and other sacred items. Representative Charles E. Bennett (D-Fla.) and Sen. John McCain (R-Ariz.) have introduced bills that are a good start in invoking the federal government's protection. However, no legislation has attacked the problem head-on by imposing stiff penalties at the marketplace, or by changing laws that make dead Indians the nation's property.

14   Some universities—notably Stanford, Nebraska, Minnesota and Seattle—have returned, or agreed to return, Indian human remains; it is fitting that institutions of higher education should lead the way.

15   Congress is now deciding what to do with the government's extensive collection of Indian human remains and associated funerary objects. The secretary of the Smithsonian, Robert McC. Adams, has been valiantly attempting to apply modern ethics to yesterday's excesses. This week, he announced that the Smithsonian would conduct an inventory and return all Indian skeletal remains that could be identified with specific tribes or living kin.

16   But there remains a reluctance generally among collectors of Indian remains to take action of a scope that would have a quantitative impact and a healing quality. If they will not act on their own—and it is highly unlikely that they will—then Congress must act.

17   The country must recognize that the bodies of dead American Indian people are not artifacts to be bought and sold as collectors' items. It is not appropriate to store tens of thousands of our ancestors for possible future research. They are our family. They deserve to be returned to their sacred burial grounds and given a chance to rest.

18   The plunder of our people's graves has gone on too long. Let us rebury our dead and remove this shameful past from America's future.

Organization and Ideas

1. Paragraphs 1 and 2 introduce the essay by presenting a "what if" situation. Why might Harjo have chosen this kind of opening?
2. Paragraphs 9–12 explain why people dig up Indian burial sites. What reasons does Harjo give?
3. Harjo explains what is being done and what needs to be done about the situation in paragraphs 13–18. What solution does she call for?
4. Considering the situation Harjo describes, the steps that are being taken to address that situation, and what remains to be done, what is the thesis of the essay?
5. If you were in Harjo's position, what additional arguments might you add?

Technique and Style

1. Describe the audience the essay is aimed at as precisely as you can. What evidence do you base your description on?
2. How would you characterize the diction Harjo uses in connection with her examples? Choose one or two examples and substitute more or less loaded words. What is gained? Lost?
3. Based on the way the essay is written, what kind of person does Harjo appear to be? How would you describe her?
4. To what extent does the essay rest its appeal on Harjo's persona? On emotion? On logic? Which appeal predominates?
5. The essay concludes with a call for action. Evaluate its effectiveness.

Suggestions for Writing

Journal

1. Imagine that you are on the board of a museum that owns Indian skeletons. Explain your response to Harjo's essay.

2. Harjo uses the term "shameful past" (paragraph 18). What other examples might Native Americans associate with that term?

Essay

1. Think of an action that was considered acceptable in the past but today is either questionable or unacceptable. Fifty years ago, for instance, no one thought much about the hazards of smoking, nor of cholesterol levels, nor of needing to inspect meat. Segregation was acceptable, as were other forms of racism. Choose a subject and think about the ethics involved and how present knowledge has changed how we live. Other suggestions:

> the sale of cigarettes
> the advertising of alcoholic beverages
> the popularity of natural foods
> the sale of diet products

2. Harjo states that "Indian relic-collecting has become a multi-million-dollar industry" (paragraph 9). Use your library or the Internet to research the degree to which relic-collecting is still a problem and what should be done about it.

Gay Marriages: Make Them Legal

Thomas B. Stoddard

What is traditional is not always what is right, or so Thomas B. Stoddard argues in the essay that follows. He calls for a redefinition of marriage that accommodates the legal status of matrimony to the present times. Stoddard is an attorney and executive director of the Lambda Legal Defense and Education Fund, a gay rights organization. Stoddard's essay was published as an opinion piece in the New

York Times *in 1989. Since that time, Canada, Vermont, and Massachusetts have legalized gay unions, and other states may follow suit. This topic continues to be hotly debated.*

What to Look For   Definition is a key element in argument. Note how careful Stoddard is to define marriage in paragraphs 4 and 5. When you write your own argumentative paper, you'll probably find it helpful first to identify the most important term and then make sure early on in your paper that you define it carefully.

1   In sickness and in health, 'til death do us part." With those familiar words, millions of people each year are married, a public affirmation of a private bond that both society and the newlyweds hope will endure. Yet for nearly four years, Karen Thompson was denied the company of the one person to whom she had pledged lifelong devotion. Her partner is a woman, Sharon Kowalski, and their home state of Minnesota, like every other jurisdiction in the United States, refuses to permit two individuals of the same sex to marry.

2   Karen Thompson and Sharon Kowalski are spouses in every respect except the legal. They exchanged vows and rings; they lived together until November 13, 1983—when Ms. Kowalski was severely injured when her car was struck by a drunk driver. She lost the capacity to walk or to speak more than several words at a time, and needed constant care.

3   Ms. Thompson sought a court ruling granting her guardianship over her partner, but Ms. Kowalski's parents opposed the petition and obtained sole guardianship. They moved Ms. Kowalski to a nursing home 300 miles away from Ms. Thompson and forbade all visits between the two women. Last month, as part of a reevaluation of Ms. Kowalski's mental competency, Ms. Thompson was permitted to visit her partner again. But the prolonged injustice and anguish inflicted on both women hold a moral for everyone.

4   Marriage, the Supreme Court declared in 1967, is "one of the basic civil rights of man" (and, presumably, of woman as well). The freedom to marry, said the Court, is "essential to the orderly pursuit of happiness."

5   Marriage is not just a symbolic state. It can be the key to survival, emotional and financial. Marriage triggers a universe of rights, privileges and presumptions. A married person can share in a spouse's estate even when there is no will. She is typically entitled to the group insurance and pension programs offered by the spouse's employer, and she enjoys tax advantages. She cannot be compelled to testify against her spouse in legal proceedings.

6   The decision whether or not to marry belongs properly to individuals—not the government. Yet at present, all 50 states deny that choice to millions of gay and lesbian Americans. While marriage has historically required a male partner and a female partner, history alone cannot sanctify injustice. If tradition were the only measure, most states would still limit matrimony to partners of the same race.

7   As recently as 1967, before the Supreme Court declared miscegenation statutes unconstitutional, 16 states still prohibited marriages between a white person and a black person. When all the excuses were stripped away, it was clear that the only purpose of those laws was, in the words of the Supreme Court, "to maintain white supremacy."

8   Those who argue against reforming the marriage statutes because they believe that same-sex marriage would be "antifamily" overlook the obvious: marriage creates families and promotes social stability. In an increasingly loveless world, those who wish to commit themselves to a relationship founded upon devotion should be encouraged, not scorned. Government has no legitimate interest in how that love is expressed.

9   And it can no longer be argued—if it ever could—that marriage is fundamentally a procreative unit. Otherwise, states would forbid marriage between those who, by reason of age or infertility, cannot have children, as well as those who elect not to.

10   As the case of Sharon Kowalski and Karen Thompson demonstrates, sanctimonious illusions lead directly to the suffering of others. Denied the right to marry, these two women are left subject to the whims and prejudices of others, and of the law.

11   Depriving millions of gay American adults the marriages of their choice, and the rights that flow from marriage, denies equal protection of the law. They, their families and friends, together with fair-minded people everywhere, should demand an end to this monstrous injustice.

Organization and Ideas

1. Stoddard's paragraphs 1–3 present an example that holds a "moral for everyone." What is it?
2. Paragraphs 4 and 5 define marriage. What point does Stoddard make about it?
3. Paragraphs 6–9 are aimed at countering arguments that can be used against Stoddard's view. Summarize them.
4. What is the effect of paragraph 10? What other paragraphs does it connect with?
5. The essay concludes with a statement of thesis and a call to action. Who should demand what, and how?

Technique and Style

1. What paragraph or paragraphs appeal to the reader's emotions?
2. What paragraph or paragraphs appeal to the reader's reason?
3. Where in the essay can you identify an ethical appeal, an appeal based on the author's persona?
4. Stoddard cites the arguments that can be used against his. Does he cite obvious ones? Is his treatment of them fair? How so?
5. Stoddard's subject is a sensitive one and his views may not be shared by many readers. Where in the essay can you find evidence that he is aware of his readers and their potential sensitivity to the issue he writes about?

Suggestions for Writing

Journal

1. Reread paragraphs 4 and 5. To what extent do you agree with Stoddard's definition?
2. Select one of the points Stoddard makes and either support or refute it.

Essay

1. Think of an issue that ought to be covered by a law or one that is governed by law and should not be. The best place to start is probably with your own experience and what irks you, but after that you'll need to do some research so that you can present your position in a more objective and reasoned way. The use of outside sources will lend more weight to your ideas. Suggestions for laws that do exist but that some think should not:
   the given speed limit
   the legal drinking age

particular zoning or IRS regulations
banning of prayers in public schools
Suggestions for laws that some think should exist but don't (varies by state):
car insurance
automobile safety seats for infants
helmets for motorcycle riders
neutering of pets

2. The word *marriage* combines religious connotations with civil rights. By legalizing civil unions, however, Vermont has split the civil contract away from the religious ceremony. Research the difference between civil union and marriage so that you can take a stand on what should or should not be legal.

High School, an Institution Whose Time Has Passed

Leon Botstein

The topic of education comes naturally to Leon Botstein, for since 1975 he has been the president of Bard College, where he is also the Leon Levy Professor in the Arts and Humanities. His administrational and teaching duties, however, have not kept him from being an active scholar and musician. He not only has continued his research in the field of history, having earned his Ph.D. in European history at Harvard, he also holds positions as Music Director of the American Symphony Orchestra, Co-Artistic Director of the Bard Music Festival, and Artistic Director of the American Russian Youth Orchestra. As a musician, he is known for his support of contemporary composers, many of whose works he has conducted in Asia and Europe as well as in this country. His two major interests are reflected in his latest books: Jefferson's Children: Education and the Promise of American Culture *(1997) and* The Compleat Brahms: A Guide to the Musical Works of Johannes Brahms *(1999). Botstein has contributed articles and reviews on history, education, music, and culture to various leading newspapers in the United States. "High School, an Institution Whose Time Has Passed" was first published in* The New York Times *and then reprinted in the* International Herald Tribune *on May 20, 1999.*

> **What to Look For**   It's a toss up to figure out which is the more difficult to write—introductions or conclusions. Sometimes, you may find that what you have as your conclusion in your draft may work as an effective introduction, but rarely is the reverse true, which is one reason concluding paragraphs present difficulties. Summaries are apt to be predictable and, therefore, dull, yet bringing in a new idea can blur your focus. One solution is to do what Botstein does: bring in an argument that can be used to counter your proposal, dismiss it, and then end by reinforcing your thesis with a call to action.

1   The national outpouring after the Littleton shootings has forced us to confront something we have suspected for a long time: The American high school is obsolete and should be abolished.

2   In the last month, high school students present and past have come forward with stories about cliques and the artificial intensity of a world defined by insiders and outsiders, in which the insiders hold sway because of superficial definitions of attractiveness, popularity and sports prowess.

3   Indeed, a community's loyalty to the high school system is often based on the extent to which varsity teams succeed. High school administrators and faculty members are often former coaches, and the coaches themselves are placed in a separate, untouchable category. The result is that the culture of the inside elite is not contested by the adults in the school. Individuality and dissent are discouraged.

4   But the rules of high school turn out not to be the rules of life. Often, the high school outsider becomes the more successful and admired adult. The definitions of masculinity and femininity go through sufficient transformation to make the game of popularity in high school an embarrassment.

5   Given the poor quality of recruitment and training for high school teachers, it is no wonder that the curriculum and the enterprise of learning hold so little sway over young people.

6   When puberty meets education and learning in the modern United States, the victory of puberty masquerading as popular culture and the tyranny of peer groups based on ludicrous values meet little resistance.

7   By the time those who graduate from high school go on to college and realize what really is at stake in becoming an adult, too many opportunities have been lost and too much time has been wasted. Most thoughtful young people suffer the high school environment in silence, and in their junior and senior years mark time waiting for college to begin.

8   But the primary reason high school doesn't work anymore, if it ever did, is that young people mature substantially earlier in the late 20th century than they did when the high school was invented. For example, the age of first menstruation has dropped at least two years since the beginning of this century and, not surprisingly, sexual activity has begun earlier in proportion. An institution intended for children in transition now holds back young adults well beyond the developmental point for which high school was originally designed.

9   Furthermore, whatever constraints on the presumption of adulthood existed decades ago have fallen away. Information and images, as well as the real and virtual freedom of movement we associate with adulthood, are now accessible to every 15-year-old and 16-year-old.

10   Secondary education must be rethought. Elementary school should begin at age 4 or 5 and end with the sixth grade. We Americans should entirely abandon the concept of the middle school and junior high school. Beginning with the seventh grade, there should be four years of secondary education that we may call high school. Young people should graduate at 16, not 18.

11   They could then enter the real world of work or national service in which they would take a place of responsibility alongside older adults. They could stay at home and attend junior college, or they could go away to college.

12   At 16, young Americans are prepared to be taken seriously and to develop the motivations and interests that will serve them well in adult life. They need to enter a world in which they are not in a lunchroom with only their peers estranged from other age groups and cut off from the game of life as it is really played.

13   There is nothing utopian about this ide~ ~ely practical and efficient, ar~ ~its implem~ ~We need to face biological ~ ~fe of a flawed inst~

Organization and Ideas

1. Botstein starts his essay with the example of the shootings at the high school in Littleton, Colorado, and then generalizes about what caused them, focusing on the notion of elitism. What is he claiming about elitism?
2. Paragraphs 5–7 explore additional reasons that high school is ineffectual and present Botstein's views on learning. Summarize his ideas.
3. Botstein sets out the heart of his argument in paragraphs 8 and 9. What reasons does he give for high school being obsolete?
4. What paragraph or paragraphs argue for Botstein's solution to the problems high school presents? State his solutions in your own words.
5. Summarize as fully as you can just what Botstein perceives as the problems with high school, together with his solution and its potential effects. Boil down what you have to one sentence for a clear statement of the thesis.

Technique and Style

1. Botstein devotes far more space to the problem than to the solution. What reasons can you find for his decision?
2. Take another look at what Botstein identifies as the problems with high school. In what order does he present them? Why might he have opted for that sequence?
3. The essay brims with assertions. Select one (paragraphs 2, 3, 6, and 7 are good hunting spots), and examine the evidence Botstein uses as support. Explain whether you find it adequate or not.
4. How would you characterize Botstein's tone? Is he blunt, condescending, reasonable? What evidence can you find for your view?
5. Reread the essay from the perspective of a high school teacher or parent. Would you find the essay offensive? Extreme? Why or why not?

Suggestions for Writing

Journal

1. Reread Botstein's solution (paragraph 10). Use your journal to record your reaction to it. Given your experience in high school and what you know about the educational system, would it work?
2. What group or groups were the "elite" at your high school? Describe them.

Essay

1. Whether you agree with Botstein or not, you probably found his essay provocative in that he makes a number of assertions about a subject you know about. Consider some of his claims:

   a. ". . . insiders hold sway because of superficial definitions of attractiveness, popularity and sports prowess" (paragraph 2).

   b. "Individuality and dissent are discouraged" (paragraph 3).

   c. ". . . it's no wonder that the curriculum and the enterprise of learning hold so little sway over young people" (paragraph 5).

   d. "Most thoughtful people suffer the high school environment in silence . . . " (paragraph 7).

   e. "At 16, young Americans are prepared to be taken seriously and to develop the motivations and interests that will serve them well in adult life" (paragraph 12).

   Use any one of these statements (or any other from the essay that you prefer) as a point to argue a "yes-but" position or to disagree with. Use the experience of others in addition to that of your own to support your argument.

2. General degree requirements and the requirements for a major are put in place by the faculty to ensure that the students who earn their degrees have a specific foundation in general knowledge and in their majors. At the same time, many students believe that requirements such as these cut into their education in ways that limit them. Review what your institution requires for your major (or as general degree requirements) and write an essay in which you argue for your opinion of what is required.

Don't Impede Medical Progress

Virginia Postrel

Virginia Postrel began her writing career as a reporter for Inc. *and the* Wall Street Journal, *moving on first to become associate editor and then editor of* Reason, *a monthly magazine that provides news, opinion, analysis, and reviews that focus on politics and culture. She is now* Reason's *Editor-at-Large, a position that frees her to spend more time on her own work. Her book* The Future and Its Enemies *(1999) examines the ways in which traditional political polarities, such as conservative and liberal, fail to deal with the major issues of our present time. She is now at work on a new book,* Look and Feel, *arguing that the idea of aesthetics is increasingly important to society and to business. In addition to writing a regular column, "The Economic Scene," for the* New York Times, *Postrel also contributes to* Forbes, IntellectualCapital, *and the* Wall Street Journal, *where this article appeared on December 5, 2001.*

What to Look For   Just as comparison and contrast essays can be organized by block or point by point (p. 176), an argumentative essay can cite a position and then counter it or break the position into points, countering each one. As you read Postrel's essay, keep track of how she lays out her argument.

1   To many biologists, the recently announced creation of a cloned human embryo was no big deal. True, researchers at Advanced Cell Technology replaced the nucleus of a human egg with the genetic material of another person. And they got that cloned cell to start replicating. But their results were modest. It took 71 eggs to produce a single success, and in the best case, the embryo grew to only six cells before dying. That's not a revolution. It's an incremental step in understanding how early-stage cells develop.

2   And it's far from the 100 or so cells in a blastocyst, the hollow ball from which stem cells can be isolated. Scientists hope to coax embryonic stem cells into becoming specialized tissues such as nerve, muscle, or pancreatic islet cells. Therapeutic cloning, or nucleus transplantation, could make such treatments more effective.

3   In theory, it would work like this: Suppose I need new heart tissue or some insulin-secreting islet cells to counteract diabetes. You could take the nucleus from one of my cells, stick it in an egg cell from which the nucleus had been removed, let that develop into stem cells, and then trigger the stem cells to form the specific tissue needed. The new "cloned" tissue would be genetically mine and would not face rejection problems. It would function in my body as if it had grown there naturally, so I wouldn't face a lifetime of immunosuppressant drugs.

4   But all of that is a long way off. ACT and others in the field are still doing very basic research, not developing clinical therapies. Indeed, because of the difficulty of obtaining eggs, therapeutic cloning may ultimately prove impractical for clinical treatments. It could be more important as a technique for understanding cell development or studying the mutations that lead to cancer. We simply don't know right now. Science is about exploring the unknown and cannot offer guarantees.

5   Politics, however, feeds on fear, uncertainty, and doubt, and the word "cloning" arouses those emotions. While its scientific importance remains to be seen, ACT's announcement has rekindled the campaign to criminalize nucleus transplantation and any therapies derived from that process. Under a bill passed by the House and endorsed by the President, scientists who transfer a human nucleus into an egg cell would be subject to 10-year federal prison sentences and $1 million fines. So would anyone who imports therapies developed through such research in countries where it is legal, such as Britain. The bill represents an unprecedented attempt to criminalize basic biomedical research.

6   The legislation's backers consider the fear of cloning their best hope for stopping medical research that might lead to gene-level therapies. Opponents make three basic arguments for banning therapeutic cloning.

7   The first is that a fertilized egg is a person, entitled to full human rights. Taking stem cells out of a blastocyst is, in this view, no different from cutting the heart out of a baby. Hence, we hear fears of "embryo farming" for "spare parts."

8   This view treats microscopic cells with no past or present consciousness, no organs or tissues, as people. A vocal minority of Americans, of course, do find compelling the argument that a fertilized egg is someone who deserves protection from harm. That view animates the anti-abortion movement and exercises considerable influence in Republican politics.

9   But most Americans don't believe we should sacrifice the lives and well being of actual people to save cells. Human identity must rest on something more compelling than the right string of proteins in a petri dish, detectable only with high-tech equipment. We will never get a moral consensus that a single cell, or a clump of 100 cells, is a human being. That definition defies moral sense, rational argument, and several major religious traditions.

10   So cloning opponents add a second argument. If we allow therapeutic cloning, they say, some unscrupulous person will pretend to
be doing cellular research but instead implant a cloned embryo in a
woman's womb and produce a baby. At the current stage of knowledge, using cloning to conceive a child would indeed be dangerous
and unethical, with a high risk of serious birth defects. Anyone who
cloned a baby today would rightly face, at the very least, the potential of an enormous malpractice judgment. There are good arguments for establishing a temporary moratorium on reproductive
cloning.

11   But the small possibility of reproductive cloning does not justify
making nucleus transfer a crime. Almost any science might conceiv-
ably be turned to evil purposes. This particular misuse is neither especially likely—cell biology labs are not set up to deliver fertility
treatments—nor, in the long run, especially threatening.

12   Contrary to a lot of scary rhetoric, a healthy cloned infant would
not be a moral nightmare, merely the not-quite-identical twin of an
older person. (The fetal environment and egg cytoplasm create
some genetic variations.) Certainly, some parents might have such a
baby for bad reasons, to gratify their egos or to "replace" a child
who died. But parents have been having children for bad reasons
since time immemorial.

13   Just as likely, cloned babies would be the cherished children of
couples who could not have biological offspring any other way.
These children might bear an uncanny resemblance to their biological parents, but that, too, is not unprecedented. Like the "test tube
babies" born of in vitro fertilization, cloned children need not be
identifiable, much less freaks or outcasts.

14   Why worry so much about a few babies? Because, say opponents, even a single cloned infant puts us on the road to genetic
dystopia, a combination of Brave New World and Nazi Germany. A
cloned child's genetic makeup is too well known, goes the argument, and therefore transforms random reproduction into "manufacturing" that robs the child of his autonomy. This is where the attack
broadens from nucleus transfer to human genetic engineering more
generally. An anti-therapeutic cloning petition, circulated by the unlikely duo of conservative publisher William Kristol and arch-techno-
phobe Jeremy Rifkin, concludes, "We are mindful of the tragic history of social eugenics movements in the first half of the 20th
century, and are united in our opposition to any use of biotechnol-
ogy for a commercial eugenics movement in the 21st century."

15   But the "eugenics" they attack has nothing to do with state-sponsored mass murder or forced sterilization. To the contrary, they are the ones who want the state to dictate the most private aspects of family life. They are the ones who want central authorities, rather than the choices of families and individuals, to determine our genetic future. They are the ones who demand that the government control the means of reproduction. They are the ones who measure the worth of human beings by the circumstances of their conception and the purity of their genetic makeup. They are the ones who say "natural" genes are the mark of true humanity.

16   Winners in the genetic lottery themselves, blessed with good health and unusual intelligence, they seek to deny future parents the chance to give their children an equally promising genetic start. In a despicable moral equivalency, they equate loving parents with Nazis.

17   Biomedicine does have the potential to alter the human experience. Indeed, it already has. Life expectancy has doubled worldwide in the past century. Childbirth is no longer a peril to mother and infant. Childhood is no longer a time for early death. The pervasive sense of mortality that down through the ages shaped art, religion, and culture has waned.

18   Our lives are different from our ancestors' in fundamental ways. We rarely remark on the change, however, because it occurred incrementally. That's how culture evolves and how science works. We should let the process continue.

Organization and Ideas

1. Paragraphs 1–3 introduce the essay. What does the introduction accomplish?
2. What are the three main arguments in favor of outlawing nucleus transplants? How does Postrel counter them?
3. How fair is Postrel to the opposition?
4. To what extent does Postrel's argument appeal to reason? To emotion?
5. To what extent, if any, does Postrel persuade you to adopt her position?

Technique and Style

1. The procedures Postrel describes are complex. To what extent does she explain them clearly?
2. How would you describe Postrel's tone? What examples best support your view?

3. What reasons can you think of for the *Wall Street Journal* publishing the essay?
4. In paragraph 15, Postrel repeats the term "they are." Why might she have done so and what is the effect of the repetition?
5. To what extent, if any, can paragraph 16 be called an ad hominem attack?

Suggestions for Writing

Journal

1. What effect would Postrel's essay have had if you knew she were a scientist? A politician?
2. What alternative titles can you think of for the essay? Which do you prefer and why?

Essay

1. Questions of ethics constantly arise in the field of medicine. Is it ethical to keep a dying patient alive? To sustain a two-pound "crack baby"? To give out clean needles at drug rehab centers? To sell organs for transplants? To use animals for research? Select one of these questions or another of your own choosing and research the topic, using your library or the Internet. Take a position and defend it in an essay.
2. Use your library or the Internet to bring Postrel's essay up to date. What is the current state of research in the United States? In England, Europe, and elsewhere? Should the laws in the United States be revised? Your answers to these questions and others that you uncover can evolve into an explanatory or argumentative essay.

One Internet, Two Nations

Henry Louis Gates, Jr.

Henry Louis Gates, Jr.'s academic credentials and awards read like a scholar's dream: educated at Yale University and Clare College of the University of Cambridge; a Mellon Fellow at Cambridge and the National Humanities Center; a Ford Foundation National Fellow and a MacArthur Prize Fellow; honored with the Zora Neale Hurston Society Award for Cultural Scholarship, the Norman Rabb Award of

*the American Jewish Committee, the George Polk Award for Social
Commentary, and the Tikkun National Ethics Award.*

*Gates chairs Afro-American Studies at Harvard University where he
holds the position of W. E. B. Du Bois Professor of the Humanities and
director of the W. E. B. Du Bois Institute for Afro-American Research.
Gates has written a number of scholarly books, of which the best
known is probably* The Signifying Monkey *(1989). But Gates is that
rare scholar who has also written for a more general audience in
books such as his* Loose Canons: Notes of the Culture Wars *(1992), his
autobiography,* Colored People: A Memoir *(1993), and* Thirteen Ways
of Looking at a Black Man *(1997), and in the PBS television series*
Wonders of the African World *(1999). He is also a regular contributor
to the* New Yorker *magazine and serves on the Pulitzer Prize Board.*

The essay that follows appeared in the New York Times *on October
31, 1999, and as its title suggests, Gates turns his attention to the electronic media and the Internet. It's an area with which he's familiar,
having coedited Microsoft's* Encarta Africana. *Most recently, Gates discovered and edited* The Bondwoman's Narrative *(2002), a fictional-
ized account of the life of Hannah Crafts, which is the first known
novel written by an African American woman who had been a slave.*

What to Look For   One way to think your way into an argumentative essay is to consider the subject from the angle of problem and
solution. You'll see that's what Gates does in his essay, using a historical perspective to back up just how important his point is. Like
Gates, you'll probably find more than one reason for the problem
and more than one solution.

1   After the Stono Rebellion of 1739 in South Carolina—the largest
uprising of slaves in the colonies before the American Revolution—
legislators there responded by banishing two forms of communication among the slaves: the mastery of reading and writing, and the
mastery of "talking drums," both of which had been crucial to the
capacity to rebel.

2   For the next century and a half, access to literacy became for the
slaves a hallmark of their humanity and an instrument of liberation,
spiritual as well as physical. The relation between freedom and
literacy became the compelling theme of the slave narratives, the
great body of printed books that ex-slaves generated to assert their

common humanity with white Americans and to indict the system that had oppressed them.

3 In the years since the abolition of slavery, the possession of literacy has been a cardinal value of the African-American tradition. It is no accident that the first great victory in the legal battle over segregation was fought on the grounds of education—of equal access to literacy.

4 Today, blacks are failing to gain access to the new tools of literacy: the digital "knowledge economy." And while the dilemma that our ancestors confronted was imposed by others, this cybersegregation is, to a large degree, self-imposed.

5 The Government's latest attempt to understand why low-income African-Americans and Hispanics are slower to embrace the Internet and the personal computer than whites—the Commerce Department study "Falling Through the Net"—suggests that income alone can't be blamed for the so-called digital divide. For example, among families earning $15,000 to $35,000 annually, more than 33 percent of whites own computers, compared with only 19 percent of African-Americans—a gap that has widened 64 percent over the past five years despite declining computer prices.

6 The implications go far beyond online trading and chat rooms. Net promoters are concerned that the digital divide threatens to become a 21st century poll tax that, in effect, disenfranchises a third of the nation. Our children, especially, need access not only to the vast resources that technology offers for education, but also to the rich cultural contexts that define their place in the world.

7 Today we stand at the brink of becoming two societies, one largely white and plugged in and the other black and unplugged.

8 One of the most tragic aspects of slavery was the way it destroyed social connections. In a process that the sociologist Orlando Patterson calls "social death," slavery sought to sever blacks from their history and culture, from family ties and a sense of community. And, of course, de jure segregation after the Civil War was intended to disconnect blacks from equal economic opportunity, from the network of social contacts that enable upward mobility and, indeed, from the broader world of ideas.

9 Despite the dramatic growth of the black middle class since affirmative action programs were started in the late 60's, new forms of disconnectedness have afflicted black America. Middle-class professionals often feel socially and culturally isolated from their white peers at work and in the neighborhood and from their black peers left behind in the underclass. The children of the black underclass,

in turn, often lack middle-class role models to help them connect to a history of achievement and develop their analytical skills.

10   It would be a sad irony if the most diverse and decentralized electronic medium yet invented should fail to achieve ethnic diversity among its users. And yet the Commerce Department study suggests that the solution will require more than cheap PC's. It will involve content.

11   Until recently, the African-American presence on the Internet was minimal, reflecting the chicken-and-egg nature of Internet economics. Few investors have been willing to finance sites appealing to a PC-scarce community. Few African-Americans have been compelled to sign on to a medium that offers little to interest them. And educators interested in diversity have repeatedly raised concerns about the lack of minority-oriented educational software.

12   Consider the birth of the recording industry in the 1920's. Blacks began to respond to this new medium only when mainstream companies like Columbia Records introduced so-called race records, blues and jazz discs aimed at a nascent African-American market. Blacks who would never have dreamed of spending hard-earned funds for a record by Rudy Vallee or Kate Smith would stand in lines several blocks long to purchase the new Bessie Smith or Duke Ellington hit.

13   New content made the new medium attractive. And the growth of Web sites dedicated to the interests and needs of black Americans can play the same role for the Internet that race records did for the music industry.

14   But even making sites that will appeal to a black audience can only go so far. The causes of poverty are both structural and behavioral. And it is the behavioral aspect of this cybersegregation that blacks themselves are best able to address. Drawing on corporate and foundation support, we can transform the legion of churches, mosques and community centers in our inner cities into after-school centers that focus on redressing the digital divide and teaching black history. We can draw on the many examples of black achievement in structured classes to re-establish a sense of social connection.

15   The Internet is the 21st century's talking drum, the very kind of grass-roots communication tool that has been such a powerful source of education and culture for our people since slavery. But this talking drum we have not yet learned to play. Unless we master the new information technology to build and deepen the forms of social connection that a tragic history has eroded, African-Americans

will face a form of cybersegregation in the next century as devastating to our aspirations as Jim Crow segregation was to those of our ancestors. But this time, the fault will be our own.

Organization and Ideas

1. Paragraphs 1–4 focus on the relationship between African-Americans and literacy. Summarize that relationship.
2. The first sentence of paragraph 4 makes a claim. In what ways do paragraphs 5–9 supply evidence for that claim?
3. While Gates presents reasons the "digital divide" exists, he is careful in paragraph 5 to discount an economic reason. Why is it important that he include it?
4. Consider Gates' subject, the problems he perceives and the solutions he proposes. In your own words and in one sentence, state the essay's thesis.
5. To what extent are you persuaded by Gates' argument?

Technique and Style

1. Gates refers to historical events in paragraphs 1–3 and 8. What do they add to his argument? To his persona?
2. In what ways is Gates' essay directed to an African-American audience? A white audience? A mixed one?
3. Where in the essay do you find Gates using an appeal to reason? To emotion? To his persona? Which appeal dominates?
4. Consider the paragraphs that both precede and follow paragraph 7. What is the function of paragraph 7?
5. Gates' last paragraph begins with a metaphor. In what ways is it appropriate for the essay's unity? For its subject?

Suggestions for Writing

Journal

1. Take a few minutes to jot down the various ways you use the Internet. What categories can those uses be placed in? Given how you use it, what effect does it have on you? If you don't use the Internet at all, explain why.
2. To test out Gates' argument, spend a half hour or so exploring Web sites that are aimed specifically at an African-American audience. Record the results in your journal, and you will have the working notes for an essay that refutes or supports his argument. If you support it, make sure your argument is a "yes-but" type so you have an assertion.

Essay

1. You can't pick up a newspaper or magazine these days without running into stories about the Internet, stories ranging from praise (useful Web sites and the like) to condemnation (Web addiction and so on) with everything in between. Think about how it has affected you and the world you live in. To get started, here are some statements to mull over, each of which can begin with "The Internet has/has not . . . "

   increased the gap between the haves and the have-nots
   contributed to ethnic diversity
   become the latest way to waste time
   spread pornography
   changed shopping as we know it
   changed education as we know it

   Like Gates, don't hold back from predicting the future.

2. Re-examine Gates' essay from the perspective of the next selection, "Internet Not For Everyone." To what extent does Gates' essay hold up? Write an essay in which you analyze the essay, given the information provided by the more recent view.

Internet Not for Everyone

Robyn Greenspan

Robyn Greenspan's career epitomizes the shift from print to electronic media that many writers have made. Starting off in advertising—copywriting, managing accounts, and running small agencies—she says she "soon realized the potential of the Internet." She now works for Jupitermedia, a company that "provides business professionals with the up-to-the-minute technology news, resources and product information that they need to do their jobs." Greenspan notes that her "decade of online experience coupled with my writing skills and marketing background resulted in a perfect fit among Jupitermedia's editorial staff." At the company, Greenspan has been a news reporter and the managing editor of CyberAtlas—a site "devoted to Internet market research and statistics . . . ranked number 1 on PC Magazine's *2003 list of "most Net-Obsessed Sites." The article included here was published electronically in <internetnews.com>, a Jupitermedia company, on April 16, 2003.*

> **What to Look For**   If used effectively, tables can illuminate infor-
> mation in ways that would be hard to follow and tedious if presented
> in prose. As you read Greenspan's article, consider what the tables
> add to it.

1   Could there be a population that time forgot? Are there people
that don't actually live by the immediacy of the Web? Apparently
so, according to research from the Pew Internet & American Life
Project that finds that nearly one-quarter (24 percent) of Americans
experience life unplugged.

2   "The truly unconnected are the Americans that those who worry
about the digital divide should understand," said Lee Rainie, director of the Pew Internet & American Life Project. "The reasons non-
users stay away from the Internet are varied and complex. Many
lack the resources to go online. Others don't live in a social world
where Internet use matters and still others have no notion that the
communication and information functions of the Internet can help
them improve their lives."

3   Pew's profile of the Internet population reveals the digital divide
clearly. From their research, the average American Internet user is
young, white, employed, well-educated, wealthier, and suburban.
Gender is balanced equally among Internet users.

Users Compared to Non-Users			
	Users	**Non-Users**	**All Americans**
Men	50%	46%	48%
Women	50%	54%	52%
Whites	77%	71%	75%
Blacks	8%	14%	11%
Hispanics	9%	10%	10%
18–29	29%	14%	23%
30–49	47%	32%	42%
50–64	18%	22%	20%
65+	4%	28%	15%

Users Compared to Non-Users *(Continued)*			
	Users	**Non-Users**	**All Americans**
Less than $30k yearly household income	18%	41%	28%
$30–$49,999	23%	17%	21%
$50–$75,000	18%	9%	14%
More than $75k yearly household income	26%	6%	18%
Not HS grad	5%	25%	14%
HS grad	23%	41%	35%
Some college	34%	21%	25%
College and grad school degree	37%	11%	26%
Rural community	21%	31%	26%
Suburban	52%	42%	28%
Urban	26%	26%	26%

Note: This table reports the share of the Internet population that comes from each group.
Base: 3,553, March–May 2002.
Source: Pew Internet & American Life Project.

4   The Pew study found that 24 percent are completely disconnected from the Internet, but some have found indirect methods for using the medium. The study defines "Net Evaders" as the 20 percent of non-Internet users who proudly reject the online world, yet they are comfortable having others pass Net-based information on to them.

5   The "Net Dropouts" are the 17 percent who once used the Internet but quit after experiencing technical or ISP problems or lost interest. The number of dropouts has risen from 13 percent in 2000.

6   The reasons most cited for the lack of connection? More than half (52 percent) said they don't want the Internet or they don't need it, and 43 percent were worried about online pornography, credit card theft and fraud. Three-in-ten were concerned that Net access was too expensive, 29 percent said they didn't have time, 27 percent thought the Internet was too complicated, and 11 percent didn't own a computer.

7   A portion of non-Internet users are socially disconnected from the Internet, with 27 percent saying that they know almost no one

who goes online, and 22 percent say they do not know of public Internet access points in their community. The report also found that almost three-quarters of disabled Americans do not go online, and 28 percent of them said their disability or impairment made it difficult or impossible to go online.

8   Amanda Lenhart, principal author of this report and research specialist at the Pew Internet Project said that approximately 30 percent of the non-users were users previously, while the remaining majority—what Pew calls the "Truly Unconnected—had no direct or indirect exposure. This group—typically older women with lower incomes and less education—had fears, worries and concerns about the Internet that could have likely come from the media, friends, neighbors or other communication channels.

9   An encouraging bit of data is revealed when respondents were queried about what they imagined the Internet to be like. The majority of both users and non-users thought the Web was most like a library—a very accurate description.

What Do You Think the Internet Is Like?	All Americans	Users	Non-Users
Library	51%	61%	36%
Meeting place	11%	10%	12%
Shopping mall	10%	10%	11%
School	6%	6%	6%
Peep show	3%	1%	5%
Party	2%	2%	3%
Bank	1%	1%	2%
All of the above	5%	4%	5%
Other/don't know	11%	5%	20%

Base: 3,533, March–May 2002.
Source: Pew Internet & American Life Project.

10   Among the non-users, 40 percent said they would eventually join the online masses, with 31 percent of that segment indicating they would most likely use the Net for research. Communicating through e-mail, IM, or chat was the draw for 11 percent of non-users, and shopping appealed to 7 percent.

11   "The Internet population shows much greater churn than most realize—a lot of people are moving in and out of the online world pretty regularly," said Lenhart. "It is too simple to talk about a digital divide based exclusively on problems with access when it is now clear that access issues change from month to month for lots of Americans. A surprisingly large number don't want to be connected even though they have tasted what online life is like or live with the Internet literally in the next room."

Organization and Ideas

1. Greenspan's article summarizes the Pew report, but it also has an argumentative edge. What is that edge?
2. How would you describe the article's organization—from general to particular, particular to general, some mixture of the two, question/answer, what?
3. What paradoxes or contradictions can you find in the results of the survey?
4. Why would the information in the article be of particular interest to the readers of internetnews.com?
5. What does Greenspan's article imply that needs to be done about the digital divide?

Technique and Style

1. How helpful and necessary are the tables?
2. The article contains lots of numbers. To what extent are they confusing? Necessary?
3. How aptly labeled are the non-users?
4. In paragraph 11 you find the word *churn* used as a noun, not the usual verb. How apt is it?
5. Take another look at the first table. How appropriate are the categories?

Suggestions for Writing

Journal

1. What in the report surprises you? Explain.
2. Think about someone you know who is "unconnected." To what extent does that person fit one of the profiles described in the article?

Essay

See the assignments listed for Gates on page 305.

ADDITIONAL WRITING ASSIGNMENTS

Using Argument

1. Choose a topic that has a direct impact on your life and take a stand: admission requirements for your institution, speed limits, collegiate athletics, bookstore policies, parking on campus.
2. Choose a topic that relates to state politics and take a stand: campaign contributions, primaries, mail-in voting, limiting campaign time, term limits.
3. Choose a topic that relates to national issues and take a stand: required ID cards, mandatory sentencing, universal health care, social security reform, welfare.
4. Choose a topic that relates to international relations and take a stand: global warming, the International Monetary Fund, the United Nations, NATO peacekeeping, free trade.

Evaluating the Essays

1. Leon Botstein argues that "the time has passed" for high school, that it's an outdated institution; in a somewhat similar line of reasoning, Thomas B. Stoddard argues that our present definition of marriage is outdated. Both argue for change. Reread the two essays to decide who makes the better case. Draw upon both to support your analysis and argument.
2. Suzan Shown Harjo argues against the mistreatment of dead relatives and their effects, and Virginia Postrel argues against the outlawing of research on nucleus transportation. Yet underlying both essays are the questions of what is moral and who should decide. Which writer answers those questions more thoroughly and effectively?
3. Both Robyn Greenspan and Henry Louis Gates, Jr. write about the digital divide, though they vary about who is on what side of the division: Gates focuses on race and Greenspan on the "truly unconnected." Reread the two selections to find a solution that would help solve both problems.
4. Suzan Shown Harjo, Thomas B. Stoddard, and Henry Louis Gates, Jr. all write about issues affecting minorities. Select two of the writers, reread their essays, and write an essay in which you argue for the more effective of the two. Make sure that you define what you mean by *effective*.

For Further

Reading:
Multiple Modes,
Varied Opinions

On College Athletics

It's almost impossible to be on a college campus and not be aware of athletics. You may be on an athletic scholarship or you may be sitting in class next to a 6' 9" basketball player or in the stands cheering for the football team. But in these days of budget pressures, college athletics are in trouble. Welch Suggs, writing for the Chronicle of Higher Education, *provides an overview of the problem aptly titled "Cutting the Field." Two possible solutions follow. Cynthia Tucker, a syndicated columnist, argues to "End the Hypocrisy on College Athletics," and Jeremy Bloom, a student and athlete at the University of Colorado, Boulder, cries "Show Us the Money." All three selections were published in 2003—Suggs' article on June 6, Tucker's column in the* Times-Picayune *on March 17, Bloom's essay in the* New York Times *on August 1.*

Cutting the Field

Welch Suggs

1 About 3:30 every spring afternoon, a college athletics department hits rush hour. Kids are getting taped up in the training room. The sharp "ping" of aluminum bats echoes from baseball and softball fields. Soccer and lacrosse and volleyball and track and wrestling and field-hockey teams are jogging, stretching, throwing balls around, getting warmed up.

2   It's a happy place, an excited place. An athlete getting ready for practice has hardly a care in the world. She leaves exams and pressures and college life behind when she walks into the locker room and puts on her cleats. He gets ready to learn some of the most valuable lessons he can get in college.

3   Why does Ben Lukowski run track for West Virginia University? "I guess for the poetic reasons—how fast can you go, what are your limits," the freshman says. "In team sports, you can kind of hide, but on the track, it's all on you."

4   Mr. Lukowski is one of the last few men wearing West Virginia track uniforms who will know that feeling. The athletics department abruptly announced last month that it was dropping its men's cross-country, indoor and outdoor track, and tennis teams, as well as its coed rifle squad.

5   The Mountaineers are hardly alone. Seven colleges this year have announced plans to drop sports, mostly men's teams and mostly the nonrevenue "Olympic" sports. Within a week of West Virginia's announcement, three other colleges also said they were trimming their athletics programs to 16 teams, the minimum required to stay in Division I-A of the National Collegiate Athletic Association (one institution has since reconsidered).

6   Having a team dropped is tough, even tragic, for individual athletes. However, the ramifications of these colleges' actions reach far beyond their campuses. If varsity sports are being pared to the minimum, what does that say about the reason colleges have teams in the first place?

7   "Why is athletics part of college?" asks Marsha Beasley, West Virginia's rifle coach for the past 14 seasons. "To me, it's because athletics offers educational opportunities you just can't get in the classroom. Teamwork, performance under pressure, concentration, all those things you and I know about.

8   "The thing is, athletics is becoming more about advertising and PR for the university. When you say Duke, what do most people think of? Basketball, not the wonderful medical school and the other things the school has to be proud of."

9   Sports wasn't supposed to be like that. But increasingly, colleges in Division I are stripping away "minor" sports and focusing on "major" ones. Football and men's basketball teams have always gotten the vast majority of budgets, despite having poorer records in the classroom than Olympic-sports teams. Now, though, the money chase is forcing colleges to give up many of their success stories.

By the Numbers

10   According to a just-released NCAA study, the number of male athletes peaked in 1984–85, two years after the association began sponsoring women's sports. That year, the association's members averaged 254 male athletes each, and Division I colleges had 318 apiece. (Both the NCAA and Division I have added numerous members over the past two decades, so using average numbers of athletes controls for that growth.)

11   By 2001–02, the final year in the study, those numbers had shrunk to 205 and 264, respectively. Over that time, the number of female athletes has grown by half, from 98 to 150 per college throughout the NCAA and from 115 to 205 in Division I. However, after exploding in the early 1990s, the growth in the number of female athletes has slowed considerably in the last few years, as has the number of teams per college.

12   The number of teams and opportunities for football players has continued to grow, while men's basketball teams have remained stable. (Over time, far more colleges have had basketball teams than football teams, and the number of players needed hasn't changed.) In other men's sports—call them minor, Olympic, non-revenue, whatever—the news has been much more bleak. Colleges have dropped scores of swimming, track, and wrestling teams, among other sports. Cynics joke that every men's gymnastics team in the country can boast of being in the top 20.

13   In many cases, this has been about colleges deciding to comply with the strictest possible standards of Title IX of the Education Amendments of 1972, the federal law prohibiting sex discrimination at institutions receiving federal funds. A "safe harbor" for Title IX compliance is having the percentage of athletes who are women be roughly the same as the percentage of undergraduates who are women, and for many institutions, the simplest way to achieve that is to get rid of male athletes. Not those in football or basketball, though. Coaches say they need 85 scholarships and 100-plus athletes for each team.

14   Now women's sports are starting to feel the pain, too. The University of Massachusetts at Amherst eliminated women's gymnastics, water polo, and volleyball in 2001. The University of Tennessee at Martin announced last month that it is dropping women's track. Women have lost significant numbers of gymnastics and swimming teams over the past decade.

15   So the problem appears to go beyond the endless debates over gender equity.

Costs and Results

16   On average, Division I-A and I-AA teams spent $4.2 million on football in 2001–02, according to data published under the Equity in Athletics Disclosure Act of 1994. They spent another $834,000 on men's basketball.

17   Neither football nor basketball teams pay their own way except at the very largest and richest colleges, the ones with huge stadiums and lucrative television contracts. Some athletics directors argue that their teams are powerful advertisements for their universities and thus should be credited for the time they spend on television, but therein lies the other problem.

18   Barely half of Division I football players earn their degrees within six years of entering college, according to the NCAA's latest report. Only 43 percent of basketball players do.

19   Yet 58 percent of track athletes graduate and so do 59 percent of all other male athletes, better by far than male students who aren't on athletics scholarships. (Female athletes are far better across the board—65 percent of basketball players, 66 percent of track athletes, and 71 percent of all other athletes earned degrees within six years.)

20   And these sports don't cost an awful lot.

A Difficult Day

21   West Virginia's athletics program has been in a cost-cutting mode for the past several years, at least in second-tier sports. Tuition costs are spiking at the university, and the athletics department pays for players' scholarships.

22   "We've made budget cuts—we eliminated some scholarships, eliminated some positions, mainly graduate-assistant positions," says Terri L. Howes, the Mountaineers' senior woman administrator. "And it got to the point where one coach said, 'If we do any more cuts, we might as well cut the program.' That really got us thinking."

23   So Ms. Howes, Ed Pastilong, the athletics director, and other senior staff members quietly began trying to trim $500,000 from the department's annual budget, which now stands at around $24 million.

24   "When we made our evaluations, we looked at every sport, with the exception of our 'priority' sports," says R. Michael Parsons, deputy athletics director, referring to football, men's and women's basketball, women's gymnastics, and women's soccer. "We looked at women's teams, and we had to look at what the impacts were going to be. We looked at the competitiveness of the program, the viability

of the sport on a local, regional, and national level, and the student impact, and obviously trying to minimize that as much as possible."

25   Without any leaks to coaches, students, or reporters, Mr. Pastilong took the plan to the university's president, David C. Hardesty Jr., and its Board of Governors in April. Upon receiving their approval, the athletics department moved quickly.

26   On April 16, Ed Dickson, West Virginia's head men's tennis coach, got a call from Ms. Howes. He was to be in Mr. Pastilong's office at 11:45.

27   "I asked her what it was about and she said, something to do with the budget," Mr. Dickson recalls. "Then other coaches started coming around, saying things like, 'I think somebody's going to get cut.'"

28   That didn't make it any easier. "I had five minutes to think about it, so I asked, 'Is this about Title IX?'" he says. "We've added a huge program [women's rowing], we're dropping mostly men's sports, so a red flag goes up there. They said, 'Yes, but there are a lot of other reasons, and basically it was a financial decision.'"

29   Then came meetings with athletes on the teams being dropped, rifle first, followed by track, cross-country, and tennis. One of Mr. Dickson's players had transferred to West Virginia from Bowling Green State University when its tennis program was dropped. "Ian said, 'I knew what was coming by the look on your face,'" the coach recalls. Some shocked members of the track team initially walked out of their meeting, though they eventually returned.

30   The thing the athletes and coaches did not understand—and still do not—is why. Was it gender equity? The cuts reduce the number of male athletes by 114, or 29 percent, based on 2001–02 figures. That would put the representation of varsity athletes at West Virginia at 55 percent men and 45 percent women. The undergraduate student body is 54 percent male and 46 percent female.

31   However, West Virginia could have made a case that it was complying with Title IX by means beyond strictly the numbers. The university has added women's soccer and rowing in the past five years, and a graduate program has done surveys of the student body and West Virginia high-school students to determine if other sports were needed, concluding that the department is satisfying the interests and abilities of female students.

32   Ms. Howes and Mr. Parsons say the cuts were made because of finances. The Mountaineers eliminated $600,000 from their annual budget by dropping the three sports. However, the cuts will be phased in over time because the athletics department will honor

scholarships for athletes who wish to remain in Morgantown until they graduate. And the $600,000 is a pittance in a sports budget of more than $24 million.

33   Some athletes think their sports were dropped to finance salaries for the football and men's basketball coaches. Rich Rodriguez, the football coach, received an extension in December to a contract that pays him a reported $700,000 a year, and John Beilein was hired to coach the basketball team last year at a salary of $550,000. Both coaches replaced legends—Don Nehlen in football and Gale Catlett in basketball—who worked, according to Mr. Parsons, "at below market" salaries.

34   "The administration hasn't been totally honest with us," says Zach Sabatino, a freshman distance runner. "They haven't given us a clear reason."

Cutting to the Bone

35   By dropping five sports, West Virginia is down to 16 teams, the NCAA minimum for Division I-A universities. Cuts at California State University at Fresno also have reduced its offerings to 16. Having the fewest sports allowable seems to be a trend.

36   "The NCAA, as the governing body of collegiate sports, must take some responsibility in the continual erosion of nonprofit, non-revenue Olympic sports," Richard Aronson, director of the Collegiate Gymnastics Association, says in an e-mail message. "So far, they have looked the other way and we continue to lose sports. And the end is not in sight."

37   Such cuts have accompanied skyrocketing costs in facilities and revenue sports, as well as in scholarship bills, nationally. Universities in the Big Ten and the Ivy League have a longstanding tradition of offering "broad based" athletics programs with scores of sports, but colleges with fewer resources are having a hard time keeping up. So they focus on the sports with some chance of generating a profit, namely football and men's basketball.

38   "We need to have a successful football team because football generates significant revenue," Mr. Parsons says. "If [the athletics department is] going to be self-sufficient, we need a winning team because that means more television appearances, bowl games, better season-ticket sales the next year. We want to compete in a lot of different sports. But in this day and age, that takes an increasing amount of resources."

39   And that's left a large portion of athletics programs at risk.

40   "Right now, in the sports culture we live in, people favor the entertainment sports over the participation sports," says Bob Fraley, track coach at Fresno State since 1980. "People are willing to spend money on entertainment, but participation sports cost money. There's very little return as far as the gate, but there are huge returns when it comes to fitness and serving the educational needs of your community. Right now, those things are not highly valued in education.

41   "When I got my start, everything had very much of an educational philosophy. You knew you had these programs that were supported by California taxpayers. They didn't ask you to make money, but they expected you to educate kids and provide a program that taught educational values, fitness, and that went all the way through the communities."

42   Fresno State announced in April that it would drop men's cross-country and indoor track. It would have dropped outdoor track as well, but Mr. Fraley agreed to retire early and coach without pay to help save the team for a few years.

43   Sports like track, tennis, and swimming, and even basketball, were started at American colleges in the second half of the 19th century as ways to train the body as well as the mind. Influenced by German theories of physical well-being as well as the "Muscular Christianity" movement that criticized Victorian effeteness, colleges began offering these sports as part of a curriculum that evolved into what is now known as physical education.

44   Football and rowing started as student clubs that were taken over by college administrations, particularly in the Northeast in the 1880s when they discovered that hundreds and even thousands of people would watch students "agitate a bag of wind," as a president of Cornell University once put it.

45   By the 1920s, both "entertainment" and "participation" sports were firmly entrenched at American colleges. Women competed in most of the same sports, but on an intramural level that usually was firmly controlled by physical education departments.

46   And nothing much changed for much of the century. Spurred by Title IX, college athletics departments created thousands of varsity teams for women in the late 1970s, but growth in women's opportunities slowed until the mid-1990s, when the threat of lawsuits and government actions prodded colleges into another expansion of women's sports. In 1998, the average number of women's teams

per Division I college exceeded the average number of men's teams for the first time. Now, top-level institutions have an average of 9.1 men's teams and 10.2 women's teams.

A Different Direction

47   Thus far, little has happened in response to the downsizing of minor sports. A few male athletes have sued colleges under Title IX, but the courts have almost uniformly been unsympathetic. In other countries, private clubs provide sports opportunities for everyone from toddlers to Olympic athletes, but very little of that exists in America.

48   A beautiful new building on the West Virginia campus provides some indication of the direction sports are taking in this country. Perhaps a mile from the university's aging Coliseum, the new Student Recreation Center literally gleams: Floor-to-ceiling windows reflect sunlight in every direction.

49   Inside the $34-million facility are seven courts for basketball, volleyball, and badminton, with high ceilings and parquet floors that amplify the bounce of balls and the squeak of sneakers.

50   A massive natatorium provides a whirlpool, lanes for lap swimming, and a huge area to play water polo or merely to play. The facility is open to all West Virginia students, and about 4,000 of them take advantage every day.

51   Varsity sports have evolved into such specialized activities that an "ordinary" student would have little chance of walking up to a coach and being allowed onto a team in any sport. As such, they seem to have evolved into irrelevance at a place like West Virginia. Recreation centers are becoming hubs of healthy activity for all students.

52   That's a little disheartening to Jeff Huntoon, the Mountaineers' head track coach. "Sure, there are numerous club-level opportunities, but that's for flag football or pickup basketball," he says.

53   "You and I can go out and play pickup basketball, but is that really top-level basketball? Of course not."

54   Intercollegiate sports offer rare opportunities for athletes to prepare mentally and physically for an all-consuming event. That's a process that teaches lessons for life, says Mr. Dickson, the tennis coach. And it pays dividends for athletes that go far beyond wins and losses.

55   "All sports teach you those things," he says. "With the individual sports, it's so obvious when you're lacking, because you can't hide

on a team somewhere. I go down the list of my players who came through here, and what they're doing now, and it's pretty damn impressive. If out of college they're teaching pros somewhere, I consider that a failure, in most cases."

Tough Timing

56　　West Virginia's timing made life difficult for many athletes. By mid-April, most other colleges had already offered all their available scholarships and team slots to other incoming athletes. So many of the sportsless Mountaineers will stay on the campus for a year, training and evaluating their options. The university is keeping the rifle range open for a year specifically for that reason.

57　　Others have arranged to transfer, and some others are done with sports, deciding to stay in Morgantown and finish their degrees.

58　　Some will feel the need to keep going at some level, even if it isn't in the professional ranks, Mr. Dickson says. They will stay in shape, they will have a better quality of life, and they will remember the intense desire and concentration it takes to be successful in life way beyond sports.

59　　In a generation, though, significantly fewer athletes could have the opportunity to learn those lessons.

End the Hypocrisy on College Athletics

Cynthia Tucker

1　　The Nebraska Legislature has half a good idea. Backed by Gov. Mike Johanns, the Legislature is considering a bill to offer stipends to athletes at the University of Nebraska, the state's largest public college. "The stipend is honest. It's aboveboard," Johanns said.

2　　Indeed. It is far better than the shenanigans that keep cropping up—secret payments to players, made-up classes with fake attendance rolls, various grade scams. No matter how many times the NCAA launches a reform effort, universities keep getting caught in athletic scandals.

3   Doesn't that suggest that reform in collegiate athletics has failed? Isn't it time to consider a more radical approach to cleaning up the corruption on campus?

4   The University of Georgia is the latest case of a university that finds itself under NCAA scrutiny following allegations of academic fraud and illegal payments in its men's basketball program. In a brutal season for college athletics, UGA is the fourth college to announce a premature end to its basketball season. UGA President Michael Adams went so far as to take the Bulldogs out of the Southeastern Conference tournament.

5   Ironically, Adams has a reputation as a collegiate athletics reformer—just another indication that the rules governing college sports cannot be refined enough to work. The rules need to be upended.

6   Giving players stipends is a start, but it only gets at one of the flimsy fictions upon which collegiate athletics is built: Players are amateurs participating for the love of the sport. There is another transparent lie that needs to be confronted: Players come to college to earn academic degrees. While that may be true of a few football and basketball powerhouses, it is patently untrue of most.

7   So the reform proposed by the Nebraska Legislature is a bold first step but would need to be joined with a major overhaul: divorcing collegiate athletics from academic programs. Ultimately, the only system that makes sense would acknowledge college athletes as the professionals they are. Pay them handsomely, and stop calling them students.

8   Oh, it may take a while—10 to 20 years—to end the hypocrisy. Fans of collegiate athletics are wedded to its traditions, corrupt though they may be. Even when the duplicity of college sports is laid out for all to see, many alumni cling to their illusions (or delusions).

9   As just one example, the most vituperative critics of affirmative action in college admissions would brook no consideration for a talented black student who scores one or two points below the school's official cut-off on the SAT. But those same critics have no problem with their alma mater's admitting a talented black football player who can barely write his own name.

10   Still, the push for cleaning up collegiate athletics may be helped by an unrelated trend: the desire of pushy baby boomer parents to have their children attend prestigious colleges and universities. At colleges such as UGA, where academic prestige is rising and admis-

sions policies are growing more selective, more and more parents will be annoyed by policies that allow prized class seats to be taken by athletes who can't be bothered to show up for class anyway. Sooner or later, those parents will start to push universities to separate their athletics departments from their academic programs.

11　　When they do, colleges will merely acknowledge what is already clear. College athletes are prized university employees who attract money and alumni support. They ought to be paid accordingly.

12　　If a few should happen to want to get a college degree along the way, they should be encouraged to do so. But nobody ought to be surprised if most are interested only in using college sports as a gateway to professional athletic careers.

13　　After all, that's the way college football and basketball players use bigtime college sports programs now.

Show Us the Money

Jeremy Bloom

1　　When I was a kid, I remember my parents telling me that going to college would broaden my horizons and give me all the opportunities in the world. What I've found out, though, is that the benefits of being a student become clouded when you add the word "athlete." That's because the National Collegiate Athletic Association not only rules college athletics, it also limits the opportunities of the 360,000 student-athletes it purports to serve.

2　　The N.C.A.A. was formed a century ago to establish rules for intercollegiate competition, and it did an admirable job. Today, however, it has become a multibillion-dollar organization that holds a monopoly on college athletics. Much of the television royalties and other revenue of college athletics go directly to the N.C.A.A., which distributes the money as it sees fit to its 1,200 member institutions. As the organization has smoothly adapted to the big-money era of college athletics, it has kept the student-athletes themselves from benefiting from the changes.

3　　Division I basketball players, for example, won't receive a dime of the $6 billion deal that the N.C.A.A. has made with CBS for the rights to broadcast its national tournament. And not only do the student-athletes not share in this wealth, the N.C.A.A. has plenty of rules to keep us from making money on our own.

4   It prohibits us from having sponsors or appearing in advertisements, even if the products have no relation to the intercollegiate sports we play. In my case, to be allowed to play wide receiver for the University of Colorado football team, I had to give up endorsement opportunities I had garnered as an Olympic moguls skier.

5   Or consider the plight of Aaron Adair, a third baseman for the University of Oklahoma who also happens to have survived brain cancer. He wrote a book about his recovery intended to help others with the disease, only to receive a call from a compliance officer informing him that his college baseball career was over because his name was attached to a "corporate product."

6   When I voice my complaints, the usual response I hear is: "The N.C.A.A. provides a free college education for these kids and that should be enough." I address that question in two parts. First, "free"? We football players get up at dawn, do an hour of wind sprints, go to classes, spend two hours in the weight room, devote a couple of hours to seven-on-seven drills, study for school, and try to have something of a social life. And this is our off-season—the hours only increase after the games start. Even if you consider the scholarships we receive to be "payment," we are recompensed at far less than the minimum wage.

7   Second, the N.C.A.A. doesn't pay for athletic scholarships, the universities do. Many universities rely on wealthy alumni who create endowments to cover tuition, room and board.

8   My solution? I have drafted what I call the Student-Athletes' Bill of Rights and have sent copies to state legislators across the country. Among other things, my proposal would allow student-athletes to "secure bona fide employment not associated with his/her amateur sport" and collect money generated by the sale of apparel that bears their names and jersey numbers. At the very least this will help student-athletes cover school-related costs, like travel and books, over and above what their scholarships pay for. Also, because the N.C.A.A. doesn't allow universities to cover a student-athlete's health insurance during the summer, the bill would assure student-athletes a full-time policy. It would also help financially burdened family members travel to post-season tournaments.

9   I am not alone in this. Kevin Murray, a California state senator, has introduced a bill along these lines to apply to all universities in his state. The athletic director at Stanford called the bill "onerous" and warned that if it passed, every athlete in California would be ineligible under N.C.A.A. guidelines.

10   But that's exactly the point: if states start ensuring that us student-athletes received fair treatment, would the N.C.A.A. really ban us all? I doubt it—I bet the organization would understand that its reign was in jeopardy and come to the bargaining table.

11   Responding to my initiative, an N.C.A.A. spokesman pointed out that the organization gives 94 percent of every dollar it receives to the universities, where it supposedly trickles back to student-athletes. I'm curious about where that other 6 percent goes—after all, 6 percent of the basketball tournament contract alone is $360 million.

12   He might also have explained the television commercials made for the N.C.A.A. I see lots of ads featuring student-athletes who say things like "I'm a swimmer, I'm a business major, I am a student-athlete." I guess it's O.K. for student-athletes to do promotional commercials so long as the beneficiary is the N.C.A.A. itself.

13   Some may say that my efforts are only self-serving—that not many student-athletes have endorsement opportunities like mine. But by the time such laws could be fully adopted I will be long gone from the college football field. My goal is to improve the circumstances of the next generation of student-athletes. That seems to be a goal the N.C.A.A. has forgotten.

On Films

After delighting many a child and adult, J.R.R. Tolkien's The Hobbit *and his multivolume* Lord of the Rings *hit the screen in a trilogy, starting in December 2001 with* The Fellowship of the Ring. *An instant hit, by early January the film had earned over 350 million dollars. Later in the year, it was nominated for 13 Oscars, winning one for best original score. As the numbers show, the public turned out in droves to see the film, eagerly awaiting the second and third installments. The critics were not unanimously impressed. Punning on the title, Sean Burns, the film critic for the* Philadelphia Weekly, *titled his review "Ringing Hollow," while Duane Dudek, Milwaukee's* Journal Sentinel *film person, took the opposite view and headlined his "Grit and Spectacle help 'Lord' Ring True." Both reviews were published in December 2001.*

Ringing Hollow

Sean Burns

LORD OF THE RINGS: THE FELLOWSHIP OF THE RING
B–
Opens Wed., Dec. 19
Director: *Peter Jackson*
Cast: *Ian McKellen,*
Viggo Mortenson, Liv Tyler, Elijah Wood

1   There's no denying that Peter Jackson's breathlessly anticipated *Lord of the Rings: The Fellowship of the Ring* is, on many levels, a staggering achievement. Years in the making and with a price tag rumored to be somewhere around $270 million, Jackson's loving adaptation of J.R.R. Tolkien's thousand-page-plus phenomenon represents one of the ballsiest gambles in Hollywood history: He dared to film an entire trilogy in a single, exhausting 18-month shoot. (The sequel, *The Two Towers*, is already slated to arrive next Christmas, with *The Return of the King* following the year after.)

2   Jackson's native New Zealand stands in for Tolkien's Middle Earth, augmented by invisible special effects so that it's a peerlessly realized fantasy world. He also has enough conviction to play this frequently cornball saga with a straight face—and it's thankfully devoid of any winking at the hipsters in the audience. For a good deal of its running time, stunning atmosphere and guileless sincerity are almost enough to carry *The Fellowship of the Ring* somewhere near the vicinity of greatness. Which makes it all the more painful to realize that, in most of the ways that really matter, the movie doesn't work at all.

3   As someone whose knowledge of Tolkien begins and ends with Led Zeppelin lyrics, I was pleasantly surprised by how understandable the screenplay (by Jackson, Fran Walsh and Phillipa Boyens) makes such complex comings and goings of hobbits, dwarves, elves, demons and wizards. I've never been able to get more than a chapter or two into *The Hobbit* without my eyes rolling back in my head, so *Fellowship* earns huge points for being accessible even to a philistine like myself.

4   It seems the ring of the title was created countless years ago by the Dark Lord Sauron and is capable of transforming all who possess it into drooling, raving madmen who use the word "precious" a

bit more than necessary. So powerful is this hunka-hunka burnin' metal that once it finds its way into the pocket of young Frodo Baggins (the blank Elijah Wood)—a hairy-footed hobbit who is for reasons unknown immune to the ring's evil spell—a bipartisan council of elves, dwarfs and other assorted short people elect representatives to make sure this very special accessory never falls in the hands of Christopher Lee's monstrous sorcerer Saruman.

5   Alas, a simple trip to the pawnshop is out of the question. The only way to destroy the ring is by taking a treacherous journey into the darkest depths of Mordor and casting it off Mount Doom. So young Frodo is led by the weed-smoking wizard Gandalf (a wonderful Ian McKellen) and several other vertically challenged badasses on a quest that will presumably take two more films to finish.

6   And that's where we run into trouble.

7   *The Fellowship of the Ring* is already earning hyperbolic comparisons to Kurosawa's *Seven Samurai*, which I guess is somewhat fitting in that both movies are very lengthy and feature characters who use swords. But the Kurosawa picture is a good 25 minutes longer than Jackson's three-hour opus, yet it seems to rocket by in half the time. Perhaps the fault lies in the source material, but *Fellowship* has no engine. It's a collection of spectacular set pieces without any sense of momentum driving them into one another. The damn thing just goes on and on. There's no feeling of progress in Frodo's journey, and every time you start to think you're finally getting somewhere, another slobbering army of wretched goblins comes charging out of nowhere. Even the most vividly rendered battle sequences begin to feel like just more of the same, and after a while you start to wonder if the movie is ever going to end.

8   By the way, it doesn't. *The Fellowship of the Ring* merely stops—practically in mid-sentence. Sure, this is only the first chapter of a trilogy, but is a wee bit of closure too much to ask as return on a three-hour investment?

9   If I sound bitter, it's because the good parts of *Fellowship* aren't just good—they're amazing. A mid-movie showstopper set in the dank mines of Moria with a troll, some monsters and a fire-breathing demon might be one of the finest action scenes ever filmed. Here, Jackson hits such an ecstatic peak of visionary frenzy so early in the game that his picture feels like it prematurely ejaculated. (There's nothing in the next hour and change that even comes close to that flaming Balrog thing.) It goes without saying that the visual splendor of *The Fellowship of the Ring* demands to be

seen and savored on the most obscenely enormous screen you can find. But in the end, it remains a movie to admire and respect, not necessarily to like much.

Grit and Spectacle Help 'Lord' Ring

Duane Dudek

1   The *Lord of the Rings: The Fellowship of the Ring* continues the dubious tradition of filling the marquee with a title so long you think you're in a bookstore rather than in a multiplex. But it does so not out of self-importance, but out of respect for the material.

2   The title alone, while a mouthful, promises a fidelity to the beloved J.R.R. Tolkien trilogy that the film itself fulfills in spades.

3   Lately, fantasy genre fans have seen heralded films fall short of their potential, in one way or another. It's as if the tools to imagine the impossible have outpaced the imaginations wielding them.

4   As a result, films that may look great have been creatively tone-deaf, causing desperate fans to embrace them despite their flaws and not because of their achievements.

5   *Fellowship of the Ring* may or may not mark the birth of a brave new world of fantasy film, but it does set a new standard against which other such films should be compared.

6   While not a slavish carbon copy of the source material, it is truer to its spirit than any line-by-line adaptation could ever be (although this opinion is spoken out of a quarter-century-old, shadowy half-memory of a text that resisted recent efforts to revisit it).

7   But in the same way Tolkien turned the developing 20th century's struggle with industrialization and war into a tale about an unlikely alliance of good souls battling an encroaching evil, New Zealand director Peter Jackson's evocative film synthesizes the traditional and the modern.

8   *Fellowship* could not have been made without the same computer-generated imagery that has run amok in the hands of less capable filmmakers.

9   The evocative environments, elaborate battle scenes and fantastic creatures require a technology that is as current as it is costly.

10   But Jackson has his roots in up-by-your-bootstraps filmmaking, and his use of miniatures, matte paintings, costumes and in-camera trickery give the film a tactile grittiness that makes the fantasy feel like reality.

11   And it is in this authenticity that the film distinguishes itself.

12   The stout-hearted *Fellowship* is closer to *Braveheart* or *Gladiator* than it is to *Harry Potter and the Sorcerer's Stone*. And its considerable violence should give parents pause. But its spectacle is made intimate and credible through the detailed conduct of its characters: the calloused, working-class hands and tired eyes of Gandalf the Wizard; the hairy-footed, clear-eyed but naive Hobbit boy Frodo, in whose untested hands the fate of the world of Middle Earth rests; and the bloody-hoofed horses ridden by the screaming wraiths that pursue them.

13   Frodo, played by Elijah Wood, has inherited a ring coveted by long-dormant evil forces. The ring has a life of its own. It wants to be found by these forces, and its evil tempts all who come near it. Led by Gandalf, played by Ian McKellen, and protected by a "fellowship" of other Middle Earth species, including elves, trolls, Hobbits and humans—played by John Rhys-Davies, Viggo Mortensen, Sean Bean, Sean Astin, Liv Tyler and others—Frodo travels into the same heart of darkness where the ring was forged to destroy it.

14   The story takes Frodo and his friends from the bucolic conviviality of the Hobbits' emerald shire and the *Lost Horizon* majesty of the elven capital, through the cavernous underworld of trolls, and into a hellish wasteland where they do battle with the things that inhabit it.

15   Although three hours long, the film ends in a cliffhanger that will be resolved in the next two films. It leaves you wanting more, but it is the same place the first book paused.

16   Jackson filmed all three stories at once, a risky tactic that offered economy of scale. But that, and shooting them in New Zealand, made the $270 million total cost of the films affordable.

17   The seams show a little after multiple viewings, but the initial impression of a vividly imagined and majestically realized journey that manages to be thrilling yet intimate is the lasting one.

18   Even if you're not a fantasy fan, *The Fellowship of the Ring* has everything you could want in almost any kind of film. It is joyous, mythic, elegiac and, most importantly, cinematic.

19   And the "ending" makes you want to read ahead to see just how
things turn out.

"The Lord of the Rings: The Fellowship of the Rings"

Stout-hearted adaptation of first book in J.R.R. Tolkien trilogy received 13
Oscar nominations, more than any film this year, including best picture, Peter
Jackson as best director and Ian McKellen as supporting actor. A majestic yet
intimate journey that is joyous, mythic, elegiac and cinematic.   (Duane Dudek,
12/18/01)

★★★1/2

Running time 2:58
Type: Action, Drama
MPAA rating: PG-13, for epic battle sequences and some scary images

Stars Elijah Wood, Ian McKellen, Christopher Lee, Sean Astin, Liv Tyler
Directed by Peter Jackson
Written by Phillippa Boyens, Peter Jackson, Fran Walsh
Produced by Peter Jackson, Tim Sanders, Barrie M. Osborne
A New Line Cinema release, 12/19/2001

Web site: http://www.lordoftherings.net/

On Torture

*A suicide bomber pushes a button, a car packed with explosives drives
into a crowded hotel lobby and blows up, a missile brings down an
airliner—acts of terrorism fill the newspapers and television screens.
Their potential targets feel anger, uncertainty, anxiety, and a general
sense of helplessness. Who will strike what? Where? When? How?
Surveillance satellites, listening devices, infiltrators, spies all provide
some information but it only goes so far. Perhaps torture could tell us
more. Under the threat and horror of terrorism, nations that pride
themselves on the rights of the individual and the rule of law are considering the idea. In the United States, lawful torture has been advo-
cated by Alan Dershowitz, attacked by Harvey A. Silverglate, and debated by Dershowitz ("Torture Should Not Be Authorized") and Philip
B. Heymann ("Yes, It Should Be 'On the Books'")—all lawyers.
Silverglate, a partner in the law firm of Silverglate & Good and author
of* The Shadow University: The Betrayal of Liberty on America's
Campuses *(1998), published his argument ("Torture Warrants?") in
Boston's* The Phoenix.com *the week of December 16, 2001. Dershowitz*

has been called by Newsweek *"the nation's most peripatetic civil liber-*
ties lawyer and one of its most distinguished defenders of individual
rights." Heymann *is a former U.S. deputy attorney general. Both*
Dershowitz and Heymann teach at Harvard Law School; their essays
were published by the Boston Globe *on February 16, 2002.*

Torture Warrants?

Harvey A. Silverglate

1   Among the unsettling effects of the September 11 terrorist attacks on New York and Washington and the anthrax mailings that followed is their triggering, seemingly overnight, of a national debate over whether the United States should practice torture—as a matter of national policy—to combat terrorism. The pro-torture camp wants to authorize law-enforcement agents to inflict intense physical pain in order to extract information from suspected terrorists (the word "suspected" is often conveniently omitted by the law's proponents) where that information might pinpoint the location of a "ticking bomb" or otherwise avert some imminent act of mass carnage.

2   So imagine the surprise of many long-time legal observers when Harvard Law professor Alan Dershowitz published an op-ed piece in the *Los Angeles Times* on November 8, arguing that "if we are to have torture, it should be authorized by the law" and that the authorities should be required to apply to judges for "torture warrants" in each case. A careful reading of his op-ed indicates that Dershowitz did not actually go so far as to say he favors torture. And in subsequent lectures and interviews he placed on record his personal opposition to torture. But the piece drew a firestorm of criticism from both liberals and libertarians, who argued that Dershowitz had indirectly sanctioned the use of torture and should now be regarded as a turncoat in the battle to preserve civil liberties.

3   Nonetheless, Dershowitz's op-ed makes a fairly powerful, though flawed, argument that torture would be ruled constitutional. Under the right circumstances, he claims, torture, while "very troubling," would pass a test the Supreme Court has sometimes used to determine the constitutionality of the government's use of an extreme law-enforcement technique: whether it "shocks the conscience."

4   "Consider a situation in which a kidnapped child had been
buried in a box with two hours of oxygen," suggests the law professor, ever the master of the difficult hypothetical. "The kidnapper
refused to disclose its location," he continues. "Should we not consider torture in that situation?"

5   Dershowitz, clearly uncomfortable with his own rhetorical question, does not quite give a direct answer. In order to avoid an ugly
answer to an impossibly difficult moral and legal question, he takes
another route. Since there is "no doubt that if an actual ticking
bomb situation were to arise, our law enforcement authorities
would torture," he says, "the real debate is whether such torture
should take place outside of our legal system or within it." The answer to this question is clear and easy for Dershowitz: "If we are to
have torture, it should be authorized by law" because "democracy
requires accountability and transparency."

6   Besides, Dershowitz argues, the Constitution poses no obstacle
to legal, court-authorized, supervised torture. That's because the
Fifth Amendment's protection against self-incrimination does not
protect against requiring someone to testify and disclose information; it merely protects against the use of such information against
the person interrogated. Thus, in the face of a court-issued "immu-
nity" order, any citizen may be forced to testify in a judicial forum,
or suffer imprisonment for the refusal to do so. Nor does
Dershowitz believe that any "right of bodily integrity" that might be
read into the Bill of Rights prohibits, say, the injection of "truth
serum," since the Supreme Court has already authorized the
forcible drawing of blood from a suspect for alcohol testing.
"Certainly there can be no constitutional distinction" he argues, "between an injection that removes a liquid and one that injects a liquid." (This particular argument is spurious, and Dershowitz should
know better: he is a long-time opponent of the death penalty,
where the current preferred method of execution is the injection of
deadly poisons into the veins of the convict.)

7   Dershowitz fails to mention altogether another amendment—the
Eighth, which states quite plainly that no "cruel or unusual punish-
ments [shall be] inflicted." The modern-era Supreme Court has ruled
that this standard, which is inherently subjective, must be interpreted
according to society's evolving standards of decency. It is likely that
the pre–September 11 Court would have ruled that techniques all
would agree constitute "torture" would qualify as "cruel" and (for

our society, at least) "unusual." But in the atmosphere created by the ghastly attacks of September 11, the Court might now rule that it is neither cruel nor unusual to torture a convict, a prisoner, or even a mere suspect, if the information that might be wrung from that person could save thousands of innocent lives. (After all, the Supreme Court did uphold the constitutionality of President Franklin D. Roosevelt's transfer of Japanese-Americans from the West Coast into "relocation camps" after Pearl Harbor, and of his using a military tribunal to try—and execute—German saboteurs who landed on our shores intending to destroy strategic targets.) War does change mindsets, even of the courts—and understandably so.

8   But leaving aside his interpretation (or neglect) of inherently vague constitutional provisions, Dershowitz's conclusion is clear: if torture is to be administered, it should require "torture warrants" issued by judges before whom the government must lay out reasons why torture—and only torture—could extract life-saving information. "Thus we would not be winking an eye of quiet approval at torture while publicly condemning it," he says.

9   Some advocates of torture justify their position on the simple ground that monsters like those who helped level the World Trade Center deserve to be tortured, ostensibly to get information that might prevent future catastrophic destruction of human life. (Of course, if the pain inflicted also goes a small way toward exacting some retribution for the WTC carnage, though the suspected terrorist had nothing to do with September 11 but is planning an entirely new attack, some would view it as a just bonus.) But Dershowitz is not in that camp. He understands that in the real world, when law-enforcement authorities have reason to believe that a suspect has information that can save lives, individual cops and agents will resort to torture no matter what. After all, we have long struggled to control the gratuitous use of torture by police on suspects from whom they seek to extract confessions, and by sadistic prison guards against inmates for no apparent practical purpose whatsoever. Can there be any real doubt that a law-enforcement officer, or, for that matter, most of us, would probably be willing to resort to the torture of a person who knew where to find our kidnapped child or where to locate an atomic bomb ticking away in some major American city?

10   So what, then, is wrong with a system that requires torture warrants—especially if an opponent of torture like Dershowitz can argue for their constitutionality? The answer is threefold.

11   First, institutionalizing torture will give it society's imprimatur, lending it a degree of respectability. It will then be virtually impossible to curb not only the increasing frequency with which warrants will be sought—and granted—but also the inevitable rise in *unauthorized* use of torture. Unauthorized torture will increase not only to extract life-saving information, but also to obtain confessions (many of which will then prove false). It will also be used to punish real or imagined infractions, or for no reason other than human sadism. This is a genie we should not let out of the bottle.

12   Second, we should think twice before entirely divorcing law from morality. There can be little doubt that until now, Americans have widely viewed torture as beyond the pale. The United States rightly criticizes foreign governments that engage in the practice, and each year our Department of State issues a report that classifies foreign nations on the basis of their human-rights records, including the use of torture. Our country has signed numerous international treaties and compacts that decry the use of torture. We tamper with that hard-won social agreement at our grave moral peril.

13   Third, our nation sets an example for the rest of the world: we believe not only in the rule of law, but in the rule of *decent* laws, and in a government composed of decent men and women who are accountable to a long tradition. There may be more efficient ways of governing, but our system is intentionally inefficient in certain ways in order to protect liberty. Our three co-equal branches of government immediately come to mind. Also, government can almost always proceed more efficiently if it is not dogged by an independent press protected by the First Amendment. But we have found from long experience that, as Jefferson famously said, if one were forced to choose between government without the press or the press without government, the latter might well be preferable. Trials by jury are long, inefficient, expensive, and sometimes lead to the acquittal of defendants whom the state is convinced are guilty and wants very much to incarcerate or even execute. Some of those acquitted are indeed guilty. Yet trial by jury remains the best (albeit imperfect) system ever devised for ascertaining truth while curbing government excess and abuse of power. Torture may sometimes offer an efficient means of obtaining information, but efficiency should not always trump other values.

14   Yet we still face Dershowitz's "ticking bomb" hypothetical. How do we deal with that? Is it really moral, after all, to insist on having

"clean hands" and to refrain from torture, when thousands or even hundreds of thousands of people could die as a result of our pious and self-righteous morality?

15   The answer to this quandary lies in a famous criminal-law decision rendered in Victorian England by the British appeals court known as the Queen's Bench. It is a case studied by virtually every American law student at virtually every law school. In *Regina* [the Queen] *v. Dudley and Stephens*, the court dealt with one of the most difficult criminal cases in English legal history.

16   In July 1884, four crewmen of a wrecked English yacht were set adrift in a lifeboat more than 1000 miles from the nearest land mass. They had no water and no food except for two one-pound tins of turnips. Three of the men—Dudley, Stephens, and Brooks—were "able-bodied English seamen," while the fourth lifeboat passenger was an 18-year-old boy who was less robust than the others and soon showed signs of weakening. As they drifted, severe hunger and thirst set in. It became clear, as the trial court found, that unless the three stronger seamen killed the boy—who by then had deteriorated substantially and was on the verge of dying anyway—and then ate his body and drank his blood, all four of them would die. "There was no appreciable chance of saving life except by killing one for the others to eat," and the boy seemed the most logical candidate since he was "likely" to die anyway, as the trial court put it. Dudley and Stephens followed this course, with Brooks dissenting. Once the boy was killed, all three partook of his flesh and blood. Four days later, the three survivors, barely alive, were rescued by a passing ship.

17   The Queen's Bench was faced with the question of whether, under English law, the three were guilty of murder, or whether the homicide was justified by a "defense of necessity." The judges concluded that they were guilty of murder and should be sentenced to death. "[T]he absolute divorce of law from morality would be of fatal consequence," they wrote, "and such divorce would follow if the temptation to murder in this case were to be held by law an absolute defense of it." Were this bright line against murder abandoned, warned the court, it might "be made the legal cloak for unbridled passion and atrocious crime." The genie, in other words, would have escaped from the bottle, with unimaginable consequences.

18   But since this case is a very hard one and the outcome—the death penalty—would strike most civilized people as excessive

under the circumstances, the judges suggested a way out of the dilemma. The judges claimed that it is left "to the Sovereign"—in this instance, the Queen—"to exercise that prerogative of mercy which the Constitution has intrusted to the hands fittest to dispense it." In other words, executive clemency offers a way to trim the harsh edges of the law in the truly exceptional case.

19   The lesson of this case for the use of torture warrants is clear. When a law-enforcement officer truly believes that a suspect possesses life-saving information, and commits the perfectly human act of torturing the suspect to obtain that information, the officer *should* be tried for the crime of violating the suspect's constitutional rights, or for some related crime such as assault and battery or mayhem (willful bodily mutilation). If the jury, acting as the conscience of the community, decides that the officer does not deserve to be convicted and punished under the circumstances, it will acquit. Indeed, under our system of unanimous jury verdicts in federal and most state criminal trials, a single juror who refuses to vote for conviction can "hang" the jury and prevent a verdict and hence a conviction. In our legal history, there have even been instances where juries, exercising what is known as "jury nullification," have refused to convict or have acquitted obviously guilty defendants. Such verdicts are hardly unknown, as in cases of mercy killings or the medical use of marijuana.

20   Further, even when a conviction has been handed down in a hard case, the government's chief executive (the president of the United States or, on the state level, usually the governor) may exercise his or her constitutional authority to commute (or terminate) the sentence and free the defendant, or even pardon the defendant and thereby wipe clean his or her criminal record. In the *Dudley and Stephens* case, in fact, Queen Victoria commuted the sentence to six months' imprisonment. This is how a civilized nation upholds civic decency and the rule of law while allowing for those exceptional situations when normal human beings break the law for some greater good or under conditions of overwhelming necessity.

21   We do not need, and should not dare to enact, a system of torture warrants in the United States. Our legal system is perfectly capable of dealing with the exceptional hard case without enshrining the notion that it is okay to torture a fellow human being.

Torture Should Not Be Authorized

Philip B. Heymann

1   Authorizing torture is a bad and dangerous idea that can easily be made to sound plausible. There is a subtle fallacy embedded in the traditional "ticking bomb" argument for torture to save lives.

2   That argument goes like this. First, I can imagine dangers so dire that I might torture or kill guilty or innocent persons if I was quite sure that was necessary and sufficient to prevent those dangers. Second, very many feel this way, although differing in the circumstances and the certainty level they would want. Therefore, the "ticking bomb" argument concludes, everyone wants a system for authorizing torture or murder; we need only debate the circumstances and the level of certainty.

3   This conclusion, leading to abandonment of one of the few worldwide legal prohibitions, leaves out the fact that I do not have faith in the authorizing system for finding the required circumstances with any certainty because the costs of errors are borne by the suspect tortured, not by those who decide to torture him. The conclusion also ignores the high probability that the practice of torture will spread unwisely if acceptance of torture with the approval of judges is substituted for a flat, worldwide prohibition. The use of torture would increase sharply if there were "torture warrants." Any law enforcement or intelligence official who tortures a prisoner in the United States now is very likely to be prosecuted and imprisoned.

4   Punches may be thrown, but anything we think of as "torture" is considered an inexcusable practice. That revulsion will disappear if we make torture acceptable and legal whenever a judge accepts the judgment of intelligence officials that: (1) there is a bomb; (2) the suspect knows where it is; (3) torture will get the truth, not a false story, out of him before the bomb explodes; (4) the bomb won't be moved in the meantime. Every individual who believes in his heart, however recklessly, that those conditions (or others he thinks are just as compelling) are met will think there is nothing seriously wrong with torture.

5   Professor Alan Dershowitz wants to bet that judges will say "no" in a high enough percentage of cases of "ticking bombs" that whatever moral force their refusal has will offset the legitimating and demoralizing effects of authorizing occasional torture. It's a bad bet.

6   Judges have deferred to the last several thousand requests for national security wiretaps and they would defer here. The basis of their decisions, information revealing secret "sources and methods" of intelligence gathering, would not be public. And if the judge refused, overrode the judgment of agents who thought lives would be lost without torture, and denied a warrant, why would that decision be more likely to be accepted and followed by agents desperate to save lives than the flat ban on torture we now have?

7   How many false positives do you want to accept? You would get six false positives out of 10 occasions of torture even in the extraordinarily unlikely event that the intelligence officers convince the judge that they were really 80 percent sure of each of the above four predictions.

8   And even if you would tolerate this number of false positives if torture were in fact the only way to get the needed information to defuse the bomb, there are frequently other promising ways (such as emergency searches or stimulating conversations over tapped phones) that will be abandoned or discounted if torture is available.

9   Finally, if we approve torture in one set of circumstances, isn't every country then free to define its own exceptions, applicable to Americans as well as its own citizens? Fear of that led us to accept the Geneva Convention prohibiting torture of a prisoner of war, although obtaining his information might save dozens of American lives.

10   As to preventing terrorism, torture is an equally bad idea. Torture is a prescription for losing a war for support of our beliefs in the hope of reducing the casualties from relatively small battles.

11   Dershowitz misunderstands my argument. I do not accept torture either "off the books" with a wink at the secret discretion of the torturers or on the open authority of the judges from whom they might seek authorization. I predict so many types of harms to so many people and to the nation from any system that authorizes torture, either secretly or openly, that I would prohibit it.

12   The overall, longer-term cost of any system authorizing torture, openly or tacitly, would far outweigh its occasional, short-term benefits.

Yes, It Should Be on the Books

Alan M. Dershowitz

1   Professor Philip Heymann and I share a common goal: to eliminate torture from the world, or at the very least to reduce it to an absolute minimum.

2   The real disagreement between us seems to be over whether the use of torture, under these extreme circumstances, would be worse if done in secret without being incorporated into our legal system— or worse if it required a torture warrant to be issued by a judge.

3   This is truly a choice of evils, with no perfect resolution. However, I insist that any extraordinary steps contemplated by a democracy must be done "on the books." Of course there is the risk of false positives and ever expanding criteria. But these evils would exist whether torture was conducted off or on the books. A carefully designed judicial procedure is more likely to reduce the amount of torture actually conducted, by creating accountability and leaving a public record of every warrant sought and granted.

4   The legal historian John Langbein has shown that there was far more torture in Medieval France than England because in France the practice was left to the discretion of local officials, whereas in England it required an extraordinary warrant, which was rarely granted.

5   Heymann suggests that "any law enforcement and intelligence official who tortures a prisoner in the United States now is very likely to be prosecuted and imprisoned."

6   I believe that a police officer who tortured and successfully prevented a terrorist attack would not be prosecuted, and if he were, he would be acquitted.

7   Indeed, in a case decided in 1984, the Court of Appeals for the 11th circuit commended police officers who tortured a kidnapper into disclosing the location of his victim.

8   Although there was no evidence that the victim's life was in imminent danger, the court described the offending police officers as "a group of concerned officers acting in a reasonable manner to obtain information in order to protect another individual from bodily harm or death."

9   Elsewhere in the opinion, they described the "reasonable manner" as including "choking him until he revealed where [the victim] was being held." These police officers were not prosecuted. Under my proposal, no torture warrant could have been granted in such a case.

10   Our nation has had extensive experience with "off the book" actions. President Nixon authorized an off the book "plumbers" operation to break into homes and offices.

11   President Reagan authorized an off the book foreign policy that culminated in the Iran-Contra debacle.

12   President Eisenhower and Kennedy apparently authorized off the book attempts to assassinate Fidel Castro.

13   The road to tyranny is paved by executive officials authorizing actions which they deem necessary to national security, without subjecting these actions to the check and balance of legislative approval, judicial imprimatur, and public accountability.

14   We are a nation of laws, and if the rule of law means anything, it means that no action regardless of how unpalatable, must ever be taken outside of the rule of law. If the action is to be taken, it must be deemed lawful. If it cannot be deemed lawful it should not be taken.

15   Unless we are prepared to authorize the issuance of a torture warrant in the case of the ticking bomb, we should not torture, even if that means that innocent people may die. If we want to prevent the death of hundreds of innocent people by subjecting one guilty person to non-lethal pain, then we must find a way to justify this exception to the otherwise blanket prohibition against torture.

16   All the evils of torture would be multiplied if we were to accept the way of the hypocrite, by proclaiming loudly that we are against it but subtly winking an eye of approval when it is done. Hypocrisy, too, is contagious.

17   Several years ago, an Israeli prime minister reprimanded security officials for bringing him "unwanted information of misdeeds by Shin Bet" (the Israeli FBI). A wise professor commented on this action in the following words: "That strategy is extremely dangerous to democratic values, because it is designed to prevent oversight and to deny accountability to the public."

18   That wise professor was Philip Heymann.

CREDITS

Page 22: "A Sandwich" by Nora Ephron. Reprinted by permission of International Creative Management, Inc. Copyright © 2002 by Nora Ephron. First appeared in the *New Yorker.*

Page 26: "Deep Cold" from *A Rural Life* by Verlyn Klinkenborg. Copyright © 2003 by Verlyn Klinkenborg. By permission of Little, Brown, and Company, Inc.

Page 28: "The Bridge" by Jason Holland. Reprinted by permission of the author.

Page 32: "El Hoyo" by Mario Suarez for *Arizona Quarterly*, Summer 1947, vol. III, no. 2. Copyright © by the Arizona Quarterly. Reprinted by permission.

Page 36: "Left Sink" by Ellery Akers from *Sierra*, 1990. Reprinted by permission of the author.

Page 55: "Designer of Audio CD Packaging Enters Hell" by Steve Martin from the *New Yorker*, April 19, 1999. Reprinted by permission of International Creative Management, Inc. Copyright © 1999 by Steve Martin. First appeared in the *New Yorker.*

Page 59: "Learning, then College" editorial by Meg Gifford, the *Baltimore Sun.* Reprinted with permission.

Page 62: "The Night of the Oranges" by Flavius Stan from the *New York Times*, December 24, 1995. Copyright © 1995 by the New York Times Co. Reprinted by permission.

Page 66: "Time to Look and Listen" by Magdoliine Asfahani from *Newsweek*, December 2, 1996. All rights reserved. Reprinted by permission.

Page 71: "The Pie" from *A Summer Life* by Gary Soto. Copyright © 1990 by University Press of New England. Reprinted by permission.

Page 83: "Chocolate Equals Love" by Diane Ackerman from *Parade* magazine, February 9, 2003. Copyright © 2003 by Diane Ackerman. Reprinted by permission of William Morris Agency, Inc. on behalf of the Author.

Page 87: "I Was a Member of the Kung Fu Crew" by Henry Han Xi Lau from the *New York Times Magazine*, October 19, 1997. Copyright © 1997 by the New York Times Co. Reprinted by permission.

Page 91: "The Handicap of Definition" from "Instilling Positive Images" by William Raspberry. Copyright © 1982 by the Washington Post Writers Group. Reprinted by permission.

Page 95: "The Myth of the Matriarch" by Gloria Naylor from *Life* magazine, Spring 1988. Copyright © 1988 by Gloria Naylor. Reprinted by permission of Sterling Lord Literistic, Inc.

Page 101: "Where Nothing Says Everything" by Suzanne Bern from the *New York Times*, April 21, 2002. Copyright © 2002 by the New York Times Co. Reprinted by permission.

Page 115: "Sweatin' for Nothin'" by Michael Barlow. Reprinted by permission of the author.

Page 119: "Stop Ordering Me Around" by Stacey Wilkins from *Newsweek*, January 4, 1993. All rights reserved. Reprinted by permission.

Page 123: "A Black Fan of Country Music Tells All" by Lena Williams from the *New York Times*, June 19, 1994. Copyright © 1994 by the New York Times Co. Reprinted by permission.

Page 128: "The Joy of Starvation" by James Gorman from the *New York Times Good Health Magazine*, October 8, 1989. Copyright © 1989 by the New York Times Co. Reprinted by permission.

Page 132: "Bananas for Rent" by Michiko Kakutani from the *New York Times Magazine*, November 9, 1997. Copyright © 1997 by the New York Times Co. Reprinted by permission.

Page 146: "The New York Walk: Survival of the Fiercest" by Caryn James from the *New York Times*, October 17, 1993. Copyright © 1993 by the New York Times Co. Reprinted by permission.

Page 150: "Always, Always, Always" by Bill Rhode. Reprinted by permission of the author.

Page 155: "The Search of Human Life in the Maze of Retail Stores" by Michelle Higgins from the *Wall Street Journal*, Eastern Edition, May 6, 2003. Copyright © 2003 by Dow Jones & Co. Inc. Reproduced with permission of Dow Jones & Co. Inc. in the format Textbook via Copyright Clearance Center.

Page 161: "The Plot Against the People" by Russell Baker from the *New York Times*, June 18, 1968. Copyright © 1968 by the New York Times Co. Reprinted by permission.

Page 165: "Desert Religions" by Richard Rodriguez from *The News Hour with Jim Lehrer*, July 8, 2002. Transcript from *Online Lehrer Newshour* by Richard Rodriguez. Copyright © 2002 by Richard Rodriguez. Reprinted by permission of Georges Borchardt, Inc., for the author.

Page 179: "Living on Tokyo Time" by Lynnika Butler from the *Utne Reader*, January/February 2003. Reprinted by permission of the author.

Page 182: "Playing House" by Denise Leight from the *Becoming Writers Journal*, Spring 2001.

Page 186: "World and America Watching Different Wars" by Danna Harman from *The Christian Science Monitor,* March 25, 2003. This article first appeared in *The Christian Science Monitor* on March 25, 2003 and is reproduced with permission. Copyright © 2003 by The Christian Science Monitor <www.csmonitor.com>. All rights reserved.

Page 192: "Two Ways to Belong in America" by Bharati Mukherjee from the *New York Times*, September 22, 1996. Copyright © 1996 by the New York Times Co. Reprinted by permission.

Page 197: "The Raven" from *Desert Notes* by Barry Lopez. Copyright © 1976 by Barry Holstun Lopez. Reprinted by permission of Sterling Lord Literistic, Inc.

Page 211: "Runner" by Laura Carlson. Reprinted by permission of the author.

Page 214: "How to Swat a Fly" from *How to Attract the Wombat* by Will Cuppy. Copyright © 1949 by Will Cuppy, copyright © 1970 by Alan L. Rosenblum. Reprinted by permission of Phyllis Feldkamp.

INDEX